Saving

Stacy

The Untold Story
of the
Moody Massacre

By Rob St. Clair

Published in the United States by Kindle Direct Publishing. For inquires, please contact Rob St. Clair at Rbstclair@gmail.com

LIBRARY OF CONGRESS CATALOGING-IN-PUBLICATION DATA

St. Clair, Rob
Saving Stacy: The Untold Story of the Moody Massacre / Rob St. Clair

ISBN: 9781791379919

Printed in the United States of America on acid-free paper.

2 4 6 8 9 7 5 3 1

FIRST EDITION

This book is dedicated to

Stacy Moody

and her father, Steve Moody, and stepmother, Audrey Moody

This book is also dedicated

to the memories of

Gary D. Shafer, Sharyl B. Shafer, Sheri Kay Shafer,

Paige Harshbarger, Megan R. Karus,

and Scott R. Moody

Foreward

If you want to commit murder and get away with it, do it in Logan County, Ohio.

– Paul Harvey, national radio broadcaster, in one of his Saturday afternoon radio broadcasts, February 1992, thirteen years before the Moody massacre

Harriot Griffin was growing more anxious by the minute. It had been almost an hour since her husband, Murray, the town marshal, had left to investigate some type of incident at Tootie Mullet's place. She knew something was wrong, and she was beginning to tremble. Now, flashing blue lights suddenly appeared out in the street, in front of her house. A few moments later came a firm knock on the door.

Crossing herself, Harriot opened the door. There stood the Logan County Sheriff with his hat in his hands.

"I don't know how to tell you this, Mrs. Griffin, but Murray's been killed."

The middle-aged woman heard the news in disbelief. Not here. Not him. In the twenty years that sixty-four-year-old Murray had served as the part-time town marshal, trash collector, snowplow operator, and street repairman for Belle Center, Ohio, nothing like this had ever happened. The $25 a week he brought home went a long way to making their $90-a-month house payment and feeding their eight children in this small town of 900 residents. How could this happen?

Just hours earlier, on Saturday, July 5, 1986, at about 11:20 in the evening, Murray and his wife were awakened by the phone ringing in their kitchen. A man reported that Phyllis

Mullet, known around town by her nickname "Tootie," had suddenly started screaming for help during the middle of their phone conversation.   The man didn't know what to do, so he called the Logan County Sheriff's Office and an operator gave him Murray's telephone number.

Thanking the man for the information, Murray hung up the phone and went to put on his boots and gun belt, telling his wife that "something was going on over at Tootie's house." Neither thought much about it. Tootie had recently separated from her husband, and Murray had already found it necessary on two or three occasions to go over to Tootie's two-story, white frame house to settle outbreaks between Tootie and her estranged husband, especially after Tootie developed a reputation for enjoying the occasional male companion, including this caller, her new boyfriend from Lima. Since Tootie lived several blocks away on the other side of the abandoned railroad tracks, Murray decided to drive, and told his wife that he would be back shortly.

Murray had just left when his wife received another phone call, this time from the Logan County Sheriff's Office with news of some type of problem at Tootie Mullet's house. The sheriff's office had just dispatched a cruiser, so Murray should wait for them to arrive.

"Too late," she told them. "Murray's already left."

Several minutes after the sheriff's office called, Murray's wife heard the police scanner in the kitchen come to life. The operator gave the code for "officer down," called for search dogs, and ordered all personnel to immediately respond to the Belle Center address.

―――

About an hour later, Logan County Sheriff Milt Watts and his lead detective arrived at Murray's house, knocking hard on the front door. In a quiet voice, Sheriff Watts explained to Murray's wife that someone had shot and killed both her husband and Tootie Mullet.

The investigation later revealed that the attacker surprised Tootie Mullet, age thirty-seven, as she spoke on the landline in her kitchen, still wet from a shower and wearing only a shirt into which she'd thrust her arms as she had hurried to answer her ringing phone. The attacker had bound her feet with a clothesline, tied her hands behind her back with a cloth, brutally beaten her, slashed her throat, and stabbed her multiple times in her chest.

Deputies found Marshall Murray Griffin upstairs at the top of the second-floor landing with four gunshot wounds: in the left knee, stomach, shoulder, and in the middle of his back – all apparently by his own revolver, which was missing. They found none of Tootie Mullet's blood upstairs and none of Marshall Griffin's blood downstairs.

A deputy sheriff called Tootie Mullet's estranged husband, who left his apartment at Indian Lake ten minutes away to head for Belle Center. When the detective interviewed him, he claimed as an alibi that he had spent all night at his apartment with his two children. He insisted that he and Tootie had settled all their marital differences a long time ago, even though he had just been served with divorce papers that day. Deputies tested his hands for gun powder residue. The test came back positive. But Tootie's husband had an answer for that. He had set off fireworks earlier that evening with his kids to celebrate the Fourth of July.

The detectives let him go.

The investigation ended there; the Logan County Sheriff's Office had no other leads.

Mrs. Griffin grieved, asking herself, "Why did we ever move to Logan County?"

———

Logan County is a forty-five-minute drive from Columbus, Ohio. Once you leave the sprawling suburbs of the state's capital, the modern four-lane highway wanders past small, local farms growing corn and soy beans, bypassing the city of Marysville, which boasts Honda's sprawling car manufacturing plant, discreetly nestled out of sight from the highway's light traffic. The gradual incline in the road is barely noticeable, but then appears the sign for "Mad River Mountain," one of Ohio's two ski resorts. Finally, the highway sign declares "Welcome to Logan County." The City of Bellefontaine, the county seat, population 13,000, is just up the road.

With more than thirty small towns and unincorporated villages scattered throughout the 467-square mile county, most Logan County residents are engaged in agriculture or are employed by Honda or one of its suppliers.

The City of Bellefontaine has the typical Midwestern town square with the spiraling clock-tower positioned on top of an 1870s-built stone and brick courthouse. The Chamber of Commerce brochure notes that the city has the shortest street in America – twenty feet long – and that Bellefontaine is only a mile or so away from the highest point in the state, at 1,549 feet.

Bellefontaine's police department needn't worry about traffic jams, protesters, or the homeless; there are none. Outside of town, the Logan County Sheriff's Office patrols more than 375 miles of roads with little assistance, other than from local town "marshals," usually one-man operations. But if necessary, the state highway patrol can be called upon for a helping hand whenever an emergency arises. In Logan County, the sheriff's office acts as the primary law enforcement agency responsible for everything outside of Bellefontaine's city limits. Due to the county's small population, deputies know just about everyone or certainly anyone deserving of suspicion.

What the Chamber of Commerce doesn't want you to know is that the citizens of Logan County know their sheriff's office has a reputation for being one of the most corrupt and inefficient departments in the Buckeye state. For years, numerous serious crimes have gone unsolved. Like barnyard dust, rumors hang in the air that some who wear the sheriff's deputy badge might be complicit in many of those unsolved crimes.

In 1986, one of those notorious, unsolved cases took place in Belle Center, population 900, a small eight-block town in northern Logan County.

———

Days after the Mullet and Murray killings, the sheriff's office received a call from a man in Belle Center identifying himself as the father of Terry Lowe, a soft-spoken, effeminate, mentally-challenged, forty-six-year-old man who had frequently babysat Tootie's two young children and served as a pallbearer at Tootie Mullet's funeral. Terry's father said his son had written a suicide note and he feared for his son's life.

Detectives arrived at the father's house and, with his permission, inspected Terry's bedroom. There they found pictures of Tootie Mullet and her children. In Terry's wastebasket they also discovered a handwritten document, the right side of the paper containing a list of names, with the names bracketed into several groupings, presumably by families. The name "Tootie," Mullet's nickname, as well as the names of Mullet's two young children, appeared on the list. The list also contained the names of other women and two other young girls who lived in Belle Center.

Terry Lowe's note seemed simple: "I can't take it anymore and I'm going to go away."

Based on what Mr. Lowe had to say about his son, detectives went to Indian Lake, ten minutes away, to look for Terry. When they arrived, they found his locked car with Terry's wallet and car keys laying on the front seat. Assuming the worst – suicide – they began preparations to drag the lake. After three days of dragging the lake, they came up empty.

After interviewing neighbors, detectives learned that Terry often had Tootie Mullet's eleven-year-old daughter and two of her friends over to his house to play. The police reports explained that the girls began visiting Terry in the spring of 1986, a few months prior to the murders. Terry knew the girls' parents, who permitted them to visit him. The girls would play together or with Terry, and occasionally they would shop together at the drugstore across the street from his home.

Some of Terry's activities with the girls had turned overtly sexual. Rumors reported that, on at least one occasion, he had shown two of the girls X-rated videotapes and explained to them what the actions in the film meant. At times, Terry watched the videos with his hands down his pants. In addition, he sometimes walked through his house in a bikini swimsuit or in underwear, again sometimes having his hands down his pants.

Shortly after the discovery of the suicide note, the sheriff's office received a phone call from the Greenville Police Department, located close to the Indiana border, seventy-five miles away. Someone had turned in a credit card belonging to Terry's father. The Logan County Sheriff dispatched two detectives to Greenville. There they found Terry in a local hotel and brought him back to Bellefontaine to question him about the faked suicide note and the homicides. He denied knowing anything about the murders. Terry told them that he worshiped Tootie.

The detectives let him go.

Amid the resulting furor, Terry moved to Nevada and became a maintenance man for an apartment complex.

———

Four years later, in 1990, a new county prosecutor, Gerald Heaton, ran on a campaign promise to clean up Logan County with a commitment to solve the notorious Belle Center case and prosecute the killer. Without any new evidence, the prosecutor indicted Terry Lowe for the murders of Tootie Mullet and Marshal Murray Griffin and had him extradited from Nevada to stand trial.

In his opening statement, Prosecutor Heaton claimed that Lowe had a plan to have sexual encounters with several Belle Center women and girls who lived in isolated areas of town. "Tootie Mullet was one of the women," he said.

The prosecutor explained that Lowe went to Mullet's home to have sex with her, but his plan went awry when she resisted, and he killed her. Lowe then killed Griffin, who had gone to the house after receiving a report of a disturbance. According to Prosecutor Heaton, "The killer's actions show the slaying was sexually motivated because Mullet's body was lying face down, in a sexual pose," though all the stab wounds were to her chest.

He then announced that the state expected to call seventy-five witnesses, two of whom would testify that they thought they saw Terry Lowe that evening walking with a bag in his hands, which might have contained, according to Heaton, "the things he would need for this night of perversion." Heaton felt sure that the bag contained the "cords with which to bind her and a pocket knife to control her."

However, the prosecutor could not produce a single shred of physical evidence tying Terry to the brutal crime. In open court the prosecutor admitted that the case rested entirely on conjecture and circumstantial evidence.

———

Many in Belle Center refused to believe the prosecutor's claim of a sexual motive for the crime.

Terry Lowe's attorney took the highly unusual step to express his own theory in open court: "Tootie's husband was upset about their divorce and losing custody of his children. He had a history of threatening his estranged wife. In addition, because of a large life insurance policy, he stood to gain financially from Tootie's death."

On February 6, 1992, the trial court rejected much of the evidence against Terry Lowe because the deputies obtained it improperly and deemed inadmissible Lowe's reported acts as to his deviant behavior with these children. Without any other substantial evidence, the judge threw out the murder charges. In July 1994, the Ohio Supreme Court upheld the trial court's decision stating that Lowe's activities with the girls failed to establish a *modus operandi* applicable to the Mullet and Griffin murders. Simply put, the prosecutor failed to establish, by the required necessary proof, a substantial link between Terry Lowe's actions with these young girls for whom he babysat and the list of names he had written out – supposedly women and girls with whom he wanted to have sexual relations – with any motive, plan or scheme to commit the murders of Tootie Mullet and Murray Griffin.

The Logan County Sheriff's Office never pursued any other suspects.

———

Years later, outside investigators and forensic analysts reviewed the case file and all other available evidence and came to some striking conclusions. Because of the position of the bodies and the sequence of killings, not one but two perpetrators had done the killings. In addition, the gunshot residue discovered on Tootie's husband's hand could not have come from setting off fireworks. Setting off fireworks would not leave any discernable chemical residue on someone's hands; even if it did, the chemicals would look distinctly different.

Marshall Griffin was shot almost in a ritualist fashion, execution style, perhaps while pleading for his life or as an act of sadism. However, the earlier conclusion that he died from his own gun proved misleading.   He died from the same caliber bullets used in most police firearms in Logan County and other similar police departments, but no one could know for sure which gun shot him, especially since detectives never found Marshall's gun.

Questions and speculation abounded. Tootie Mullet and her husband had separated after a contentious relationship. Tootie had started dating a man who lived in Lima, a thirty-minute drive away. Her husband knew this. Served with a complaint for divorce that day, did he want to drive over to Belle Center and catch his wife in a comprising situation? Did he take a friend with him, maybe to serve as a witness? Did that account for the second set of footprints later found outside of Tootie's window, but never identified?

Why didn't the prosecutor believe an elderly lady's testimony stating that she saw a deputy sheriff leaving the house the evening of the shooting, even identifying the deputy sheriff by name?

If anyone had a motive, Belle Center citizens believed Tootie's husband did. Even though the prosecutor may have believed otherwise and thought the Terry Lowe case a "slam dunk," no one in Belle Center thought that Lowe would ever kill. He might have had mental challenges and demonstrated deviant behavior, but that didn't mean he would ever commit murder.

When Terry Lowe walked free of the homicide charges, the community outrage grew exponentially after the trial judge highlighted the incompetency of the sheriff's office in conducting its investigation. Even worse, some members of the community speculated that deputies knew all along who had committed the murders. Rumors ran rampant that the sheriff's office protected the true murderer: one of their own, a deputy sheriff and good friend of Tootie's husband.

In the coming years, this sleepy, rural county would see more unsolved murders. Did they have a grossly incompetent prosecutor and sheriff's office? Or did the blame lie in something more sinister, maybe involving rogue deputies and their friends?

That question would be answered thirteen years later when the Moody massacre took place.

Chapter One

It was a rampage. This is going to stun our community. Nobody deals with something like this. I don't care where it happens; it's hard. These are the most tragic shootings I've ever seen in my thirty-one years here.

– Sheriff Michael Henry, press conference, May 29, 2005

When fifteen-year-old Stacy Moody returned to consciousness that Sunday morning, Memorial Day, 2005, she clutched to a fleeting hope that the eerie silence meant that everyone else lay asleep. She prayed that her face still looked normal, that her eyes hadn't swollen almost shut, that the sweet stench of blood didn't hang over the room, and getting her outfit exactly right for her brother's high school graduation ceremony that afternoon remained her biggest problem.

The party last night for the entire Riverside High School senior class, all fifty of them, had seemed like a lot of fun at first, especially to those not in the graduating class, like herself. But her brother had left early, inviting several of his friends to come over to their house to continue to celebrate, so she'd left also.

The trio that Scott invited to their home, all the types who'd probably one day marry, have kids, work the farms and small-town jobs that kept the state going, and spend their lives attending potluck dinners at churches and community events, looked wholesome, happy and healthy in their yearbook pictures. They'd trooped into Stacy's home, watched an Arnold

Schwarzenegger movie, and spent the rest of the night playing pool and talking about friends and school and everything else.

As Stacy slowly drifted back to consciousness that Sunday morning, while she still assumed that she'd had nothing more than a spectacularly vivid and horrible nightmare, she lay in her cozy upstairs bedroom in the farmhouse that had been in her family for generations. She vaguely wondered when she needed to start getting ready for that afternoon's graduation, when her older brother would march down the auditorium aisle to "Pomp and Circumstance" while her divorced mother and father took pictures from opposite sides of the room, and her grandparents sat uncomfortably on hard chairs and she tried not to get too bored.

Stacy didn't think that bad things could happen in rural Ohio, and certainly not in the white, two-story, wood-framed farmhouse where she lived with her mother and brother, or in her grandparents' home just down the road on the same dairy farm. She'd grown up walking the quarter mile between the two houses that both lay on the south side of a state road about two miles west of Bellefontaine, the Logan County seat.

The steep roof on Stacy's house used to be red but now had faded. An old-fashioned milk can sat on the porch. Her mother had decorated the sprawling home with funky colors mixed with antiques. Stacy had watched the births of most of the calves. Her 4-H club certificates and awards decorated her room.

Stacy and Scott had grown up with stern warnings to stay away from the two-lane state highway that brought traffic past their front yard, but for the most part her mother Sheri Kay hadn't worried too much about the kind of trouble her children might get into because they stayed busy with chores. A hired hand helped, but Sheri Kay, Scott, Stacy, and their grandparents handled most of the endless tasks that started early every morning when their twenty-five cows needed milking and their chores continued throughout the day over the 425 acres that needed tending.

Mainly Stacy's mother didn't worry because the family lived in a small community where everyone knew everyone else and word of teenage hijinks got back to the parents quickly. Sheri Kay had far more pressing concerns after her second divorce. She'd married young the first time, but trying to run the farm with her husband, Steve Moody, had proven a challenge. Without him, the cows still calved, and someone still needed to plant and harvest. With the tenacity of those who work the land in Ohio, with its flat, endless beauty and sunsets and fertile soil, along with the snow and ice and droughts and unpredictable weather that randomly hindered or helped make possible lavish harvests, she'd reverted to her maiden name Sheri Kay Shafer – everyone called her Kay – and taken a job with the Ohio Department of Transportation.

At age thirty-seven with two almost-grown children, Sheri Kay's life started to look better. She had met yet another new guy. Her oldest son had just finished high school; her daughter Stacy had only a few years left. Her kids, especially Stacy, had become friends with their father's new family, not that this made Sheri Kay very happy.

————

Stacy's hopes that another ordinary day had begun vanished as the pain that woke her exploded. She stumbled to her feet, dimly aware that her clothes seemed stiff.

They stank.

Her face throbbed.

Her lustrous shoulder-length chestnut hair felt sticky.

She couldn't see too well. She couldn't think.

One thought kept resurfacing.

Mama?

Mom?

It didn't take long for Stacy to reach her mother in her bedroom.

She tried hard, shaking her mother, but Sheri Kay wouldn't wake up.

Black splotches kept appearing before Stacy's eyes. She felt so dizzy.

She hurt.

A lot.

It took a while for Stacy to make it down the stairs into the kitchen where there was a mess her mother would never have tolerated.

A long time later, Stacy drifted back to consciousness, found her cell phone, and fumbled with the flip-top as she dialed again and again until she finally reached her stepsister.

———

A sleepy Nikki Vagedes answered, not hiding her irritation at an early Sunday morning call. The two stepsisters had no biological relationship but had grown close after Stacy's father married Nikki's mother.

Nikki hadn't attended last night's pre-graduation party for her stepbrother, but Scott would only celebrate the completion of high school once. So, Nikki had followed his plans and now she planned to attend that afternoon's ceremony and watch him receive his diploma. Nikki and her boyfriend, Jeff Kueterman, had spent the evening at a race track in nearby Waynesfield, with Jeff driving the course for hours in one of his souped-up hot rods until he'd ended up crashing it.

Last night around midnight, just ten hours or so earlier, Nikki and Jeff had stopped at a Shell station in Russell's Point to call Stacy's family to let them know about the accident and to find out how the party was "shaking out." Stacy had answered the phone. Her grandfather had agreed to handle the next day's milking so the family and a few friends who'd stayed over could all sleep in. Everything had seemed normal to Nikki, at least over the telephone. Stacy hadn't slurred her words or seemed intoxicated. She hadn't indicated any problems with the guests her brother invited: Paige Harshbarger, Bret Davidson, and Megan Karus.

Scott had included Paige Harshbarger because he couldn't leave out his new girlfriend of about ten days. He had broken up with someone a few weeks earlier, but it hadn't bothered him too much because he quickly began dating Paige, an extremely popular fourteen-year-old who'd just completed her freshman year at Riverside High School. Her fresh-scrubbed looks and dark blonde hair that she liked to wear in a bun couldn't hide the four-year age difference between them, but Scott liked her a lot.

Like everyone else at school, Scott had known her long before he began to notice her, just as he'd known his closest male friend since infancy, Bret Davidson, who'd just completed his junior year at Riverside. Bret had risen with Scott in the ranks of Future Farmers of America to the point that they now judged show cattle together at FFA events.

Bret had the tall, athletic physique of someone who did hard work every day. He knew how to hunt and fish, could hold his own in a fight, had the patience of one responsible for animals, and ignored his typical Midwestern good looks, wearing his brown hair short on the sides and without a part. Because he wasn't going to graduate for another year, he had tickets to a Cincinnati Reds baseball game the next day which meant he'd attend Scott's party but planned to miss the commencement ceremony itself.

The third friend that Scott invited, Megan Karus, also a graduating senior, came to the party wearing a Bluffton College sweatshirt to celebrate the school where she planned to start on a scholarship in the fall. It was her last weekend before the job she had lined up started Tuesday at the Ameristop Shell station, where the manager thought of her as a good kid. Short and a little heavy, she wore her dark, shoulder-length hair down. It showcased her great smile.

Stacy had invited a friend as well, and her mother's boyfriend was on hand. Everything had seemed fine to Nikki when she hung up the phone.

What had happened?

———

Even after Nikki groggily woke up, she could barely hear Stacy's faint, scratchy voice. Not until her stepsister implored her for help for the third time did it register with Nikki.

"Please hurry," Stacy begged in a strange, wobbly voice. "My mom's been beaten up, and I can't wake her."

"I'll be there as soon as possible," Nikki clipped, now wide awake. "Hang on."

Divorced and the mother of four young children, Nikki, age twenty-nine, pushed her boyfriend Jeff awake and told him to help gather the kids and get them ready to leave for the farmhouse.

Normally a twenty-minute drive over flat, country roads, Nikki knew ways to shave off a few minutes. They traveled from De Graff, a small farming town in southwestern Logan County, to Stacy's home on State Route 47 West, just outside of Bellefontaine. On the way, Nikki and Jeff discussed last night's party. With just a few kids, and with Stacy's mom as the so-called chaperone, what could have happened?

Nikki took a deep breath before they pulled into the gravel driveway of the two-story, white-framed farmhouse. "Stay in the car," Nikki told her children, and she scrambled out of her minivan with Jeff in tow. They crossed over the side-door threshold, pressed open the unlocked kitchen door, and gingerly stepped into the kitchen.

The counters held stacks of dirty dishes.

Trash lay strewn across the floor.

A red stain seeped across large sections of the cream-colored linoleum.

Flies buzzed.

The room stank of garbage, stale food, and something else, something bad.

The red stain looked like blood. It had spread everywhere.

The downstairs bathroom door creaked open.

Stacy stumbled out.

Blood was spattered like a Pollock painting all over her sweatshirt and jeans. Bruises and marks covered Stacy's swollen, ashen face. Zombie-like, Stacy dropped into a chair.

"Call 911," Jeff ordered. "I'll check the rest of the house."

Nikki called Emergency Services and spoke to radio dispatcher Dawn Hubbard, a thirty-year veteran with the Logan County Sheriff's Office, who put down her magazine and wheeled around in her chair to note the time and day: 10:35 Sunday morning, May 29, 2005.

Nikki didn't like talking about Stacy as though she wasn't there, but she got the words out over the phone as best she could. "My stepsister's covered in blood. She looks like she was badly beaten up."

The dispatcher used her neutral, professional voice, the one that usually calmed even the most frantic, to tell Nikki she was "going to get a squad and an officer right up to that residence."

"Now," the dispatcher continued, "I need to know the address."

As Nikki stared at Stacy, she couldn't think. Address? It was the white farmhouse down from Stacy's grandparents' house. She had no idea what street number they used. She asked Stacy but didn't get a response.

Jeff yelled from upstairs, telling Nikki to come quick.

Stacy just stared, seated and unmoving at the table.

Nikki, still clutching the phone, stumbled up the stairs to

where Jeff stood in a bedroom doorway. Stacy's mother, Sheri Kay Shafer, lay in her bed as though asleep. Jeff tentatively stepped into the room, approached the bed, and nudged her.

Nothing.

Jeff felt for a pulse.

No movement.

Nikki had followed Jeff into the bedroom, then abruptly stopped while still cradling the cell phone in her hand. She wailed into the receiver. "She looks dead! Stacy's mom looks dead!"

The dispatcher responded soothingly. "What's the address, honey? Can you go outside and look at the mailbox?"

Nikki screamed to Jeff, "Go outside and check the mailbox. Tell me what the address is!"

The two backed out of the bedroom.

Jeff hesitated.

He stared up and down the hall, swallowed, and signaled to Nikki that they should check out the rest of the upstairs.

One behind the other, they tiptoed into the bedroom of Stacy's brother, Scott Moody.

They recoiled from the blood.

Scott and a teenage girl lay together on his single bed with Scott halfway down the bed with his feet firmly planted on the floor. The girl, Paige, seemed to be propped up but slumped against the wall. Neither moved.

Jeff noticed a rifle on the bed between the two bodies. Nikki saw only her eighteen-year-old stepbrother and his girlfriend. Now crying, she lifted the phone to her ear.

Nikki: Oh my God! My God! The son – my stepbrother –   and his girlfriend are dead, too!
Operator: What?
Nikki: I found Sheri Kay's son and his girlfriend. Oh, my   God.

Operator: What's the matter?
Nikki: Oh, my God.
Operator: What's going on, honey?
Nikki: Sheri Kay's son and his girlfriend are beat up, too.
Operator: The son and the girlfriend?
Nikki: (Unintelligible.) I've got to get off the phone and call   my mother.
Operator: I need the address, honey.
Nikki: (Unintelligible) . . . is the only one awake.
Operator: There's only one awake?
Nikki: Yes. My stepsister, Stacy.
Operator: How many people have been beat up?
Nikki: Four, four.
Operator: Please, what's the address?

In a panic, Nikki turned to Jeff. "What's the number on that mailbox? They need to know."

Jeff raced down the stairs, bypassed the motionless Stacy, and ran out the kitchen door.

The mailbox. Where was it? Across the road.

He blindly tore across the state highway, barely registering the screech of tires as two cars slammed on their brakes to avoid hitting him. Jeff jumped back, let the cars pass, glanced at the painted numbers on the mailbox and then ran back inside to give the address to Nikki. As he started to yell upstairs to her, he glanced into the living room. His words died in his throat.

Another body lay slumped on a loveseat in the family room.

Nikki stumbled down the stairs to implore Jeff for the address but halted when she noticed Jeff's fixed gaze. She stiffened, then yelled in a higher-pitched shrill scream into the phone: "Oh, my God! There's one in the living room. There's another one on the couch," she said. Nikki then shouted out the address to the 911 operator. "Please hurry!" she cried. "Everyone's been beaten up."

The sheriff's office was a little more than a mile away from the farmhouse, up State Route 47 toward Bellefontaine, then north a few hundred yards on County Road 32. From the back door of their home, Stacy's family could have seen the far end of the county jail exercise yard, if they'd wanted to look. Deputy Wirick had on-call duty that Memorial Day weekend, so he took the dispatch for a possible assault at a local address. He flipped on his siren and started the flashing lights. On the way, the dispatcher radioed new information: multiple victims and one of the victims had no pulse.

As the deputy approached the farmhouse, Nikki's boyfriend Jeff ran down the driveway toward the two-lane road, flailing his arms to flag the police cruiser down. The deputy pulled into the driveway, spraying gravel, and slammed his car to a stop as Jeff frantically came up to the cruiser.

Between gasps for air, Jeff explained that several people had injuries, with one person still "up and speaking."

His hand gripping his holster, the deputy ran toward the farmhouse and through the open doorway where a teary Nikki sat protectively beside Stacy at the kitchen table. Nikki'd just hung up the phone after calling her mother and fumbled now, not sure what to do. According to the deputy's official report, Stacy appeared "dazed with a large amount of blood on her neck and face."

The deputy demanded that Stacy tell him what had happened, but Jeff interrupted and grabbed him by both shoulders, spinning him around in the process. "There are more upstairs. You need to check the ones upstairs."

Deputy Wirick rushed up the steps and hesitated in the hall as sunshine traced the floor. Jeff followed and pushed a shaking finger toward the left bedroom. The deputy tentatively approached the doorway and saw "a white female laying supine in the bed."

Jeff waited a moment. "That's Stacy's mother, Sheri Kay

Shafer."

The deputy later recorded that "she was covered up with a blanket neatly tucked under her chin. Her right hand was laying half way above her head with the palm up and open." At first, Deputy Wirick thought she might have fallen asleep, but he quit that hope. He noted that she appeared "grey and blue and not breathing."

Jeff swallowed hard, but got out the words to the deputy that Stacy's bedroom lay off to his right. Deputy Wirick stepped inside and scrutinized the room, especially the large amount of blood on the sheets and pillow, searching for a body, but nobody lay there.

Still panicked, Jeff nudged him to the bedroom over the stairwell, the one that belonged to Stacy's brother Scott. Tentatively entering the room, Deputy Wirick took a deep breath and discovered "a white male laying on the bed with a long rifle in his right hand with his thumb on the trigger." Scott "was laying supine on the bed with his feet and legs below the knees off of the end of the bed." In addition, the deputy would write in his report of a "white female laying on the bed on her right side, facing the wall of that bedroom."

Deputy Wirick pulled out his walkie-talkie and radioed his superior officer that he needed backup for a shooting. He then headed back down the steps to update the dispatcher. Jeff interrupted him and pointed to the loveseat in the living room. The officer edged near the furniture and discovered another female victim, Megan Karus, lying on her left side. She "also appeared to be blue, grey with no sign of responsiveness . . . and had what appeared to be swelling to the left side of her face."

The deputy returned to the kitchen with Jeff where the sobbing Nikki hovered next to the unmoving Stacy.

Deputy Wirick pulled out a pad of paper, cleared his throat, and started to question Stacy.

"What's your name?"

A long pause, then a quiet mumble. "Stacy . . . Moody."

"How old are you?"

Another reply, slower this time. "Fifteen."

Those answers pretty much ended the interview. As Deputy Wirick pressed for more information, Stacy's eyes glazed over, her answers growing more and more incoherent. It didn't take long for the Deputy Wirick to conclude that Stacy couldn't register his words, but he kept trying.

—————

"Stacy, what happened?" The deputy prodded.

No response.

"Do you have any idea who did this?"

After a long moment, a slow whisper. "No."

Sirens in the distance grew louder and louder, then stopped, mid-wail. Deputy Wirick's supervisor, Sgt. Dodds, emerged from his car, grimly assessed the situation, and started to secure the crime scene.

More sirens. An ambulance pulled up.

After Jim Collins, a paramedic with the Bellefontaine Fire Department, heard what the sergeant had to say, he fumbled for his bulletproof vest, strapped it on, and cautiously entered the house, followed by his partner.

They found Stacy at the kitchen table, bloody, her eyes unfocused, her face swollen and bruised. The paramedics started protocols to stabilize her. When finished, they went from room to room to examine the victims. None had any pulse or signs of respiration. All felt cold to the touch. The paramedic's report would cite the rifle in Scott's bedroom: "We found . . . a male victim with a rifle within arm's reach of him," a statement that would differ significantly from Deputy Wirick's official report.

The chief of the Bellefontaine Fire Department arrived after the EMTs had strapped Stacy onto a gurney and transported her to a waiting ambulance. Chief Holycross approached the back of the ambulance and tried to learn from Stacy if she knew who had done this to her.

Dazed, she said, "No."

A grim consultation followed. Stacy had two gunshot wounds to her face and neck, a shattered neck vertebra, and had lost a significant amount of blood. Something seemed wrong with her thinking and speech. The decision to take Stacy Moody to a local hospital via an ambulance changed. The paramedics began preparing her for a life-flight to Columbus, some forty-five miles away.

———

Stacy survived the trip. She arrived at Ohio State University's Medical Center where physicians determined that she'd been shot twice, lost a significant amount of blood, that the main artery to her brain had been severed, and that the gunshot wounds had damaged her vocal cords. Surprised that she'd lived through so much, they gave her a grim prognosis.

Chapter Two

You could clearly see small gunshot wounds behind the ears of both Shafers. The gunshot wounds appeared to be from a close distance, possibly even contact wounds. I believe the wounds are consistent with the victims at the other house.

– Detective Jon Stout's report on discovering the bodies of Gary and Sharyl Shafer, the grandparents

Over his twenty years of service in the sheriff's office, Detective Jon Stout had developed a strong track record for drug busts and solving random crimes that plagued Logan County's 467 miles of farmland and small towns. He'd spent his entire career in local law enforcement, starting at age eighteen, and had traveled the endless county roads many times.

At age thirty-eight, he'd grown used to the long hours that helped precipitate his recent divorce. Three-day weekends tended to give law enforcement plenty of traffic accidents, so he hadn't taken his four children anywhere that Memorial Day weekend. He grew anxious as he pulled up the gravel driveway to the farmhouse just after the paramedics gave up hope of any survivors except Stacy.

Stout quickly stepped out of his unmarked car, greeted Sgt. Dodds and Deputy Wirick, and acknowledged the quick briefing. A professional, he didn't rush into the house, but immediately began his preliminary investigation of the crime scene, starting with an overview of the site itself.

Sheri Kay Shafer's home at 2647 State Route 47 West lay approximately one-quarter mile west of her parents' home on the same road. Both stood on the south side of the road, just two miles west of Bellefontaine's city limits. Both homes stood on the same dairy farm, a family-owned business.

Sheri Kay's residence, a typical Midwestern two-story wood-framed farmhouse, had a barn out back with a fifth-wheel camper parked between the house and the barn on the gravel driveway. A gray Honda Civic LX and a silver Ford F-350 pickup truck sat in front of the barn.

As church bells rang from the town two miles away, Detective Stout, along with Sgt. Dodds, entered the house to record the crime scene itself. According to Detective Stout's later report, "there was blood on the kitchen table and floor. More blood splatters could be seen in the dining room." While in the living room, he noted a recliner with the foot rest open, a blanket or quilt rolled off to the left side, and a large amount of blood on top of the left arm rest.

In another corner, Megan Karus, a family friend who had attended the party and spent the night, lay on a loveseat on her left side with her buttocks against the back of the loveseat, covered by a multicolored comforter with only her head and right hand exposed. She wore a gray hooded sweatshirt with "Bluffton" written across the front, faded blue jeans, and white socks. She had blood stains on her right hand. Blood oozed from the area of her right ear.

The officers found a .22 caliber cartridge casing on the floor near the north wall of the living room. They also noticed more bloodstains on a blue reclining chair near the west wall and on a red and blue sleeping bag lying on the chair. Blood covered the floor between the chair and an end table. They also found a bloody tissue on top of a magazine rack attached to the end table.

Detective Stout and Sgt. Dodds checked out the stairwell where they noted blood drops and smeared handprints.

Upstairs in the master bedroom, Sheri Kay Shafer lay on her back with blankets pulled up to her chin. Her left arm stuck out from underneath the blankets. Her right arm was bent at the elbow so that her right hand rested on her chest. Her legs and feet lay straight with her feet approximately twelve inches apart. Stout guessed that her legs and feet had assumed that position due to posturing because of a head injury. She wore a blue pajama top designed with pink stars and black and white cows and gray sweat pants. Just in the hairline of her right temple, Stout discovered a possible contact gunshot wound. Both eyelids had blackened and swollen. Blood had run from her nose, mouth and left ear; dried blood stained Sheri Kay's neck and both of her hands.

A .22 caliber cartridge casing lay on the bedroom floor resting next to a work boot on the east side of the bed. The officers noticed footwear impressions deposited in the dust on the floor next to the bed's headboard.

In Stacy's bedroom, Stout found bloodstains on both the bed and bed clothing, a .22 caliber cartridge casing on the bed, another .22 caliber cartridge casing on the floor on the east side of the bed, and a bloodstained, red "Ohio State" hooded sweatshirt lying on the bed. According to Stout, the sweatshirt appeared to have several bullet holes. As he examined it, a bullet fragment fell out onto the bed. He recorded bloodstains on the sheets, blankets, pillows, floor, a chest of drawers, and on a TV screen, and a bloody handprint on the face of a large antique mirror hanging on the south wall.

Detective Stout and Sgt. Dodds found the bodies of Paige

Harshbarger and Scott Moody in the third bedroom, both lying on Scott's single bed, which had only box springs and a mattress. Paige lay on her right side facing the wall with an orange-colored blanket pulled up tightly around her, although it did not cover her head and right hand. Her right hand rested against the wall, in front of her face, with the palm toward her face. She wore a gray, hooded sweatshirt. Blood had run from her nose, mouth and an area near her left ear. They noted bloodstains on her right hand and on the wall near her right hand. Her left eyelid had grown dark and swollen.

Scott Moody lay on his back on top of an orange blanket to the right of Paige, positioned so that his lower legs hung over the end of the bed, his feet touching the floor. He wore blue jeans and a pair of clean, white socks. A .22 caliber rifle lay by his right side between him and Paige. According to Stout, Scott's right hand was on the rifle, with his right thumb through the trigger guard and on the trigger. The tip of the barrel rested on his right shoulder. His left hand lay on his left hip. His right pant leg had hitched up to about the top of his sock, while his left pant leg had pulled up to just below his knee. Scott had blood running from his mouth and nose, and his left eyelid was blackened and swollen. Stout noted bloodstains on both his hands and a pair of work boots on the floor at the foot of the bed.

Stout recorded two distinct blood stains on the north wall, a .22 caliber cartridge casing lying on the floor near the foot of the bed, a second .22 caliber cartridge casing on the bed under Scott's body, and a third .22 caliber cartridge casing wrapped in the bottom edge of a curtain of a window on the east wall.

Wirick, the deputy who had first arrived on the scene, would state in his official report that the teenage girl in Scott's bedroom, Paige Harshbarger, "appeared to be grey, blue and unresponsive, that Scott had a large amount of blood on his face, that there was blood on the bed and a blood spatter mark on the wall at about the height of Paige's waist." Further, Wirick's report stated that "Scott lay on his back and did not have shoes or a shirt on, while Paige was completely dressed and neatly covered with a blanket pulled up to her neck."

When Detective Stout finished, he went outside and began to interview Nikki regarding Stacy's telephone call and what she and Jeff had discovered when they first arrived. Stout asked Nikki to list the family members and other victims in the house and clarify how everyone knew each other.

For whatever reason, he never asked Nikki for a written statement.

———

A little after eleven o'clock that morning, as stragglers filed into church services that bright sunny day in Bellefontaine, Detective Stout's supervisor, Sgt. Cooper, arrived. He entered the farmhouse with Stout, went from room to room recording his observations, including that Scott held a .22 caliber rifle, and then called Logan County Prosecutor Gerald Heaton who came to the scene with a deputy county coroner.

As Detective Jon Stout continued his interview of Nikki, her mother and stepfather arrived, breathless from the frantic ride and long walk from their parking space behind the lines of vehicles parked on the road. Nikki's stepfather, Steve Moody, ex-husband of Sheri Kay Shafer and father of Scott and Stacy Moody, grimly listened to Stout and Cooper. He then asked Detective Stout about Sharyl and Gary Shafer, Stacy's grandparents, who lived just a quarter of a mile down the road. Stout explained that he had heard they'd gone out of state.

Steve abruptly interrupted, "No, they're back. If they're not here, then something's wrong."

Detective Stout turned to Deputy Koehler and instructed him to take another unit and check out Gary and Sharyl Shafer's home. If no one answered, he instructed, they should force their way in.

Ten minutes later, Koehler radioed Stout to tell him they had found both grandparents, Gary and Sharyl Shafer, dead on their kitchen floor.

———

Detective Stout and his partner, Mike Brugler, drove over to the property to investigate this new crime scene. Entering the kitchen, they discovered Sharyl Shafer, age sixty-six, lying face down on the kitchen floor, fully dressed and wearing slippers, with household mail under her body. Gary Shafer, age sixty-seven, lay draped over her mid-section, face down, a large pool of blood surrounding his head. Stout could clearly see that each had small gunshot wounds behind their ears, which appeared to come from a close distance, possibly even from point-blank contact.

Stout recorded that the wounds seemed consistent with those of the victims at Sheri Kay Shafer's house. Gary Shafer's glasses had fallen to the floor between his legs. Three rounds of ammunition within twelve inches of each other lay around Gary Shafer's left boot. Fully dressed, he still had his barn boots on.

Stout reported, "There were two chairs at the kitchen table where it appeared people had been sitting. On both sides there were glasses of juice with bowls and medication ready to be taken. Breakfast interrupted, four pieces of bread were lying on top of the toaster. The bread was buttered. Next to the sink, a knife stuck out from a tub of butter. On the stove there were two eggs ready to be placed into a skillet."

Stout and Brugler returned to Stacy's home to begin photographing the two crime scenes. Alerted by police scanners, local media swarmed to the crime scene, asking questions and interviewing anyone who would offer a statement.

Although Stacy, the lone eyewitness, lay in an intensive-care unit in Columbus in critical condition, the media and rumor mill quickly found others in the community who'd participated in the small pre-graduation celebration the night before, starting with Sheri Kay Shafer's boyfriend, Jason Sutherly, who had come over to the farmhouse but left early in the morning.

And there was Stacy's friend, Andrew Denny, who had enjoyed the movie and played some pool but had also left early the next morning.

And Bret Davidson, who had stayed up talking with Scott until four a.m., slept for two hours on the living room couch next to the loveseat where Megan Karus slept, woke up around six a.m., and left to go home and help with his family's milking. Sheri Kay Shafer had walked him to the door and offered to fix him breakfast if he decided to return. He got the news of the deaths in a phone call during the fourth inning of the Reds baseball game he attended in Cincinnati that day.

The staff at Riverside High School heard the rumors and contacted the sheriff to ask him to withhold public news of the tragedy until after the graduation celebration for the now forty-eight seniors who would receive their diplomas.

The sheriff requested the services of a local pastor to help with counseling.

In the face of more and more media converging on the crime scene, Logan County Sheriff Mike Henry issued a press release shortly after 11:00 a.m. that Sunday morning, sending it by fax to several local and national news sources, announcing that he would hold a formal press conference at his office later that evening.

Despite the intended silence, rumors of the tragedy spread like wildfire, including new ones that the police had already solved the case: Scott had shot everyone and then shot himself in the face. By noon, Reverend Jones, the pastor that the sheriff had asked to help with counseling, heard on his police scanner that the sheriff had closed the investigation. "Declared closed already, only a few hours after the shootings!" he said to himself.

———

A very somber graduation ceremony took place at Riverside High School that afternoon with two missing students and a very diminished crowd. Some of the students arrived unaware of the tragedy, but one by one faces changed during the ceremony as whispers spread.

That afternoon, speculation abounded among neighbors, the community and media. Family secrets leaked. The farm had stayed in the family for decades, but the Shafers didn't have clear title to it because the great-grandmother had left a bad will. The farm had gone downhill. The police had visited the house several times, never about anything too bad except things like loud music, but still.

The story spread that Scott had often fought with his grandfather and didn't plan to stay on the farm.

At 7:00 Sunday evening, Logan County Sheriff Michael Henry straightened his wrinkled tee-shirt, adjusted his Dale Earnhardt, Jr. ball cap, and stepped before a crowded group of reporters representing local, state and national media outlets. Facing the glare of the blinding spotlights, he began, his voice choking: "It's tough on us. We knew these people. We're familiar with these kids. I feel so badly for these families, this community."

The reporters stayed silent, with mikes tuned to the sheriff's every word.

He continued, "You can't imagine what it's like to deal with this. When you have six victims, it's very horrendous. It was a rampage . . . These are the most tragic shootings I've seen in this county in my thirty-one years here because of the sheer numbers and all the young victims."

Sheriff Henry waited a moment before he explained the details. He estimated that between 7:00 and 10:00 a.m. Sunday morning, eighteen-year-old Scott Moody got out of his bed, loaded a .22 caliber semi-automatic rifle, walked a quarter-mile to his grandparents' home, and shot them as they made breakfast. Investigators had found Gary Shafer, age sixty-seven, and his wife, Sharyl Shafer, age sixty-six, dead on their kitchen floor.

The sheriff went on to say that Scott most probably crossed back over crop fields to his adjacent house, reloaded the rifle, and went from bedroom to bedroom, shooting people as they slept. The sheriff commented that he believed the sequence was that Scott first shot Riverside High School student Megan Karus, age nineteen, then his mother, Sheri Kay Shafer, age thirty-seven, then his girlfriend, Riverside High School student Paige Harshbarger, age fourteen, his sister, Stacy Moody, age fifteen, and finally himself.

"There was no sign of a struggle at either of the two houses, and it appeared that all of the deceased victims at Sheri Kay Shafer's house were killed while they slept," he said.

The big question remained, "Why?"

The sheriff had no answer.

With only the department's written reports to finalize, Sheriff Henry announced that he'd closed the case: "The suspect is one of the deceased."

———

The Sunday interviews conducted by investigators and the press neatly wrapped up the motive: A disturbed young man, relied upon by his mother and grandparents to help the family through its mounting farming and financial problems, had felt overwhelmed by the difficulties that lay ahead of graduation.

Case closed.

———

As the only eyewitness, Stacy Moody fought for her life during the next three days. She drifted in and out of consciousness, unaware of the funeral plans for her mother, brother, grandparents, and friends, or even that they had died. She didn't know that the police had declared the tragedy a murder-suicide.

After three days, Stacy's physicians finally gave officials permission to interview her.

The sheriff's office didn't send anyone to Columbus, but Logan County Coroner Dr. Michael Failor, needing to complete his paperwork, made the drive. He came to Stacy's bedside and introduced himself to Stacy, her physician, and Steve Moody's attorney. As a formality, and anticipating the answer, Dr. Failor asked Stacy, "Who shot you?"

Still unaware that her mother, brother and grandparents had died and that the Logan County Sheriff had identified her brother as the shooter, Stacy replied in a quiet, raspy voice that she didn't remember what woke her on Sunday morning, but that she opened her eyes to a man standing over her bed holding a gun. She described the gun as having a "huge barrel." Stacy continued that the man shot her in the neck and she just lay there.

According to Stacy, the man walked out of her bedroom and then she heard two more shots. A few moments later, he came back into her room. While the man stood over her with the gun a second time, she tried squirming to get out of the way, but he shot her again. That's when she felt a horrible pain. She lay there as he finally walked out. She then heard two more shots.

The coroner expected her to describe the assailant as someone who resembled her brother. Eighteen-year-old Scott Moody had stood at five-feet-eight, weighed 135 pounds, and had worn his light-brown hair short. All the detectives unanimously stated that Scott was not wearing a shirt of any kind when they discovered his body.

When prompted again by Dr. Failor, Stacy paused for a moment, trying to clear her thinking. Looking at Dr. Failor, she then described the intruder as older with short gray hair. He wore a blue shirt. She didn't remember whether he had any facial hair, and she couldn't remember any other descriptive details other than that he appeared to have a bigger build.

As she struggled to stay conscious for the interview, she whispered adamantly that she had never before seen the man who tried to kill her.

Because Stacy was feeling weak and drifting in and out of consciousness, Dr. Failor agreed to cut the interview short. He asked Audrey and Steve Moody, who had been waiting outside Stacy's hospital room in the hallway, to contact him as soon as Stacy felt up to talking again.

Dr. Failor was worried: How could he reconcile what Stacy had just told him with the police reports he had studied? His facial expression said it all: "What the hell is going on?"

Chapter Three

Wilma wasn't sure what to do. She simply couldn't pass everything down to her daughter Sharyl. Her daughter was just too sweet, a kindergarten teacher. Sharyl was much more interested in children than farm finances, crops, and dairy cattle. So, Wilma needed to do something creative, ensuring that the family farm would be passed down to future generations.

– Ron Shafer, Gary Shafer's brother, commenting on the Buroker-Shafer family farm and the difficulties his brother Gary had in dealing with Wilma Buroker

Most in the community knew the bizarre history of the Buroker family farm, including all the scandalous gossip and various family feuds that had taken place over the years. Most thought that the trouble started during Stacy's childhood, when her great-grandmother, Wilma Buroker, decided to get her affairs in order.

As Wilma sat on the massive front porch of her stately white farmhouse staring with rheumy eyes at the flat, endless fields, birds sang nearby, and the wind whispered in the towering trees near the chimney that had once made the house seem the epitome of wealth. Wilma had a decision to make and this seemed like the best place to think things through, but her mind kept drifting off to that day in her girlhood when she'd played beside these same trees that her grandfather had planted.

An only child, she'd just collected her dolls when her grandfather started talking to her parents in the living room. It hadn't meant anything to her at the time, that her father would inherit the entire farm, but that night her parents, Homer and Lola Fuson, sat down at the kitchen table and started to draw out plans to enlarge the barn. Her parents hadn't relaxed too often before that day, except on Sundays of course, but they began working even longer hours after that.

As Wilma shifted in her seat, trying to catch the nice breeze, she looked around at the pastures and fields of crops and the barns that housed a successful dairy operation and felt a shiver of pride that all that endless hard work had grown the business into a Logan County landmark, one that had lasted for more than 100 years.

She shook her head. Nobody knew how hard things had looked at times. Wilma had married Ralph Buroker in the height of the Depression, and in 1939 she had her only child, Sharyl. They'd gotten through it all. They'd raised their daughter in the local Methodist church and paid for Sharyl's college education at Findlay College some fifty miles away.

A family picture taken in Wilma's old age showed her standing behind her daughter and son-in-law, her hair nicely permed, a broach pinning her blouse, the picture of stylishness for an elderly woman in the 1990s.

Wilma didn't look quite that nice today, but she always tried to stay prepared in case company dropped by, so she waved from her porch as a car pulled in from the highway and pulled around the quiet-U-shaped compound her house shared with several other buildings.

Her large estate included not just the farm, but also various properties and rental homes. Entering from the highway to her home, the driveway formed a large "U" shape along the western side of Wilma's house. Traveling west from Bellefontaine, drivers would use the first part of the "U" to turn left into the compound. But to be safe, when people left the property, they used the back side of the "U" because of the dips in the two-lane highway and the inability to see oncoming traffic.

Directly behind Wilma's family home lay two smaller properties that Wilma rented out. Around the curve of the driveway rose the barn, with "Fuson-Buroker" proudly stenciled above two twelve-foot sliding barn doors.

Wilma waited a moment, but the car drove past her and finally stopped. Wilma's son-in-law, Gary Shafer, strode out from the barn and bent over the window to talk to the driver. Wilma settled back in her chair and nodded her head. Her daughter Sharyl might lack gumption, but she'd done a good thing at age twenty when she married a local farm boy, Gary Shafer. He'd gone to college too, over in Indiana, and worked for some time as a draftsman. They moved into one of the houses on the property and Sharyl got a job teaching school. Nine years later, in 1968, Wilma's only grandchild, Sheri Kay Shafer, came along.

———

According to family lore, Wilma's daughter Sharyl and her husband Gary Shafer had only one child because Wilma insisted on it. This mandate would eliminate any sibling rivalry, typically the cause of family members feuding when parents died. Friends remember Wilma saying, "One child is simply enough for each generation, allowing each family in turn to prosper without unnecessary arguments."

Rumor maintained that Wilma hinted strongly that her daughter Sharyl should demand the same of her own child.

Wilma's son-in-law Gary looked up from leaning over to

talk with the driver of the car, caught sight of Wilma, and waved his right hand. She nodded back. Although he might sometimes have seemed stubborn and strong-willed, he usually deferred to his wife's wishes, which meant Wilma's desires and plans. Wilma's daughter's job as an elementary school teacher took most of her time and interest, and she didn't usually argue with her mother's plans for the land.

Wilma settled back in her chair. After Gary married her daughter, the sole heir to the Buroker farm, he'd worked the place for his in-laws for decades. Now he managed the entire enterprise. He attended the nearby Methodist Church in Bellefontaine, like his wife and mother-in-law, joined the Logan County Marathon Bridge Club like his wife, stayed active in the local Masonic Lodge while Sharyl belonged to Eastern Star, worked on occasion as a draftsman, and raised show horses and prized cattle that he displayed with his family around the state and even in the Tournament of Roses Parade in Pasadena.

———

Gary finished his conversation and turned away as the car pulled out to the road. A walk along the gravel driveway to the right revealed another small outbuilding used for storage, with Gary and Sharyl's house at the end of the "U." Their view of nearly five hundred acres stretched out behind and to the west of the compound, abundant with soy beans and wheat. The plantings ended a quarter mile down the road at the western edge of the farm, anchored by another farm house rented by tenants.

Wilma sat back in her chair and pursed her lips as she watched the car leave and Gary head back into the barn. Gary Shafer had worked for decades without any kind of legal agreement that he or his wife would inherit the place. But who else would?

However, Wilma had started to take a hard look at her oh-so-sweet, easily-manipulated daughter Sharyl and at her granddaughter Sheri Kay Shafer, who kept making one poor life choice after another. Wilma concluded that she couldn't trust them. Her parents had worked too hard and it mattered too much that the farm remain in the family. As Wilma sat on the porch that day, she conceived a plan that she hoped would keep the farm in the family for her great-grandchildren. She wanted to make sure that neither her daughter nor her granddaughter could sell the land, but that it would pass down through her daughter and then through her granddaughter so that eventually Sheri Kay's children, Scott and Stacy, would inherit the place.

Her loving husband, Ralph, had died in 1987. Now, seven years later, Wilma, who was eighty-eight and in declining health, knew it was time to finally revise her Last Will and Testament.

―――――

Wilma summoned the family lawyer to prepare a draft of a new will, but he retired before she could finalize her thoughts and properly execute it, so she asked around for recommendations and finally went to Howard Traul, Bellefontaine's new city law director who also maintained a private practice.

He suggested some fundamental changes, but Wilma had made up her mind. She was adamant, "The farm is going to stay in my family."

On September 9, 1994, Wilma went to Attorney Traul's law office and signed what the probate court would later call a poorly drafted and confusing will. It contained complicated life estates and tried to establish a charitable foundation to recognize Wilma's parents, Homer and Lola Fusion, Wilma's husband and herself, and even her daughter, Sharyl Shafer. It also requested that the court appoint trustees to carry out her wishes.

The probate judge called it the most unusual will ever to be filed in Logan County. Unfortunately, it would take more than fifteen years after Wilma's death in 1995 to settle her estate, many of those years being spent in expensive, contentious litigation among members of her family.

In changing her will, Wilma assumed that if she used life estates she could then control the family farm for the next few generations. Wilma Buroker's father had done something like that. In 1937, Homer had created a simple, two-page will, leaving everything to his wife, Lola, for the "term of her natural life" and, after his wife's death, passing everything to Wilma.

Wilma decided to do something along those same lines; she just needed a lawyer to write it up and make it legal.

In her new will, Wilma dictated the customary gifts to keep everyone happy: $3,000 to her granddaughter, Sheri Kay Shafer; $3,000 each to her two great-grandchildren, Scott Moody and his sister, Stacy, but to be held in trust by Sharyl and to be used only for higher education purposes; and $3,000 to the First United Methodist Church of Bellefontaine.

The will continued: All livestock, machinery and equipment, all crops, either growing or stored, all her jewelry, household goods and furnishings, including silver, and the "car that I am driving at the time of my death" would go to her daughter, Sharyl.

That left the remainder of her estate, including the family farm of 475 acres and several other parcels of real estate, the total worth about two million dollars according to recent appraisals. Wilma was determined to pass one-half of the family farm to future generations by life estate, but the other half she wanted sold in order to establish a charitable foundation.

Wilma continued devising her plan. Her daughter Sharyl would inherit one-half of the farm, but only as a life estate; she could never sell it or give it to anyone else. Upon Sharyl's death, her life estate would pass to Wilma's granddaughter, Sheri Kay Shafer, again as a life estate. Upon Sheri Kay's death, her children Scott and Stacy Moody would inherit the land free and clear, to share and share alike.

The magical legal term "to share and share alike" meant that each great-grandchild would receive one-half of their mother's interest, or one-fourth of the family farm. However, the will omitted a critical phrase, "or to the survivor of them." Wilma didn't think it necessary. If anything should ever happen to either of her great-grandchildren, that child's family should receive something. After all, these young children would probably have stable families and children of their own by then. Certainly, by that time they would have had an attorney draft wills for themselves and their spouses, protecting their own families.

Wilma hoped that by then, maybe fifty or sixty years in the future, Scott and Stacy Moody would appreciate the importance of keeping the farm in their families.

––––––––

Wilma's new will continued with instructions to sell the other half of the farm to fund an education foundation: "The Fuson-Buroker Memorial Trust." That had a nice ring to it. The foundation would award scholarships annually in Wilma's parents' names, her and her husband's names, and even in the names of her daughter and her husband, Sharyl and Gary Shafer. Everyone would remember Wilma Buroker's generosity, and for years to come the family name would retain the respect and prestige it had enjoyed for more than 100 years.

The plan seemed foolproof, at least to Wilma.

However, her new will created problems she hadn't foreseen,

besides the trouble of probating it. After Wilma's death and the "reading of her will," and learning that he'd never own the land he'd worked for decades, her son-in-law Gary Shafer lost a lot of motivation to struggle as hard to run the property. With thirty years of teaching, his wife would soon retire, and she could be of more help. But as the two grew older, the physical labor would get more difficult for both of them. Without constant upkeep – the buildings were slowly falling into disrepair – the work would be piling up. The farm's productivity would decrease dramatically. As the estate settlement dragged on and on, Gary's wife, Sharyl, not that interested in farming in the first place, struggled to manage the paperwork.

––––––––

These last five years had been difficult for Wilma. In 1985, she watched her seventeen-year-old grandchild, Sheri Kay Shafer, fall in love with a twenty-year-old farm boy she had met at the Logan County Fair and, against her wishes, marry him. She feared that this marriage to Steve Moody was destined to fail, but Wilma knew she would help any way she could, probably providing a home for this young couple to live in and encouraging her son-in-law, Gary Shafer, to hire Sheri Kay's new husband to help on the farm. Now, looking back, she knew she would regret it.

Wilma knew that her granddaughter, Sheri Kay, was having more troubles than anyone could imagine. To Wilma, the word "irresponsible" came to mind. For whatever reason, she couldn't keep a job, or a boyfriend. And work wasn't Sheri Kay's strong suit either. She would apply for menial paying jobs, then quit within a few weeks. She liked to party, and men were always around the house at all hours.

Now, to her chagrin, Wilma had two great-grandchildren

from Sheri Kay's marriage to Steve, Scott and Stacy Moody. All of them were living in Wilma's house. With a growing family, Sheri Kay needed a larger house, and Wilma agreed that she and her family could move into the larger farmhouse a quarter of a mile down the road. In Wilma's opinion, maybe the move would help solve the marital problems that Sheri Kay and Steve were having, or at least put their fighting out of earshot.

But Wilma's first concern was that Sheri Kay was vulnerable. Anything she received from Wilma's estate would, unfortunately, be taken away by others. Sheri Kay would never be a farmer, but maybe her son, Scott, would. In addition, young Stacy loved farm animals and both she and Scott were future 4-H'ers. If Wilma's great-grandchildren were ever going to inherit the family farm from a life estate, Sheri Kay needed to be financially secure. Thankfully, the new provisions in Wilma's Last Will and Testament would provide for that.

————

There was no doubt that Wilma wanted to control the family farm, but she never could have imagined what would take place that early Sunday morning on Memorial Day weekend ten years later, ruining her plans for her own daughter and her husband, Sharyl and Gary Shafer, her granddaughter, Sheri Kay Shafer, and those two beautiful great-grandchildren, Scott and Stacy Moody.

Chapter Four

Sheri Kay's troubles would continue. No one claimed to know where she was getting the drugs that kept showing up at her home. Too many men were dropping by to visit, too many good times. One of the reasons I moved out was because I could no longer tolerate Sheri Kay's erratic behavior.

– John Martin's statement to detectives, May 29, 2005

The family troubles started years before Wilma revised her will. Different people remembered different dates, but for the most part all agreed that the problems started for sure in 1990 when then twenty-two-year-old Sheri Kay decided she needed a lawyer.

It didn't take much prompting for Sheri Kay to decide to drive past Bellefontaine's proud stone courthouse to head to Dayton for an attorney. On her way, she reflected on her recent visit to a local Bellefontaine lawyer, sort of a preliminary interview to talk about her case. She'd arrived a little late for the appointment because a woman had stopped her in the parking lot to reminisce about first grade when Sheri Kay's mother, her teacher, liked to read a story just before recess every day.

After Sheri Kay hurried away and entered the law firm's ornate front door, the receptionist recognized her immediately since she'd visited Sheri Kay's grandmother time and again for a donation for one cause after another. Last year, the Boy Scouts needed funds; before that, the softball team had to have better equipment; before that, a fire had destroyed a family's home.

With a courteous but strictly neutral face, she took Sheri Kay immediately past the waiting room and into the attorney's office. As Sheri Kay waited, an aide came in to offer coffee. The two had known each other since childhood, when they'd played hide-and-seek in Sheri Kay's huge yard before they would tiptoe into the house to stare agog at the family trophies and then out to the barn to see the prized cows and show horses. In the aide's nervousness during the long silence while waiting for the attorney, she began babbling stories about high school friends and their different majors in college until she trailed off in embarrassment when she remembered that Sheri Kay hadn't gone to college.

As Sheri Kay left to go home to her six-month-old baby Stacy and her three-year-old son Scott, she ignored a whiff of disapproval and the feigned politeness of the attorney and his staff. Didn't they know that times had changed? Sheri Kay cancelled her next appointment with that local lawyer and instead found a divorce attorney in Dayton.

Sheri Kay had married at age seventeen to twenty-year-old Steve Moody, a local farm boy she met at the Logan County Fair. Her grandmother Wilma hadn't approved, but she let the newlyweds move into her large home to give them a place to stay, and she ordered her son-in-law Gary Shafer to give Steve a job. The marriage had obvious strikes against it, but Wilma came from an earlier generation when teenage marriages lasted for life. She assumed that this would work. Sheri Kay stood to inherit a farm and Steve Moody liked working the land. They knew each other's families and friends.

In August 1986, twelve months after her marriage, Sheri Kay gave birth to a son she named Scott and followed that three years later with a daughter, Stacy Marie Moody. Wilma soon moved the very young parents and their children to one of the farmhouses on the property to get them out of her home and to give them more room.

Sheri Kay now had her own place. It could have used a new roof and some repairs, and Sheri Kay didn't have much time for housecleaning, but she had great fun decorating the place.

Over her new husband's objections, she painted their master bedroom bright pink and their living room teal. It had hardwood floors. Her closets overflowed with clothes. She and Steve had a barn out back and plenty of room for the cows her family raised for exhibitions. Wilma took the long view: If Sheri Kay could make this marriage work, if Steve Moody continued to work the farm, her granddaughter would have no reason to struggle the rest of her life.

But six months after Stacy's birth, Sheri Kay called it quits. In March 1990, she filed for divorce.

———

According to courthouse observers, what followed during the next few years grew into one of the ugliest divorce battles ever to take place in Logan County. Sheri Kay's parents and grandparents and great-grandparents might have spent their lives worshiping at the First Methodist Church and building strong business ties in the community – and keeping their family's dirty laundry secret – but Sheri Kay wanted to make Steve suffer. During their divorce, Sheri Kay and Steve used every weapon they could find against each other: screaming matches, broken promises, allegations of gross neglect of duty and extreme cruelty. Each party publicly called the other an unfit parent.

Between fights, Sheri Kay and Steve Moody tried everything: reconciliation, separation, dating again, counseling. At one point, Pastor Scott Griswold of the Lewistown United Methodist Church wrote a letter to Sheri Kay's attorney stating that both Sheri Kay and Steve had come to him for counseling. Pastor Griswold added, "It became evident that the suggestions I offered were not going to be followed. I came to the conclusion that the counseling I offered would be of no benefit. I suggested that their situation was beyond my capacity as a minister. At that time, I suggested they seek more professional counseling."

As the divorce proceedings dragged on, Sheri Kay found herself in the same home but in a very different life. She now had to find a babysitter if she wanted to go out with her high school friends, but she didn't have much in common with them any more since they talked endlessly about their husbands or their upcoming weddings. She didn't really fit in at church, either. Sheri Kay wanted to grasp her youth, which meant she wanted to party and have a good time, but the guys she knew tended to marry young and stay married or they didn't want to get too serious with someone who had two small children. As an only child of an only child, Sheri Kay didn't have any sisters or cousins. And in a small, rural farming community, she didn't have too many other options for friends unless she wanted to hang out with people that her mother didn't like.

———

Sheri Kay started a casual relationship, or so she thought, with John Martin, age forty-four, a local farmer who leased property directly behind the Buroker farm. Eventually, Martin moved in with Sheri Kay and her kids during Sheri Kay's separation from

Steve Moody. Having such an obvious affair embarrassed her soon-to-be ex-husband. It didn't help that Sheri Kay failed to make wise choices or resolve her venom toward Steve.

Sheri Kay's new friend John Martin lived with her for some time before he claimed that he couldn't handle her erratic behavior. Soon after he moved in, Sheri Kay grew suspicious of Martin's dealings with her son, Scott. Rather than kick him out, she reported an incident to Logan County Children Services, the first of many complaints that she would file, always alleging misconduct by others.

Logan County Children Services followed up with her complaint, writing to say, "Dear Sherry [sic]: For your information, we saw and spoke with Scott about a report that John Martin had hit the child. We found no evidence of abuse, nor do we intend to pursue the allegations further."

Sheri Kay lost that case, but she found a new weapon in her arsenal against Steve. In the courthouse of this small, enthralled county where nothing could stay secret, Sheri Kay filed numerous motions accusing Steve of sexual abuse of the children. And by god, she had the medical records to prove it! According to Sheri Kay's attorney, she could document the dozen times she had taken her children to hospital emergency rooms to be examined.

Sheri Kay would continue to file her complaints, but the responses remained the same: "Dear Ms. Moody: In response to your phone contact this date, emergency removal [removing the children from Steve's home during his court-approved weekend visitation] has to go through the courts or through law enforcement."

Sheri Kay turned to her father for help with her legal bills. With his approval, she hired Lawrence Henke, an older Dayton attorney, to represent her in her divorce from Steve. However, the attorney eventually withdrew from her case, writing to Sheri Kay complaining about her hostile behavior.

Sheri Kay responded to Henke's letter by calling him, saying, "You had better get off your ass and start working for us instead of Mr. Moody!" Sheri Kay then hung up the telephone on him, fuming that Henke had sold her out.

Finally, on May 2, 1991, after the parties had filed numerous motions regarding child support, visitation, real and personal property appraisals, and a host of other issues, the court began the final hearing to resolve the various pending motions and issue the parties' decree of divorce. After an unheard-of twenty-four witnesses testified over four hearing days, which stretched out over several months, the judge finally signed a divorce decree, effective August 31, 1992.

That didn't stop the fighting.

––––––––

Sheri Kay did her best to sabotage her children's relationship with their father. On one occasion, she claimed the kids had pink eye and couldn't visit with Steve under the directive of a physician. No doctor's orders ever came to light, and Scott even went to school the following Monday.

According to Steve's attorney, writing in a letter to Sheri Kay, "I want to assure you that Steve intends to make certain that every right to which he is entitled under the Local Court Rules, under the Decree of Divorce, and the laws of the State of Ohio, are complied with by you in their entirety. There will be no more warnings; if you disobey any further order of the Court, the next step will be a contempt citation."

The problems continued.

In early 1993, Sheri Kay attempted to file criminal charges against Steve for sexual abuse of then three-year-old Stacy.

After Children Services investigated Sheri Kay's complaint, they responded, "Dear Sherri [sic], In speaking with Detective Kelly with the Logan County Sheriff's Office, he informed me that unless we have a better statement of the incident by Stacy, the charges are likely to be dropped."

A few months later, Steve contacted Children Services for help with visitation. Courthouse observers didn't hesitate to offer an opinion: "There is simply no end in sight to halt the battle between these two parties."

Children Services notified the Court: "Dear Judge O'Connor: The defendant, Steven Moody, has twice contacted this agency regarding visitation on July 26 and again on August 9. Plaintiff, Sheri Moody, has not contacted the agency to date. Therefore, the agency has been unable to arrange for the ordered two supervised visits."

Subsequently, court-ordered supervised visits took place. According to Children Services, "Overall, the parental child interaction, although strained by the restricted environment, seemed nurturing and healthy. No areas of concern were noted which would be sufficient enough to warrant discontinuing supervised visits."

————

Without an education, Sheri Kay had few job skills. The farm that had sustained her family for generations found itself facing new challenges. After Steve Moody (and his labor) left and Sheri Kay discovered that child support didn't go very far, she began a habit of applying for menial paying jobs, then quitting within a few weeks. That continued for years until she finally landed a job that paid well, or at least better than minimum wage, with the state's transportation department. Just as things started to look up, a car crash resulted in a shoulder separation that left her in long-term chronic pain and forced her into disability.

When she finally returned to work, one of her evaluations from the Ohio Department of Transportation (ODOT) had a couple of unsatisfactory remarks: "I do not feel Sheri is doing the amount of work I expect of her. She has in the past refussed [sic] to do a job (mowing) I asked her to do. In some of her other jobs she tends to stand around and let other people do the job for her."

Regarding Team Effort and Cooperation, "Sheri is not getting along with some of our people because of her refusall [sic] to do a job and the fact that she does not jump in and help on many of her other jobs. I receive many complaints often about her cooperation. I counceller [sic] her after she refused to mow and she took an extended lunch."

On one occasion, Sheri Kay filed an interesting response: "I have a problem with this because I believe he is basing this evaluation on hearsay, not on what he has witnessed for himself." She laid out her defenses, but one paragraph stood out: "I was assigned to mow at State Routes 68 and 508. In the past I had an altercation with an ex-employee's wife who has threatened me with bodily harm if I was ever seen near her home.

"At the time I had notified my superiors of the situation and was informed by them if I felt threatened or afraid if asked to work in the mentioned area I was to say something about it and I would not be held in disfavor."

In December 1994, at age twenty-six, another car struck Sheri Kay's vehicle in the rear end. She returned to the emergency room again and again with pain in her right shoulder. The physicians eventually diagnosed her with soft tissue injury with cervical strain, or strain to her neck, and she saw a neurosurgeon from January through March of 1995. Between emergency room visits and treatments, she racked up $5,722 in medical bills. She sued the driver who'd hit her and won, but she spent months on pain pills. Unfortunately, when her doctors refused to prescribe more, she learned that she could easily find drugs elsewhere.

Sheri Kay continued to stay angry and resentful of her ex-husband, especially after Steve Moody remarried and moved on. His new wife, Audrey, brought two children to their marriage, including a daughter named Nikki who grew close to Sheri Kay's daughter Stacy. Audrey and Steve Moody would go on to have three more sons.

———

Sheri Kay's frequent drug use, a stream of male visitors, and occasional visits from the police grew more and more obvious to her grandmother who lived right down the road. Saddened by Sheri Kay's behavior, on September 9, 1994, Wilma Buroker finally signed her new Last Will and Testament, written to keep her daughter Sharyl and granddaughter Sheri Kay from selling the farm. Wilma died seven months later on July 15, 1995, at peace because she'd done all she could for her family, especially her great-grandchildren.

———

The Logan County Probate Court appointed Wilma's daughter, Sharyl Shafer, as executor of her estate. She, in turn, hired the one who'd drawn up the will, Wilma's attorney Howard Traul, to assist her in administrating her mother's affairs.

Wilma's estate originally contained approximately 475 acres spread out over eleven parcels, including a residential property located in Bellefontaine. Although at one time the land was valued at more than two million dollars, disputes came up regarding the appraisals of the property for estate tax purposes. The original appraisal for all the properties came in at $834,110, less than the Logan County Auditor had the properties assessed for taxation purposes.

Sharyl failed to correct these important issues in a timely manner. As a result of her negligence, she was late in filing the estate's Ohio Estate Tax Return, which was due nine months after the date of death. (Later, the tax return was amended and the family paid $33,915.06 in additional taxes and penalties.)

Frustrated with her mother's struggles in handling Wilma's estate, and because of her need for money, in January 2001 Sheri Kay started researching all of Wilma's properties, wanting to know their correct values. Finally, in February she contacted an attorney in Columbus regarding the possibility of representing her interests in Wilma's estate in probate court. Sheri Kay now had real concerns about the estate gifts due to herself and her children and how her mother, Sharyl, was failing to handle her duties.

The Columbus attorney referred Sheri Kay to a probate litigation attorney, but before doing so she carefully explained to Sheri Kay the situation regarding life estates. The attorney was careful to explain, "Your interest in a life estate in one-half of the property occurs when your mother and then your father (who has a successive life estate in one-half of the property) dies or your father remarries. After your death, your two children together receive one-half of the farm, what you and your father had. After your parents' death (or the remarriage of your father), the other half of the farm goes to fund the trust your grandmother created by her Last Will and Testament."

Sheri Kay spread out her court papers over her kitchen table and then began researching legal terms in her borrowed library books, searching for definitions of "tenant," "transfer of interest of a deceased survivorship tenant," "sale of entailed and other estates," "recording and filing notices of federal tax liens," "purchase of tax certificates," "delinquent tax contracts," "valuation of qualified farm property," and anything else she thought might be helpful.

In the spring of 2002, Sheri Kay hired another attorney, Terrence Flahive, to initiate a lawsuit and represent her interests in Wilma's estate.

She told others, "It's time to finally do something if I ever want to see my money."

Because Sharyl Shafer had failed to file an account with the probate court when required, Attorney Flahive wrote a letter to Attorney Howard Traul asking for an explanation for the failure to file an account in a timely manner with the court. Traul responded to Flahive stating, "Sharyl Shafer could not find various monthly checking account statements and had made several deposits into the estate checking account but didn't remember the source of those deposits."

Sheri Kay didn't care; long ago she'd lost sympathy for her mother's problems.

In May 2002, Sheri Kay filed a motion with the court seeking the removal of her mother as the fiduciary of the estate "on the grounds that the beneficiary [Sheri Kay] believes that numerous items in the Last Will and Testament of Wilma F. Buroker have not been complied with and that this estate has been going on for seven years without any of the wishes of Wilma F. Buroker being complied with."

With Sheri Kay's motion to remove her mother as the fiduciary of Wilma Buroker's estate still pending, on September 5, 2003, Sharyl Shafer, as executor, filed a "complaint" with the court seeking help with interpretation of the will and instructions on how the assets of Wilma' estate should be distributed.

Several months later, Sheri Kay lost all patience with her mother and the court. In a "To Whom it May Concern" letter filed with the probate court, Sheri Kay complained that distribution of the assets from Wilma Buroker's estate had still not happened. Further, she claimed that the estate's executor (her mother) had not paid the federal or state estate taxes, although Wilma had died in 1995.

As Sheri Kay explained, "The parties involved in the control and distribution of [the estate] are committing illegal acts and misuse." Sheri Kay alleged that her mother, Sharyl Shafer, was "not carrying full replacement insurance on the properties, does not repair or take care of the buildings on the properties, has failed to pay all real estate taxes, including more than $20,000 in back taxes, and has committed waste [neglecting the buildings, failing to plant crops], thereby forfeiting her life estate."

According to Sheri Kay, one of the tenants owed two years of back rent at $350 per month, another sign that her mother had failed to manage the estate properly. A spreadsheet would show eleven parcels with a 1995 valuation by the county auditor of $836,090, but a new 2004 evaluation of $1,213,650, an appreciation of $377,560.

Sheri Kay wanted to know: "When would the estate be settled!?"

———

In early 2005, the parties finally agreed on a resolution and entered into an Agreed Judgment Entry to distribute the assets of the estate in the following manner: The court's entry set aside $375,000 for the establishment of the Logan County Education

Foundation, which would start no later than December 31, 2007, requiring the sale of land.

The residential property located in the City of Bellefontaine would go on sale with an agreed lowest-sale price of no less than $50,000. The residential and farm property located at 2285 State Route 47 West, consisting of 115 acres, would go on sale with a minimum price of no less than $300,000. Sheri Kay's home, located at 1882 State Route 47 West, consisting of a house, barn and adjacent one acre, would go on sale with a minimum sale price of no less than $90,000. Sheri Kay had the first right of refusal to purchase her home, and she had until April 1, 2005, to do so.

As all this dragged on, Sheri Kay's second marriage unraveled. She had married Steve Wolfe in 1998, but they divorced in October 2003.

Looking back, Sheri Kay realized that over the past few years she had raised two children, Scott and Stacy – even in her own late adolescence, survived family fights over her grandmother's estate, struggled with two accidents and her subsequent drug use, watched the decline of the family farm, faced career struggles, endured through some "maybe-a-mistake" relationships, and now two failed marriages. But the kids had turned out fairly well, or so Sheri Kay thought. Both had friends in school, stayed active in Future Farmers of America events and 4-H clubs, continued the family history of raising show animals, and exhibited their carefully bred milking cows at the Logan County and Ohio State fairs. Both visited their grandparents whenever they chose and their father and his new family on more occasions than she wanted.

Stacy, at age fourteen, looked like a typical athletic teenager, with long blond hair she parted in the middle and a too-tight sweater that didn't hide her beautiful figure, while Scott, with his short, dark hair, lack of interest in fashion, and muscular build, mostly looked like a regular kid. To Sheri Kay's mind, she'd done a good job as a parent, especially since she had needed to deal with so many issues all their lives.

––––––

In April 2004, with all of Wilma's estate problems still pending in probate court, Sheri Kay and her second husband Steve Wolfe had their own post-divorce problems. Wolfe had failed to remove his personal property from Sheri Kay's house, and he kept calling her about getting his belongings and money that he thought he was owed. Finally, Sheri Kay went to the Logan County Sheriff's Office seeking a restraining order to keep Steve Wolfe from entering her house without her permission and bothering her in any way.

Sara Wolfe, Steve Wolfe's daughter, had been close to Sheri Kay. Although Steve Wolfe and Sheri Kay divorced in early 2003, Sara continued to live in Sheri Kay's house until she graduated from high school that spring. Sara enjoyed living with Sheri Kay, and she became a good stepsister to Stacy and Scott. In fact, on the back of her senior picture she wrote to Sheri Kay: "Mom, Hey! I know that we don't see that much of each other, but I still love you! I'm sorry for everything that I have put you through. I love you! And I miss you so much. You always will be my mother especially over my mom. I love you! -L- Sara."

But it didn't take long for Sheri Kay to ruin yet another relationship. In another note written by Sara a few months later, she describes another side of Sheri Kay: "Kay, I'm just going to tell you that you have no FUCKING idea what you are doing to your own daughter [Stacy]. She is laying in her bed crying and you expect me not to ask her what is wrong? That is fucking shallow. Since I came back I have been through nothing but

HELL! Why don't you grow the hell up and face your problems like an adult? I don't care if you do get mad, take care of your daughter! Sara."

———

On May 10, 2005, Logan County Children Services notified Sheri Kay that Scott's child support would be terminated on May 29 because of his graduation from high school and the fact that he had turned eighteen. Steve Moody's child support for Stacy would be set at $128.04 per month, effective June 1, 2005.

It would never be paid.

Chapter Five

When asked, Sutherly explained to the detectives that he had slept with Sheri Kay in her bed last night. Then, without prompting, that reminded him of something else: "The reason I originally started wandering over to Sheri Kay's house was because of Stacy. I wanted to date Stacy." Because fifteen-year-old Stacy refused his advances, he decided to start seeing her mom.

– Jason Sutherly, age twenty-five, one of Sheri Kay Shafer's casual boyfriends

Sheriff Henry knew from the moment he got the call about this unimaginable tragedy that he would need to put all his department's resources on the case. In his rush out the door that Sunday morning, he immediately began formulating a plan. When he arrived at the scene, he found Jon Stout already on site conducting an investigation. Stout, the department's most experienced detective and rising star, had a great track record, including a knack for breaking up drug deals. In addition, he'd recently broken up one of the largest chop shop operations ever seen in Ohio. The sheriff figured that Stout could wrap this case up quicker than anyone.

Stout and the rest of the investigators concluded among themselves almost right away who did it and what happened, and Sheriff Henry soon concurred, but rumors of all kinds spread. Within minutes of arriving at the scene, the sheriff faced a media circus.

Sheriff Henry needed to piece together the horrors of Saturday night and the early hours of Sunday morning. Stacy, in a half-lucid moment, claimed that some stranger did it, a statement the detectives quickly dismissed as unlikely and unbelievable, but they needed to conduct the right interviews and establish Scott's motive to close the door on any speculation that someone else, some unknown psychopath, haunted the community and might randomly commit another atrocity. All the detectives from the Logan County Sheriff's Office would have their work cut out for them.

The detectives' division at the sheriff's office consisted of seven officers headed by Detective Sergeant Jeff Cooper. Sgt. Cooper understood Sheriff Henry's instructions for that critical Sunday so he dispatched one detective to Columbus to talk to Stacy's doctors, interview her family, obtain her medical records and, if possible, obtain Stacy's statement. Cooper assigned other detectives to coordinate with Ohio's Bureau of Criminal Identification & Investigation (BCI), log evidence, and disseminate information. He ordered Detective Stout to continue to conduct interviews, partnering with Mike Brugler, a new detective still on probation. This would give Brugler a chance to learn from the best. The sole remaining officer in the department would have responsibility for everything else that happened that Sunday in Logan County.

After Detectives Stout and Brugler surveyed the crime scene at Sheri Kay Shafer's house, they interviewed Stacy's stepsister, Nikki Vagedes. She reiterated that she had received a phone call from Stacy that morning. She went on to describe their room-by-room findings when she and Jeff first arrived at Sheri Kay's home. She added that Stacy told her that she didn't know what had woken her up, but when she did wake up, she said, "There was an older guy with gray hair standing there with a gun, and I tried to push the gun out of the way."

Stout seemed to dismiss Stacy's comment; he knew he needed more information from Stacy, but he wouldn't be able to get it until her medical condition improved and her doctors permitted her to be interviewed. Now he wanted to focus his attention on Nikki's relationship with the victims and learn about the family dynamics. As Nikki explained to the detectives, Scott and Stacy didn't get along with their father, Steve Moody, or with Nikki's mother, Audrey, who had married years earlier. But Nikki thought of someone else who might be important, Sheri Kay's current boyfriend, Dave Cusic.

The detectives called Cusic and asked him to come to Bellefontaine as soon as possible to answer their questions.

Once Stout and Brugler completed a final walk-through of Gary and Sharyl Shafer's home, they talked to tenants, neighbors, and curiosity seekers who had gathered at the property. Apparently, the detectives were not short on people to interview as many were well acquainted with the family. Stout and Brugler quickly conferred and decided it would be best to continue taking statements at the sheriff's office later that afternoon. They told everyone at the scene that if anyone had any information to please come down to the sheriff's office later that afternoon to give a statement.

————

When Stout and Brugler returned to the sheriff's office that Sunday afternoon, they found Dave Cusic waiting for them with a ready alibi: He had spent Saturday night at home with his wife. Cusic had lived with his girlfriend for approximately eighteen years, speaking of her as his "wife." She knew nothing of Cusic's fling with Sheri Kay.

In a taped interview, Cusic explained his relationship with Sheri Kay. They had met three years ago through a mutual friend while buying and selling cattle. Sheri Kay recently helped him out financially by hiring him to work the farm and remodel her home.

"Sheri Kay was a close family friend as were our children," Cusic offered. "Our relationship evolved after spending so much time together," he added. "Plus, she was sexy."

Cusic said about Sheri Kay, "We always got along together; we never had the slightest of any disagreements."

According to Cusic, he last saw Sheri Kay the previous Friday evening, May 27, around 6:00 p.m. when they sat at her kitchen table and shared a beer. They kissed a little and made small talk. She mentioned that she had just gotten approved for a loan to buy her share of the farm and she seemed genuinely excited. After he left, she called him on his cell phone and reminded him that he had to pick up flowers for his wife's mother's funeral.

The detectives turned to the subject of Scott. Cusic claimed that he and Scott had always gotten along, but Scott sometimes seemed a little "backward." And no, he didn't know of any problems between Scott and his mother or with his grandparents. Yes, they had some shotguns inside the house; he knew that because he and his family hunted together during deer season, but he hadn't heard of Scott or anybody else owning a .22 caliber rifle and he had never seen one inside of Sheri Kay's home.

Cusic said he had called Sheri Kay's cell phone sometime between 10:30 and 11:00 Sunday morning to remind her that he couldn't attend Scott's graduation that afternoon because of his wife's mother's funeral.

"Stacy answered the phone," he said, "but she was incoherent."

Cusic could tell something was wrong, but he attributed it to their late night graduation party.

He could hear in the background that Stacy was also talking to someone else on her own cell phone, which made it more difficult to understand her.

Cusic said he hung up with Stacy and tried calling Gary Shafer's cell phone several times to see if he knew what was going on, but he never got an answer. He then called Stacy back on her cell phone and asked for her mom. Stacy, in a raspy voice, simply told him that her mother was in bed, nothing more.

Cusic needed a drink of water before answering any more questions. After a brief pause, he continued. "I hung up again with Stacy and I kept trying to call Sheri Kay's cell phone. Finally, Nikki's boyfriend answered, 'really panicky,' and told me 'it was bad, and I might want to come up as soon as possible.'"

The next time he spoke to anybody, he insisted, came after the sheriff's office called him and told him to come in ASAP for an interview.

"Hey, I still had no idea what happened. Me and my wife were at a friend's cookout Saturday night in New Martinsburg," Cusic declared, "from around six until one or two in the morning. We were together the entire time. After we left the cookout, we went straight home and went to bed." According to Cusic, that's all he knew.

Detectives would later calculate the drive time from New Martinsburg to Sheri Kay's house: one hour and fifteen minutes. As other leads developed, they would learn more about Dave Cusic and his dealing in drugs.

With the interview concluded, Dave Cusic hurried out of the station.

One of the patrolmen at the blocked-off intersection of State Route 47 and County Road 32 radioed Cooper. "I've got a man here, Jason Sutherly, who says he was at the Shafer house last night."

Cooper looked at Stout and told him to go talk to the man. Stout drove the mile to the intersection, introduced himself to Sutherly, and asked him to go to the sheriff's office for the interview.

At 4:00 that afternoon, detectives began taping their interview of Jason Sutherly, age twenty-five. He said that about a year ago he'd become involved with one of the renters on the farm, Misti Martin, who was John Martin's daughter. John, who leased the land behind Sheri Kay's home, had lived with Sheri Kay off and on for a few years, but things never worked out between them. They remained friends, and his daughter Misti now rented one of the Shafers' farmhouses.

Eventually, Jason Sutherly soon moved in with Misti, his new girlfriend, and he quickly became friends with the grandparents, Gary and Sharyl Shafer, as well as with Sheri Kay and her kids. Sutherly thought Stacy was cute and often stopped by to say hello to the family. After a short period of time, Sutherly and Misti Martin split up.

The detectives listened patiently as Sutherly explained that Sheri Kay had called him Saturday night wanting to know if he would like to go out to dinner with her. He said sure, and around five-thirty he and Sheri Kay went to the Red Lobster in Lima, about thirty miles away. Afterwards, they went to a local Wal-Mart to get Scott a graduation card. While shopping in the store, they got a call from Scott and Stacy telling them that they'd invited a few kids from the graduation celebration to come back to their house.

According to Sutherly, Sheri Kay had a reputation as a "cool mom," meaning that she let the kids party. She would buy beer for the kids, but she would never let anybody leave if they'd had too much to drink.

When Sutherly and Sheri Kay arrived at her house, Scott said a few of them were hungry, so Sutherly and Sheri Kay left for Wendy's to pick up some burgers and then stopped at a beer and wine carry-out for a case of beer.

Stout asked Sutherly, "Who was there Saturday night?"

"As far as I know, there was Sheri Kay, her two kids Scott and Stacy, and Scott's girlfriend, Paige [Harshbarger]. There was another girl there, a girl Scott was graduating with, and some other guy I think the kids went to school with. Around midnight, some other guy showed up that Stacy invited. He was a farmer from Urbana. He was driving a real nice Dodge truck outfitted with smokestacks."

Sutherly said he didn't remember his name but said that he seemed like a real nice guy.

"He came in late, and as soon as he arrived, Stacy and that guy went upstairs to Stacy's bedroom." He added that later Scott and his girlfriend went up to another bedroom and he thought that the other two kids passed out downstairs on two of the couches.

Detective Brugler encouraged him to continue.

Sutherly said that he and Sheri Kay stayed up until three or 3:30 in the morning and then he decided to leave. He walked past the living room where Megan Karus was asleep on the loveseat and Scott's friend Bret Davidson was sprawled on the couch. The recliner was empty. Sutherly thought Scott and his girlfriend had stayed upstairs.

"The other guy that showed up to be with Stacy was still with her in her bedroom," he said.

Sutherly explained to the detectives that he had slept with Sheri Kay in her bed last night. Then, without prompting, that reminded him of something else: "The reason I originally started wandering over to Sheri Kay's house was because of Stacy. I wanted to date Stacy." Because fifteen-year-old Stacy refused his advances, he decided to start seeing her mom.

When he was getting ready to leave, Sheri Kay walked him downstairs to the side door. At the time, she was wearing jeans, shoes and a low-cut, long-sleeve white shirt.

The detectives brought up the question of guns in the house. Sutherly didn't remember seeing any guns. No, he hadn't shot any weapons recently. Nobody in the house had shot any guns that night.

Did he remember any history of them having guns?

Sutherly had to think. During the time he had lived with Misti Martin, Sheri Kay had given two handguns to Misti's father, John Martin, because while going through her divorce, "Sheri Kay was concerned that her then-husband, Steve Moody, might come in and shoot her in her sleep."

Sutherly had only seen those two weapons, the two handguns given to Martin, although he knew that Sheri Kay's father Gary Shafer had some guns.

Sutherly paused, then continued talking about the evening. "There were no problems at the party that night. It was kind of a last minute thing. Scott's official graduation party wasn't scheduled until June 18. Everyone was just kicked back and having a good time. We were all having a good time riding the four-wheeler out back."

Brugler asked if Sutherly had ever visited the inside of the grandparents' house.

Sutherly nodded. "Yes, when I was living with Misti." He remembered that "they kept their house locked up tight, they kept everything secured."

"What time did the grandparents do the milking?"

Sutherly thought for a moment, then explained, "As far as Gary, he would try to be out in the barn by six in the morning, but neither of them really had a set schedule."

Sutherly was distraught about what had taken place. He said that when he left about 3:30 that morning everyone was asleep. Regarding the drinking, Sutherly said, "As far as I know, Sheri Kay didn't have a drop. I had two beers at supper. I think I saw Scott take two swigs out of his girlfriend's beer."

Sutherly offered that Paige had gotten intoxicated. "She had slurred speech and all that." He thought Stacy might have gotten drunk, too, but not as badly as fourteen-year-old Paige.

Earlier, when they had returned from town with the burgers and beer for the party, Sutherly saw Scott's friend, Bret Davidson, sick on the floor, passed out. "He must have got up and moved to the couch at some point because he was on the couch when I left."

Detective Brugler asked what they did that night and Sutherly talked about the four-wheeler. Scott took it out first; several rode on it. Paige kept wanting Sutherly, not Scott, to take her on rides. He asked Scott if he minded his girlfriend riding with him, but Scott said it was okay. When the four-wheeler started to get low on fuel, Scott put it away.

Then the detectives came to the real question: Did Sutherly know any reason why Scott would go on a killing rampage?

Sutherly hesitated. "Personally, no." However, Sheri Kay had once told him that Scott could blow up at any time and that he had a very hot temper, like his dad. But Sutherly insisted that Saturday night Scott seemed excited about graduating, although his girlfriend might have made him a little upset.

"She was a lot to handle. She was really drunk," he said.

Had Scott had too much to drink?

"No. Scott told me he did not want to walk down the aisle at graduation with a hangover."

The detectives asked about drugs.

Sutherly shook his head and replied that when he and Sheri Kay returned from dinner, the kids had a bottle of vodka out. "The kids ran out of beer, so we went into town and got them a case of Bud Light from the Oasis."

Sutherly knew that Sheri Kay had been dating another guy by the name of Dave Cusic for the last year-and-a-half or so. "I've never met the guy. Although he scares me. He's in to drugs, big time. He's probably a dealer. This guy is pretty rough. He has another woman that he just had a baby with. In fact, he just started accusing Sheri Kay of messing around with other people. Sometimes I worried for her safety."

Stout asked Sutherly, again, to explain what time he left and what time he got home. Sutherly repeated that he got home about 3:30 that morning. When he arrived, he turned off his alarm system and then he slept until noon. He finally got up and cooked some steak for breakfast, and then he got a phone call telling him the news.

Chapter Six

He's not the person I thought would flip their lid. I thought it would be Gary [Shafer]. I do know that Scott was doing something drug-wise. I know when I lived there, Scott would be fine one day and not the next. But I still don't believe that Scott could have had that kind of rage in him.

– Steve Wolfe, Sheri Kay Shafer's second and former husband, who lived with the family for six years until their divorce in 2003

After Detectives Stout and Brugler completed their interview with Jason Sutherly, the sheriff requested that they come into his office so that he could learn the status of their interviews. He had one main question. The graduation ceremony was over. He planned to announce at seven that evening that he'd closed the case. He was naming Scott as the perpetrator. Had they found anything that meant he shouldn't do that? They updated him on their interviews and what they had learned.

Sheriff Henry grimly rubbed his eyes. He didn't want to deal with the countless phone calls for days and weeks on end from scared citizens who saw shadows lurking. If his team had solved the case, he wanted to wrap up this nightmare.

An officer knocked on the door to inform the detectives that Steve Wolfe, one of Sheri Kay's former husbands, was waiting in the hallway to speak with them. Stout and Brugler glanced at the sheriff, then got up to leave.

————

The detectives brought Wolfe into the institutional interview room, sat him down on one of the steel chairs, the one that didn't rock, offered him coffee, explained about the recorder, thanked him for voluntarily coming in, and started in with a few background questions.

Wolfe shifted in his seat, took a deep breath, and explained that he and Sheri Kay had married in 1997 and divorced in 2003. They didn't have any kids together. After their divorce, Wolfe described his relationship with Sheri Kay as rough at first, but now he described it as "friendly."

He seemed to grow a little nervous as he recounted that recently he'd broached the subject of what she still owed him from their divorce, some $15,000 in cash and other property. The last time they spoke, approximately four months ago, she'd agreed to begin settling things.

He waited for some sort of a comment.

The two detectives nodded.

Nervous, Wolfe took another deep breath and went on. Because of where he lived, he'd always go by the two Shafer farmhouses on his way home from Bellefontaine, not that he tried to keep up with his ex or anything like that. Saturday night, while on his way home from a late movie with his girlfriend around 12:15 or 12:30 a.m., he drove past the Shafer homes and noticed a few lights on at Gary and Sharyl Shafer's house and all the lights on at Sheri Kay's. He saw someone riding a four-wheeler in Sheri Kay's driveway.

Detective Stout asked Wolfe if his female friend had spent the night with him last night. Wolfe said, "Yes, but she left this morning around 9:30 or 10:00."

Wolfe tended to monitor his police scanner and heard an operator earlier that morning calling for a med-flight from Sheri Kay's house. Wolfe called his friend John Martin to see if he or his daughter, Misti Martin, who rented one of the Shafer farm houses, knew what had happened. Martin told him that he had received a call earlier from Stacy, but he didn't think she or Sheri Kay had any problems.

The detectives listened with their faces professionally neutral. What did he know about the tragedy? As Scott's stepfather for so many years, what kind of an opinion had he formed about him?

Wolfe didn't seem to have expected the question. He paused and reflected. "He's not the person I thought would flip their lid. I thought it would be Gary [Shafer]. I do know that Scott was doing something drug-wise. I know when I lived there, Scott would be fine one day and not the next. He would get belligerent, mouthy and aggressive. Grandpa Gary acted that same way, but worse. I was always watching my back when I lived there."

Brugler asked if he'd seen any rifles or handguns in the house.

Wolfe said Sheri Kay had two handguns, but he didn't know anything about a .22 caliber rifle. "Grandpa Gary had all the guns."

Stout asked about the grandparents locking their house.

Wolfe replied, "They were all about keeping things locked."

After a long silence, Wolfe began to insist that he knew his ex-stepson Scott well. Wolfe had lived with Scott for six years until his divorce from Sheri Kay in 2003. Even after their marriage ended, Scott and Stacy had stayed close with his own two children. "They were here about a month ago, all playing board games," he said. Wolfe added that, ironically, his daughter Sara would have gone to the party, but she'd gone out of town last night. He hesitated, then adamantly declared that he didn't believe that Scott "could have had that kind of rage in him."

Shifting to a different subject, the detectives asked about the rumor of Scott's decision to quit seeing his father.

"You know how teenagers are. There wasn't any real animosity there."

Stout asked what caused Wolfe's divorce from Sheri Kay in 2003.

Wolfe seemed a lot less nervous and cautious as he moved onto safer topics. The split came about "mostly over money." But Wolfe put at least part of the financial blame on Sheri Kay's parents, Gary and Sharyl Shafer. "We were struggling with trying to keep her parents afloat," he said. "We shared the bills for the farm, but it got to the point where we were paying more than they were."

Wolfe said he could never understand the family's declining fortunes. The Shafer family had successfully raised shorthorn dairy cattle in Logan County for more than 150 years.

"Sheri Kay and I made a good living when we first had a herd, but milk prices went down, and things got a little tighter."

Over the past several years, the two Shafer farmhouses had come to look worn down and in disrepair. Wolfe thought sometime around 1997 the grandparents had quit paying real estate taxes on the farm, eventually running up $56,000 in arrears. However, the family had recently headed off foreclosure when they negotiated with the county treasurer for a payment plan that included selling off part of the farm, which was apparently valued at $1.3 million.

Wolfe doubted the official motive, that Scott couldn't handle the stress and was overwhelmed by family responsibilities.

Wolfe said that Scott wasn't worried about the future. Scott had "worked the ground" that spring, planting feed crops for the family's growing herd.

"At the time, they had twenty-two cows, and several of them were going to give birth in the next two or three months." Wolfe said Sheri Kay had taken out a loan to repair the tractor and planned on buying more cows.

Wolfe conceded that Scott and his grandparents may have disagreed over how to operate the farm, but he doubted it could have triggered such a violent reaction in Scott. Family disagreements over the farm "had been a thing for at least thirty years," he said.

He had never seen a rifle in the family home when he lived with Scott and his mother, and Scott had only a passing interest in hunting.

The detectives looked at each other, then agreed that they had no more questions.

Wolfe hesitated, unsure if he should ask, but he finally blurted out the thing that kept nagging him, the issue about the rifle. "Where did it come from?" he wondered.

————

As the air-evac helicopter transported Stacy to Columbus, Detective Robinson followed by car with orders to interview her once the physicians permitted it. He spoke with Stacy's father, Steve Moody, as they waited Sunday afternoon at the Ohio State University Medical Center to learn Stacy's prognosis.

Steve explained that the weekend before he had arranged to pick up Stacy for visitation, but no one answered the door when he arrived to get her. Wednesday night he and Audrey again went over to pick her up and, as before, no one answered the door or the phone.

According to Moody, "Stacy told us at different times that Dave [Cusic], Sheri Kay's then boyfriend, brought marijuana into the house."

Moody acknowledged that his relationship with Scott had deteriorated, and he had not seen Scott for two or three years for visitation.

Detective Robinson asked if he knew of any firearms in Sheri Kay's house.

Moody replied, "Not specifically, but they were hunters."

During the long afternoon in the hospital's waiting room, Audrey Moody, Steve's current wife and Stacy's stepmother, corroborated that in the past Stacy had come to their home for regular visitations, and that she and Steve saw Stacy for the last time a week before on Wednesday. They had tried to pick her up the weekend before, but no one came to the door or picked up the phone.

"We tried several times, but we never received an answer," she said.

According to Audrey, "Stacy has been under a lot of stress lately. Apparently, there has been a lot of yelling and fighting at Sheri Kay's home. There has been a lot of drinking and parties lately. Her mom was out of control."

Audrey said she knew of drugs in the house. She also said that Stacy had told her that Scott had been very angry at his mom the last couple of years, often cussing at her.

As the evening news caught their attention, the Moodys glanced up at a wall-mounted television in the waiting room. At 7:00 that evening, they watched Sheriff Henry begin his press conference and declare the case closed. "Simply put," the sheriff stated, "Scott was the gunman, the one responsible for this terrible tragedy."

However, the investigators still needed to wrap up their

paperwork with a few more interviews.

————

Detectives Stout and Brugler began the next day with John Martin's daughter, Misti Martin, age twenty-three. She had lived in one of the rental farmhouses across from Gary and Sharyl Shafer's home for several years.

According to Misti, she saw Gary and Sharyl Shafer walking to their house after milking their cows Saturday night at approximately 6:30 or 7:00 p.m. She spoke with Sheri Kay briefly on the phone at about 7:20 p.m. to verify that Sheri Kay would babysit Misti's son; however, Sheri Kay couldn't because things had come up with Scott's graduation.

At 10:05 Sunday morning, Misti missed a call from Sheri Kay's cell phone. When she played the message, Misti couldn't understand Stacy's hoarse whisper. She assumed Stacy had left the message as a joke, so Misti erased it. Shortly thereafter, she heard the sirens and went outside where neighbors congregated as they tried to figure out what had happened.

————

Melby Ober, age forty-nine, who lived in Cable, Ohio, came forward and volunteered to give a written statement to the detectives that he had met Sheri Kay six or eight years before. Sheri Kay had purchased thirty-two cows from him in 2003, agreeing to pay him $900 a month for five years on their $57,000 contract. According to Ober, she'd fallen six months behind on her payments; however, he did get a check from her on May 1, the first one he'd received from her in five months.

Sheri Kay had gotten a loan on Friday, May 27, and shared the news with him that she wanted to buy out her mother and father from the farm. Sheri Kay also mentioned that Scott planned to attend a diesel mechanic school after high school and that things were beginning to look optimistic. According to Ober, Sheri Kay never mentioned that Scott was stressed or unhappy about the future of the farm.

———

On Sunday evening, just as Sheriff Henry concluded his press conference to explain the timeline of the tragedy, Kelly Stevens called the sheriff's office stating that she thought she might have an important tip. She and her husband had driven past the Shafer homes that morning on their way to Mary Rutan Hospital in Bellefontaine.

Kelly explained to an officer that at approximately 10:42 Sunday morning, as she headed eastbound on State Route 47 following her husband, they approached Sheri Kay Shafer's house. A white male ran from the house toward the road. She gave an accurate description of him: approximately five feet nine inches tall, medium build, early 30s with a goatee, wearing a blue ball cap, a white tee-shirt with writing on it, and blue jeans. According to Kelly, the man nearly ran into the path of her husband's car, forcing him to slam on his brakes. The man stopped momentarily while the cars passed, then ran north across the road.

Kelly told the operator that as she and her husband approached the intersection of State Route 47 and County Road 32, she saw a marked sheriff's car running with its lights and sirens on, traveling westbound on State Route 47. She later heard of the shootings and wanted to call and report what she had seen.

On Monday morning, May 30, Detectives Stout and Brugler conducted a taped interview with Kelly Stevens. She explained what she had seen the previous morning. She said it had seemed strange at the time, but she hadn't thought too much about it. After she got to work, she learned of the shootings. Later that evening, when talking with her husband, they realized the shootings had taken place in the house they saw the man fleeing. They thought it odd because of the timing and that the man appeared to have run from the rear of the house toward the roadway.

The detectives explained to her that the sheriff's office received the call of the shootings at 10:44 Sunday morning from Stacy's stepsister, Nikki. During that time, she couldn't remember the address of the house and told her boyfriend to run outside to find the address on the mailbox. The detectives explained that Nikki's boyfriend had dark hair and a goatee. Based on the timeline, they concluded that she and her husband had seen Nikki's boyfriend running. Kelly agreed that it made sense.

———

Andrew Denny, age nineteen, was another piece of the puzzle as to who had been at Sheri Kay's house Saturday night for the kids' informal graduation party. Stout and Brugler interviewed him late Sunday afternoon.

According to Denny, Stacy had called him around midnight Saturday and wanted him to come over. Denny traveled from Xenia twenty miles away and arrived at Sheri Kay's home around 1:00 Sunday morning in his Dodge pickup truck, which was outfitted with distinctive smoke stacks.

When he got to the house, he met several people, but he didn't know anybody except Stacy until Scott came up to him and introduced himself. According to Denny, everybody seemed drunk except for Sheri Kay and her friend, Jason Sutherly. Denny told officers that he didn't see any problems with anybody and everybody just seemed to be having a good time. No one mentioned guns, and nobody shot any weapons during his time there. He was told that Megan Karus passed out around midnight and fell asleep on the loveseat.

"We hung out for a while and drank a couple of beers, and then me and Stacy went upstairs to her bedroom and 'made out.'"

Denny explained that he had to get up early because he and his father had work to do, so Stacy set the alarm clock for six o'clock. When it went off, said Denny, "Stacy hit the snooze button several times." He finally woke up around seven o'clock, running late.

Denny said that when he left, he walked out past closed bedroom doors, so he wasn't sure who was sleeping there. However, he remembered seeing Megan on a loveseat downstairs and a guy asleep on the big couch, but he didn't know his name. Nobody in the house seemed awake as he hurried out. He had to stop and think about the time he left, and finally figured he left around 7:15 Sunday morning.

––––––––

Was everyone now accounted for? Where was John Martin? Were the detectives missing something? Stout and Brugler knew there were inconsistencies in the witnesses' statements when compared to the homicide/suicide statement issued by the sheriff.

So, what needed to be changed so that these stories would come out straight? Unfortunately, the facts weren't falling into place as easily as some had hoped. Days after Sheriff Henry declared the case closed, the detectives sat down to list the inconsistencies in the various interviews.

Chapter Seven

*I played pool with him for – I don't know how
many hours – and he just acted like himself. I
know I'm lucky, I left . . . I could have ended up
dead like the rest of them.*

– Bret Davidson, age eighteen, one of Scott
Moody's closet friends, who spent the night after
the small party and left about an hour before
authorities believe the shootings began Sunday
morning

As soon as Sheriff Henry's evening press conference
ended its broadcast on national television, telephone
calls, faxes, and emails started pouring in with opinions,
suggestions, and comments. Many suggested that investigators
were too quick to reach judgment and should look for possible
motives, not only for Scott but for others as well. All had to be
taken seriously, to a point. In between their other duties, the
detectives had to read all the correspondence, and follow up on
some.

Sheriff Henry picked up an unusual one that had been
printed by one of his deputies. It came from Mara, a visionary
in Las Vegas.

"Okay," thought Sheriff Henry, "I'm game. Maybe she has
something of significance to offer."

Mara admitted that people tended not to take visionaries too
seriously, "yet this incident is very serious." She explained that
she had watched many events as a remote viewer and

clairvoyant. And, for whatever it's worth, she wrote that "she is a mother and grandmother."

"The young man Scott Moody," she offered. "It feels as if he was in a dilemna [sic] of sizeable proportions. The rifle seems to be a hunting rifle, probably deer. I sense other weapons around and more ammo than weapons. Some things in old trunks contain munitions of some sort. There may have been a conflict between Sheri Kay Shafer and the girl Megan Karus that included Scott Moody. It appears that he may have lost it, gone trigger-happy before he realized what was happening, looked at his sister and wounded her, left her to make the call, then went and shot the elder victims, back to the others where he knew his sister would survive, or he thought, then shot himself.

"It seems a conflict of wounds and weapons used. He may have looked for a hand gun to use on himself. From what it appears, he laid the victims out almost reverently. It also seems he may have had some water that he used to do some type of blessing that he crossed their foreheads with. He may have been into a group of some type. Perhaps gothic or something a bit different.

"It also seems they are not far from water, a body of water perhaps within the area."

Mara said that this was all that she saw for now, but she would look again later. She explained that "bits and pieces usually come in a little at a time, depending on the situation." However, if she saw anything else, she would let the sheriff know. She left her telephone number.

———

Rick Schott, identifying himself as a chemist and engineer, wrote to the detectives. "The Scott Moody murder-suicide has the earmarks of being caused by a psychiatric drug, such as Ritalin, Prozac or Zoloft. Recently, the FDA mandated a 'black box' warning on all prescriptions of SSRI's (the group of drugs including Prozac and Zoloft among others), warning that these drugs can cause teenagers to commit suicide."

The sheriff's office received scores of letters with advice, all striking this same common theme. "Your Moody case bears many similarities to a number of cases where the shooter was on or recently on an antidepressant like Prozac, Zoloft, Paxil, etc. The shooters at Red Lake and Columbine were on those drugs."

Ernest Ryan, another interested sleuth, wrote to Sheriff Henry that he had followed and investigated these types of murder-suicide cases since 1994. According to Ryan, "The trademark signature of this type of case is the senseless committing or attempting to commit murders of one's family, school mates or fellow employees. This is always followed by suicide or attempted suicide."

Some of the emails were not so helpful and offered more of a critique. From an anonymous email received by the sheriff's office shortly after Sheriff Henry's evening news conference:

"I WAS JUST A WITNESS TO THE MOST HORRIBLE SHOW OF A NEWS PRESS CONFERENCE GIVEN BY YOUR ELECTED SHERIFF THAT IS UN-MATCHED IN ALL NEWS VIEWING I HAVE EVER SEEN. YOU GOT 6-8 PEOPLE DEAD IN TWO SEPARATE FARMHOUSES AND THE IDIOT HAS TO GO GET HIS DALE EARNHARDT JR. CAP AND A TEE-SHIRT THAT LOOKS LIKE IT JUST CAME OUT OF THE WASH TO GO ON NATIONAL TELEVISION AND

*TRY TO EXPLAIN THE INCIDENT. HAD TO
GET HIS FIX ON I GUESS. WHERE IN THE
HELL ARE YOU PEOPLES' MORALS. BOY I
TELL YOU, YOU FARM GROWN EATIN'
BUCKEYE LOVING FOOLS ARE THE
WORST OF THE WORST. WHAT A GROUP
OF INDECENT JERK-OFFS . . . PLEASE
FORWARD THIS TO YOUR SO CALLED
BEST OF THE BEST SHERIFF. I
WOULDN'T ELECT, OR EVEN ASSOCIATE
WITH A LOW LIFE CALIBER PERSON
SUCH AS THAT . . . WHAT-SO-EVER. YOU
PEOPLE NEED TO GET A LIFE!!!!!!!!"*

———

After the press conference that Sunday night, Detectives Stout and Brugler drove over to the home of one of Scott Moody's closest friends, Bret Davidson. He'd taken many classes with Scott at Riverside High School and the two had teamed up in Future Farmers of America together. Both helped run their family dairy operations.

Sitting awkwardly in the family's small living room, eighteen-year-old Bret answered the detectives' questions, pausing now and then before he continued in a sometimes choked-up voice. He'd gone to Scott's house Saturday night to hang out and fell asleep around four in the morning. Megan Karus was passed out on the downstairs loveseat, so he took the couch. Yes, he felt pretty sure that at that time Jason Sutherly hadn't left yet and that he still remained upstairs. Bret said he woke up around six in the morning.

"I just shot right up. I woke up out of a dead sleep. It was kind of weird because I went to bed late."

Davidson said he tiptoed upstairs to tell Sheri Kay good-bye.

"She was asleep, but I whispered to her that I was going to get on home because I had chores to do. She got up and walked me to the door, unlocked it, and told me I was welcome to come back for breakfast later once I was done with my chores. She locked the door back up as I left. There was nothing wrong with anybody. Nothing weird."

Stout asked if he felt sure about the time he'd left.

"Yes," Bret said, "I looked at my cell phone."

"What about the Dodge pickup?"

Bret nodded. "Yes, it definitely was there. It had the smoke stacks."

Could he tell them any more about who slept where in the house?

Bret sat back and brushed a hand over his face, reflecting. When he went upstairs to wake Sheri Kay, her door was open. He thought Paige was in bed with Scott. He couldn't remember if anyone was in bed with Stacy. When Bret fell asleep, the guy driving the truck hadn't arrived. When he woke up, he saw the Dodge parked outside. Nobody was asleep in the recliner.

Bret explained that he, Scott, Paige and Stacy had gone to a couple of graduation parties Saturday evening and then went to Scott's house around 9:30 or 10:00 p.m.

"Everybody was fine. Everyone drank a few beers. Scott and Paige were okay, but Paige was hanging on me a little bit," he said.

Bret said that Scott didn't get mad.

The detectives asked if he'd had anything to drink. After a short hesitation, Bret said that he had two beers and then got sick.

As the questions trailed off, Bret sat up straight and stated emphatically that Scott couldn't have done this. "He wouldn't hurt his grandparents or his mother or sister." He went on that Scott showed no signs of feeling troubled in the days before graduation. "He rarely lost his temper and was generally quiet, except when he was talking about farming."

Bret insisted that Scott had not had any alcohol to drink at any of the graduation parties.

While at Bret's home, the detectives interviewed Lee Anderson, Bret's stepfather. Shaken and pale, he told them that when Bret showed up that morning he'd scolded his son for staying out all night without telling him, but he saw no signs that Bret had done any drinking.

"I told him he'd better get his butt moving," Anderson said. "He had bloodshot eyes, but he appeared to be normal when he got home. He appeared to have had a full night of sleep. He didn't appear to be anything but normal."

After Bret Davidson finished his chores that Sunday morning, the family had left for Cincinnati to watch the Reds play baseball.

———

On Monday, May 30, J.T. Splawn and his wife, Diana, arrived at the sheriff's office saying that they thought they could offer valuable information to the detectives. Ex-tenants of one of the farmhouses, they said they knew the family fairly well.

Diana Splawn explained to Detectives Stout and Brugler that she'd had several discussions with Scott where he stated that he wanted his grandma and grandpa dead.

She added, "Scott wasn't very fond of his mother either. Everyone was always fighting since Grandma and Grandpa kept the milk checks."

She paused. Stout nodded for her to continue.

She said that her son, Dustin, and Scott had stayed best friends until they moved out of the Shafer's rental house the previous summer. "Well, we then had a falling out with them." She explained, "Two years ago, Sheri Kay had a little party and got my kids drunk."

Did she know anything about the .22 rifle used in the killings?

She thought that the weapon belonged to Grandpa. "That was the gun Dustin and Scott went out hunting with." Because Scott was afraid of guns, "Grandpa would always keep all of the guns and ammunition at his house. The only gun Scott owned was a double barrel shotgun, but he was afraid to shoot it."

Detective Brugler asked if the grandparents kept any weapons at the barn.

Diana explained that her son Dustin stored his BB gun there.

J.T., Diana's husband, added that sometimes the Shafers had a .22 down at the barn to shoot rats.

Detective Stout asked, "Do you know what kind of .22 rifle it was?"

The couple looked at each other and shrugged. Diana said, "Dustin would know. He milked for them for three months before we moved out of there."

The detectives would never follow up in asking Dustin about the rifle.

Stout asked if she knew about any disputes concerning the property.

"It was a war, an all-out war," she said. Grandpa Gary Shafer and Sheri Kay got along to a certain point, but "Sharyl Shafer's mother [Wilma Buroker] left all of the property to Sheri Kay and that is why there's been this ongoing dispute." According to Diana, "Gary and Sharyl Shafer thought they should have gotten the farm since they worked it all those years."

"About the time we moved in, Sheri Kay found a bank that would lend her the money. No one was paying taxes on the farm. They weren't paid since her great-grandma [Wilma Buroker] died."

What caused the fights?

Diana snorted and answered in one word: milking. Gary and Sharyl Shafer refused to milk, and so did Sheri Kay. That left Dustin and Scott to do all the milking.

"Dustin and Scott were late last year several times for school. Dustin would stay and help Scott just to get it done," said Diana.

The detectives asked how Scott got along with his grandparents.

Diana answered that Scott hated his grandfather. Scott would come over to their house several times and say he "wishes the SOB would just drop dead."

In Diana's opinion, Scott had a love-hate relationship with his grandparents. They would go out and buy him something new and everything would be okay for a while, but Scott would end up destroying his gifts. "They bought a new mower. He would take it out and tear it up. He would spitefully tear up all of their equipment, ruin it. They would make him bail hay and he would tear up the equipment."

Diana went on, rambling, "Scott and Sheri Kay didn't get along very well, either. Scott would stay with his mom for a while and then get in to it with her and move in with his grandparents. He would get in to it with them and then move back in with his mom. If you ask me, they kind of tugged him back and forth. Mom would buy him a pickup truck and the grandparents would buy his graduation pictures."

"Interesting," Stout said in a bored tone.

Diana continued, "Stacy always stayed tight with her mom though."

Detective Brugler asked if Diana's son Dustin and Scott remained close.

Diana shook her head. "Oh no. Once they had a falling out, they were pretty much enemies, but Stacy and Dustin remained friends."

"You didn't like the family much now, did you?" Stout asked.

"Well, Gary Shafer had called the police and got J.T. [Diana's husband] arrested for lying. They were hateful and spiteful. They would lie at any cost."

Diana said that they'd rented Wilma Buroker's house after she passed. Sheri Kay always had them pay her the rent until Gary Shafer came over and demanded that the Splawns pay it to him.

J.T. Splawn interjected, "Grandpa would keep all the guns and ammo. If Scott had a gun, he had to go down to his grandpa's to get it. Scott probably blew up since he knew he was graduating and everyone was going to make him do all the work."

Diana agreed. "Stacy and Scott had a typical brother and sister relationship. Scott was sometimes jealous of Stacy due to her and Sheri Kay being so close. Scott would sometimes get mad at Stacy when she sided with her mother. When we first moved in, Scott basically lived with us. He didn't get along with his mom or grandparents, so he stayed with us."

"Thanks. That's all," Stout clipped, as he got up from the table and prepared to leave. There simply wasn't any credibility here.

The Splawns were surprised. They looked at each other. Just like that, the interview was over.

———

The detectives requested that the Logan County Children Services director provide any history of the victims and their families. A search of their records revealed that between May 1990 and February 1993, during one of the most contentious divorces to take place in the history of Logan County, the agency processed fifteen reports regarding Scott and Stacy Moody, their mother, Sheri Kay Shafer, and their father, Steven Moody, ranging from alleged child abuse and neglect to alleged sexual assault. No investigator ever substantiated any of the charges, but those old reports kept Steve Moody's name on the detectives' list of people of interest.

Then out of the blue, Detective Cooper received a telephone message from Cheryl Garland-Briggs, the director of New Directions, a local counseling service, stating that Sheri Kay Shafer had come to her office seeking counseling approximately three months before the tragedy because Scott Moody had been abusive. Sheri Kay worried that Scott might kill her and her daughter, Stacy.

Ms. Garland-Briggs thought that the detectives should know this, that it might be important. It certainly fueled the fire for Scott's motive.

Chapter Eight

One night we were all sitting at the kitchen table. Misti and Sheri Kay were talking about things Scott used to do when he was a kid. We were all laughing, but then he just blew up on us. Scott was laughing one minute and then just blew up the next. He would sometimes just blow up for no reason.

– Amanda Arthur, age eighteen, who dated Scott almost her entire senior year, breaking up with him just two weeks prior to graduation

Wanting to help with the ongoing investigation, others came forward. The detectives waded patiently through endless calls filled with speculative conversations about the family that so many in the community knew. Amanda Arthur, Scott's former girlfriend, and her parents met with detectives on Tuesday afternoon, two days after the tragedy.

Amanda explained that she had dated Scott almost her entire senior year, but they broke up two weeks prior to graduation because Scott started acting "really weird." She didn't feel comfortable with him anymore. She also had found someone else.

She shifted her weight awkwardly in the vinyl chair. "I found someone I felt happier with, someone that didn't make me feel as scared."

She explained, "One night we were all sitting at the kitchen table. Misti and Sheri Kay were talking about things Scott used to do when he was a kid. We were all laughing, but then he just blew up on us. Scott was laughing one minute and then just blew up the next. He would sometimes just blow up for no reason."

She recalled, "Thursday night before graduation, the school had a senior awards banquet. Scott was acting really strange. He was acting really withdrawn. Apparently, he was mad at his mother and Stacy."

When asked if Sheri Kay liked her, Amanda said that Scott's mom liked her a lot. It was his grandparents that didn't like her. "They thought Scott could do a lot better than me."

Detective Stout asked about guns in the house.

"There were some guns in the house," she nodded. "There was a gun in the corner by the microwave. It was a brown long gun."

"When was the last time you spoke to Scott?" Stout asked.

Amanda hesitated, then replied, "After graduation practice I talked with Scott, and he said he was happy with his new girlfriend, Paige. He said he was happy that I had someone else, too. He told me he just wanted to be friends and get along."

She paused and thought, then said that during the past year Scott had told her that his mom wanted to buy the farm, and he would own it when his mom passed away.

"He also told me he got along with his grandparents, but Scott did get into it with them sometimes because they were always wanting him to work."

She went on. "He had a lot of stress on him with the farm. His grandparents were always on him. They didn't want him to have a life outside of the farm. Some of the time he talked about killing himself.

"Scott always told me that if we ever broke up he was going to commit suicide. He would always say he was going to hurt himself and cut himself."

Amanda told the detectives that Scott had said several times that the world would be a better place without him. Just a few weeks before, when everyone went to Cedar Point, Amanda said, "Scott said what he'd always said, 'If you break up with me, I will hurt myself in some way,' but he always said he would never hurt me or his family because he loved us. He told me he would never end up like his dad because his dad cheated on his mom."

The detectives asked about Scott's routine.

Amanda explained, "Scott didn't milk in the morning. He always did it at night. But he hadn't done it for a while because he had hernia surgery. His grandma didn't want him to do anything due to his surgery. He did help out some, but not much."

Amanda said that Scott had changed. He hadn't acted like this when they first started dating. "Scott just became real emotional recently. Sometimes he would just blow up and other times he would call me crying for no reason."

Amanda's parents had also thought about Scott. They told the detectives about Thursday night's awards banquet where Scott appeared to be really withdrawn. They said Scott would keep putting his face in his hands. He would not eat.

———

Roger Tangerman was the last tenant living in one of the farmhouses that the detectives needed to interview. He willingly answered questions. Yes, he remembered Sunday morning vividly. It had seemed like a normal day, other than the lack of routine sounds that usually carried from Gary and Sharyl Shafer's place when they did their milking.

"You could have set your clock by what Gary and Sharyl were doing or places they were going, especially around milking time."

That day, he had put up some fencing while his live-in girlfriend Mary and her son were assembling a table and chairs in the yard. His own son was asleep inside. His daughter had just come outside when they heard the first sirens. As the sirens grew louder, they realized something was going on down at Sheri Kay's house. Unaware of exactly what was happening, they couldn't drive down to see because law enforcement vehicles were blocking the road. Tangerman ran inside to get his binoculars for a better look.

Until then, it had seemed like a typical Sunday morning. Tangerman stated that he and Mary went to bed around 11:30 Saturday night, later than usual because Mary's son came over to visit. They woke up around eight in the morning and Tangerman went outside by 8:30 or nine, later than normal for him. He never saw Gary or Sharyl that morning because by the time he made it outside they would already have returned to their house to eat breakfast.

According to Tangerman, Gary and Sharyl Shafer usually began milking around five or 5:30 in the morning and then again around 4:45 in the afternoon unless they had somewhere to go. They would usually finish milking in the morning around 7:30 or eight.

"It just depended on whether or not Scott was there to help with the milking." However, lately he had not seen Scott.

Tangerman said he had lived in the rental property for about seven months, since October 2004. He and Gary and Sharyl Shafer had always gotten along. Almost every night he would go down to the barn and visit with Gary. He thought of both of them as good friends.

"They were like a second set of parents. I never had any problems with Gary or Sharyl as landlords."

The detectives asked about Sheri Kay.

Tangerman explained that he never had any regular contact with Sheri Kay.

"She really never came down to the farm much except to visit with Misti Martin [John Martin's daughter] or her parents." Tangerman said that when he first moved in, he and Scott became friends. But as time went on, he said, "Scott quit hanging out as much and started hanging out with his friends more. Typical teenage behavior, I guess."

Tangerman added that he recently had a small run-in with Scott after Scott passed him in his truck and nearly ran him off the road. He later confronted Scott about the incident, but Scott and his friend got pretty mouthy with him.

"I didn't want any problems with him, but I told Gary and Sharyl about the incident. They said they would take care of the problem."

Tangerman said he never really heard Scott and Gary get into any arguments and described their relationship as typical. Gary never talked or complained too much about Scott. Tangerman paused, then continued saying that, of course, he would never ask about something that was none of his business.

Detective Stout wanted to know what kind of relationship Sheri Kay had with her parents.

Tangerman thought that they had a normal relationship, but he really didn't see Sheri Kay enough to comment further. Since her recent shoulder surgery, she didn't help much with the milking. He added that he heard rumors about Sheri Kay and her parents' relationship, but he didn't listen much to them.

"According to rumors, it sounded like Sheri Kay and her dad were getting along because they were working together, trying to get the farm's finances worked out."

"What about guns?"

Tangerman said that he'd seen Scott doing some shooting in the past using shotguns he kept for deer hunting. He didn't know of Scott having a .22 caliber rifle, but it wouldn't surprise him if he did have one to go groundhog hunting.

After a moment of silence, Tangerman volunteered that it was his and his family's opinion that they didn't believe Scott did the shooting because of the way it happened.

"I know things might have been bad, but I don't believe Scott would've taken out his entire family."

Tangerman said, thinking back, that he remembered early Sunday morning looking out his front window and seeing a car pull into Gary and Sharyl's driveway. Two men got out. One went to the front door of the house to knock, the other, a gray-haired man, went around the side of the house, toward the barn. Tangerman thought it a little unusual because the second man was wearing only a tee-shirt and it still felt a little chilly out that morning.

Tangerman went into his kitchen for a few moments to make himself a cup of coffee. When he returned to his living room, he looked outside and noticed only one of the men getting back into the car and leaving the Shafer's home.

Yes, he felt certain. Only one man got back into the car and left. Tangerman didn't know if the men had gotten lost and needed directions, but it seemed strange. He recalled that he thought he might have seen one of the men at the funerals. "He could have just been a family member."

The detectives never asked what time he saw the men at Gary and Sharyl Shafer's home, nor did they follow up with Tangerman, looking for more details.

———

It had been a long three days for Steve and Audrey Moody – camped in the hallway outside of Stacy's hospital room in Columbus at the Ohio State University Medical Center – listening to doctors expressing their opinions about Stacy's prognosis and her intensive care treatment, answering questions from the police, being constantly interviewed by members of the local and national press, and worrying about their own three young boys back home in De Graff. They thought it couldn't get any worse.

Chapter Nine

Stacy, lying in her hospital bed with her head and face wrapped in white bandages, had started talking, even if in a raspy voice. According to her taped interview with detectives, when asked who shot her, Stacy replied: "The man had short gray hair and was wearing a blue shirt."

– Stacy Moody, three days after the shootings, being interviewed by detectives in her hospital room at the Ohio State University Medical Center

S teve and Audrey Moody didn't know how much longer they could keep up this pace. Exhaustion was overcoming them, traveling back and forth from the hospital in Columbus to their home in De Graff, an hour away, several times each day for the past three days, tending only to urgent family matters requiring their immediate attention.

That night, June 1, detectives from the Logan County Sheriff's Office finally would interview Stacy. That afternoon, Steve returned to De Graff to attend Scott's funeral, leaving Audrey at the hospital by herself to watch over Stacy. Alone and tired, Audrey reflected on that past Sunday, three days ago, knowing that many lives would be changed forever.

"That day was like a puzzle, all the pieces were there but we couldn't put them together."

Audrey thought of her relationship with Steve and his two

children, Scott and Stacy, remembering how difficult the past several years had been. Steve and Sheri Kay Shafer were married in August 1985. Scott was born in August 1986 and Stacy three years later, in September 1989.

Audrey recalled their long, nasty divorce, which was full of accusations and mudslinging. De Graff and Bellefontaine were two small towns, and everyone knew about the Shafer-Moody divorce. The court docket had been overflowing with scheduled hearings alleging child abuse, neglect and sexual assault.

But by August 1992, Sheri Kay and Steve were finally divorced.

Audrey stood by Steve during that long, terrible process. When it was over, they decided to celebrate by marrying the next month. At the time, Audrey's two teenage girls were living with her, Kristel, age eighteen, and Nikki, age sixteen. Kristel had graduated from high school, and Nikki was helping Steve with his farming. All of them were looking forward to a new beginning.

———

Sheri Kay was looking for someone else, too, and John Martin and his two children moved in with her a few months after she and Steve had separated. But try as she might, things didn't go too well. After two short years, Sheri Kay asked John Martin to leave.

Without missing a beat, Sheri Kay soon had another man living with her, Steve Wolfe, bringing his three kids with him. Sheri Kay and Wolfe would marry in 1997, but their marriage would end six years later in 2003. To Audrey, it seemed like a revolving door of men.

Audrey tried not to be bitter. Although Steve's marriage to Sheri Kay had been over years ago, their battles continued.

Visitation was the issue. Steve wanted to see Scott and Stacy, but Sheri Kay would do everything she could do to throw up roadblocks.

As Scott and Stacy grew older, Steve and Audrey hoped visitation would get easier. But it was not to be.

In the fall of 2002, they received a telephone call from Scott saying that he would no longer be coming to see his father. It was very upsetting to Steve and Audrey, but Audrey realized it was completely understandable. They were now raising their own three young boys.

They believed then – and still do – that children need to have guidance and rules in their lives. Audrey felt this was something Scott and Stacy didn't receive from their own mother.

The older Scott and Stacy became, the more freedom Sheri Kay was giving them. Drinking and smoking were not allowed in Steve and Audrey's home. Sheri Kay seemed to feel otherwise, especially thinking that drinking was okay.

Audrey enjoyed the times when Scott and Stacy would visit with them. They were sweet times, watching the kids grow older, playing board games, going out to the movies together, or sometimes driving to Dayton or Columbus for special events. Those days were now distant memories.

————

Although disappointed, Audrey and Steve were not surprised when Scott decided he no longer wanted to visit his father. After all, he had a mother who still hated Steve and discouraged any visitation. Audrey and Steve were glad that at least Stacy enjoyed coming over to see them and their three boys, visiting every other weekend and on Wednesday evenings.

But this would soon change. By late summer of 2004, it was becoming obvious to Audrey and Steve that fourteen-year-old Stacy was having troubles. You could see it in her school work and in her behavior. They thought the lack of supervision in the house was becoming a real problem. Sheri Kay couldn't control herself, let alone her children. As a result, Stacy was acting out with alcohol, drugs and men.

In August of 2004, Steve received a disturbing call from Stacy.

"Guess where I am," Stacy said. "I'm in a semi, with my new truck-driver friend, in Tennessee."

Steve asked her if she was with her mom.

She hesitated, then said, "No. I'm with a guy friend."

When Audrey and Steve saw Stacy the next time, she said, "Please don't tell anyone I called you. Mom doesn't want you to know where I went."

Visitation just got worse after that. Stacy wouldn't be home for the Wednesday pickup, and she wouldn't answer her phone. Audrey and Steve made several attempts to contact her over the next few days, only to be given the option of leaving messages on her cell phone.

With deep regret, Audrey and Steve accepted the fact that weekly visitations with Stacy were coming to an end.

During the time that Scott stopped coming over for visitation, Stacy told Audrey that Sheri Kay had become involved with a man who was selling drugs from Sheri Kay's home. Audrey had heard through the grapevine that Sheri Kay was suddenly losing a lot of weight and having physical problems. She also knew that Sheri Kay was fighting with her own mother and father, Sharyl and Gary Shafer, over farm problems.

In 1995, Sheri Kay's grandmother, Wilma Buroker, had died. Wilma, of course, had been the owner of the entire farm and had exercised complete control over it since it had been in her family for years. Now, nine years later, Wilma's estate was still pending in probate court, not even close to being settled.

Everyone knew that Sheri Kay and her parents couldn't agree on anything. As per court order, the farm was being controlled by trustees appointed in Wilma's Last Will and Testament. To the chagrin of those who were familiar with the situation, the farm buildings and equipment of this once prosperous farm were slowly deteriorating. County records indicated that real estate taxes for some of the parcels were delinquent.

As Audrey explained, "This was a 24/7 party house. The kids knew that as long as mom was having disputes with her parents, Sharyl and Gary Shafer, they could do whatever they wanted. Sheri Kay knew it was important to keep them happy. She hated the idea that they might live with their father."

A few months before, Sheri Kay had visited Nikki, Audrey's daughter. Sheri Kay asked Nikki if it was possible for Nikki to get a loan so that Stacy could have a truck when she started driving. Nikki told Sheri Kay that she didn't have very good credit, and she "couldn't see this happening."

Audrey was confused by what Sheri Kay was asking of her own daughter, Nikki. Not only did the request seem inappropriate, but just recently Sheri Kay had been telling people that she had been approved for a bank loan and was planning to pay the farm's back real estate taxes. Now she needed more money, and she was asking Audrey's daughter for help?

Hospital hallways are dreary places to wait, especially when the time spent is full of anxiety and trepidation. Steve was in De Graff attending Scott's funeral, and Audrey had been daydreaming. She was startled by the doctor approaching her, smiling.

"It looks pretty good," he said. "Stacy's awake, and I think she's able to talk a little bit." Although overwhelmingly concerned with Stacy's health, Audrey had a burning desire to find out what had transpired Saturday night and early Sunday morning.

Audrey had already pieced together some of the events leading up to Sunday morning. On Thursday evening, May 25, Scott, Stacy, Sheri Kay and her parents, Gary and Sharyl Shafer, went to Riverside High School for a senior banquet and awards ceremony. After the banquet, Stacy, Scott and Sheri Kay picked up Scott's new girlfriend, Paige, and then went over to Nikki's house.

Sheri Kay had previously talked to Nikki about some issues concerning Stacy. That night, Sheri Kay had asked Nikki if she would take care of Stacy and let her live there if anything ever happened to her.

It was an unusual request, and a troubling conversation. Apparently, Sheri Kay told Nikki that she believed Stacy was upset about something, and Sheri Kay wanted Nikki to talk to Stacy about it after graduation on Sunday. She never said what it was.

———

Stacy, lying in her hospital bed with her head and face wrapped in white bandages, was talking, even if in a whisper. She attempted to tell Audrey what had happened on Saturday, the day before she was shot.

Audrey explained to others what Stacy had told her: On Saturday, May 28, Stacy and Sheri Kay went uptown in Bellefontaine to go shopping. Later that day, Scott, Stacy and Sheri Kay went to a graduation party at Tom Coy's house in the afternoon. The kids ended up taking Sheri Kay home. They then stopped at Amy Hall's house for a short time.

Scott and Stacy left to pick up Paige, who was going to stay with them at their house for a few days. Paige's father was going to be out of town, apparently hunting in Michigan with friends, and Sheri Kay had agreed to have Paige stay with them.

The three of them then went to a party at a friend's house. This turned out to be a big party, a graduation party for classmates Wes Clem and Parker Robinson. Everyone who was going to graduation was invited

After an hour or so, Scott and Paige left the party to get some supplies while fifteen-year-old Stacy remained to party with Scott's friends. When Scott and Paige got back, the party had gotten too large, so they decided to leave and invite just a few close friends over for a "party at the Moody house." Megan Karus and Brett Davidson followed them home.

Audrey wanted to continue the conversation with Stacy, but Stacy was simply too tired and needed to rest. Audrey quietly walked out of Stacy's hospital room only to discover visitors in the hallway wanting to talk with Stacy.

———

Now, Wednesday, June 1, at 10:30 at night, Detectives Stout and Brugler with the Logan County Sheriff's Office wanted to conduct a taped interview with Stacy in her hospital room. Not wanting to upset her, no one had yet told Stacy that her mother, brother and grandparents were dead and that her brother, Scott, was the main suspect in the murders.

Stacy was tired and confused. Where was Mom?

Unbeknown to the detectives, Dr. Michael Failor, the Logan County Coroner, had just left a few hours earlier. He and Steve Moody's lawyer had argued in the hallway. Dr. Failor wanted to be alone with Stacy, not wanting any interference from the lawyer, but the lawyer refused. "If you want to ask Stacy, a minor, questions, a parent representative is going to be present." At this point, Stacy needed representation.

Unfortunately, now with the coroner and lawyer gone, Stout and Brugler were able to enter Stacy's hospital room to conduct their own interview without any interference.

According to their taped interview, Stacy stated that on Sunday morning she didn't remember why she woke up, but when she did, there was a man standing over her bed holding a gun. She described the gun as having a "huge barrel." The man then shot her in the neck and she just laid there, dazed.

Prompted by Stout, Stacy continued, "The guy walked out of my bedroom and then I heard two more shots." She hesitated, trying to catch her breath.

"The man then came back into my room and shot me a second time. He then walked out, and I heard two more shots." She seemed unsure but thought the man had left.

———

Stacy described the man as having short gray hair and wearing a blue shirt. She was unsure if he had any facial hair and couldn't remember any other descriptive details other than that he appeared to have a bigger build.

After she was shot the second time, Stacy, confused and in shock, believes that she passed out. When she came to, she went to find her mom. Scared and unsure of what all had just happened, Stacy found her mom in bed with blood coming out of her mouth.

Stacy then went to her brother's room. She remembers seeing Scott with what she thought was a .410 shotgun in his hand, pointing up toward his face. There was blood splattered on the wall. She then went downstairs and saw Megan Karus on the loveseat, but she wasn't moving either. Stacy said she started screaming at her to wake up, but Megan wouldn't move.

Going downstairs after being shot, she recalled, was difficult. Finally, in the family room, she knocked a bunch of "stuff" over before she collapsed into the recliner and fell asleep. She didn't remember having any pain.

After waking up, she thought she used the bathroom and that's when she saw the injuries to her face.

At first, she thought somebody was playing a joke or prank on her and thought it might have been her friend, John Martin. But after she realized that she had been shot, she knew it wasn't him. He would never do that to her because he was like a second dad. Stacy said it just looked like him because the guy was older and had gray hair.

Stacy then began trying to call people, but she didn't know who to call and everybody she tried wouldn't pick up their phone. She finally called her stepsister, Nikki. The next thing she remembered was seeing Nikki and her boyfriend, Jeff, at her house and hearing sirens.

When asked by the detectives, Stacy said that her family owned three shotguns: a .410, a 12-gauge and a 20-gauge shotgun. The .410 shotgun was under her mom's bed, and the 12-gauge and 20-gauge shotguns were in the corner by the microwave. The detectives asked if she knew about a .22 caliber rifle. She thought that if a .22 caliber rifle was involved, it probably belonged to her grandfather, Gary Shafer.

Stacy was tired, and the detectives concluded their interview twelve minutes later.

———

The next day, at approximately 10:30 in the morning, the detectives returned to Columbus to conduct yet another interview with Stacy in her hospital room. Stacy was still in the intensive care unit at the Ohio State University Medical Center, but her condition had been upgraded to fair. She was also experiencing significant pain and was having some difficultly speaking.

The detectives again asked her who had done this to her. Stacy repeated that she didn't know. She was tired of them asking the same questions again. Did they not believe her, or could it be they didn't want to hear what she had to say? Like the evening before when she was interviewed by these same two detectives, she affirmed that the man who shot her "had gray hair, was wearing a blue shirt, and was older," but she couldn't approximate his age. It was like a dream, a very bad dream.

Stout then asked her a leading question, "Describe the gun you saw your brother holding."

Stacy was confused by the question. She said that the gun that shot her looked like a pump gun that had a huge barrel with a wood stock. She said she thought it looked like the gun she had seen Scott using when they had gone deer hunting together.

Once more, without prompting, Stacy repeated that she was unaware of what woke her up, but that when she woke there was a man standing over her holding a gun.

Frustrated with the questioning implying that Scott was the shooter, in an exasperated voice Stacy repeated, *"The man I saw was not my brother!"*

In her mind, she was positive the man who shot her was an older man with gray hair.

Stout and Brugler agreed to cut the interview short with Stacy because her condition was worsening. She was drifting in and out of sleep. Going back out into the hallway, they told Steve and Audrey to contact them as soon as Stacy felt up to talking again.

———

Friends say Scott Moody was never violent, but Sheriff Henry maintained that Scott, for whatever reason, was somehow driven to kill his grandparents, mother and two visitors and shoot his sister twice before killing himself.

"What drove this eighteen-year-old to lash out may never be known," Sheriff Henry said. Still, he had instructed his detectives to continue looking into the case, trying to find a motive.

According to some people, the answer may be traced back to the acrimonious divorce between Scott's parents fifteen years before and strife over the family farm. Some said as young children both Scott and his younger sister, Stacy, exhibited strong negative feelings about their mother, her relationship with her parents, and her relationship with their father. Their parents' three-year battle involving unsubstantiated claims and counterclaims of abuse and neglect had taken its toll on Scott and Stacy.

According to John Holtkamp, the director of Children Services, by 1993, the year the divorce was finalized, the complaints finally ended.

"That doesn't mean it didn't continue to be a very difficult time for these children. The divorce case file includes a notation that Sheri Kay was overly dependent on her family."

According to Steve Wolfe, Sheri Kay's second husband, "This was partially due to the car accident, but Sheri Kay always had trouble holding on to a job."

"We were spending money faster than we were making it."

Court records support that assertion. There were no mortgages on the properties, but taxes on two parcels had been delinquent since 1996. Most of the ten parcels were current, but by the end of 2004 the two delinquent properties would be about $45,000 in arrears.

Yet, there was no threat of foreclosure according to Logan County Treasurer Dara Wren.

"It's been in probate, and we can't foreclose on it," she said. The county treasurer was told by the attorneys involved in the estate that there was a plan to pay off the delinquent taxes.

Neighbors and friends said the family disagreed about everything, but primarily about how to operate the dairy farm that was producing little milk.

According to neighbor Clifford Kelly, "The farm is in disrepair. It's a sad, sad situation. What was once a well-established farm has really deteriorated over the last few years." Clifford Kelly didn't elaborate, only saying that the family had been working to restore the farm's prominence.

––––––––

Angel Wolfe, Sheri Kay's former sister-in-law, told the *Columbus Dispatch* that Sheri Kay felt her parents couldn't handle the work on the farm. Angel said Sheri Kay told her that they were behind on taxes and that her parents didn't agree with her desire to modernize the farm.

The estate remained in probate while the family tried to iron out how best to divide the land.

According to Angel, "Three years ago, Sheri Kay attempted to have her mom removed as executor of the estate." She continued, "But the Shafer family started to come back together after the 2003 divorce, and apparently they worked out a plan to resolve the back taxes."

"What's so bizarre is that everything was finally going positively for the Shafers and Sheri Kay," said Sharyl Shafer's attorney, Howard Traul.

"The probate court plan involved selling part of the estate holdings to pay off back taxes and allow Sheri Kay to inherit a part of the farm while purchasing another part to continue operating the twenty-two-head dairy farm."

"Wilma Buroker's Last Will and Testament said the family could stay on the farm as long as they wanted," Traul said. "But in the event it was sold, approximately one-half of the proceeds would go to establish an educational scholarship, the other one-half to Sharyl Shafer and her daughter, Sheri Kay Shafer."

"One property in Bellefontaine had already been sold," Traul said, "and the family was moving ahead to clear up another property for Sheri Kay. In addition, they were ready to establish a scholarship with the Logan County Education Foundation."

According to Traul, "Nothing major was to happen immediately as Sheri Kay was continuing to line up financing for her portion of the agreement."

The sale plan, which was filed with the Logan County Probate Court, focused on retaining most of the farm land in the family, much of which was rented out, and selling off only unneeded homes or other parcels.

———

With everyone dead, Stacy was now the beneficiary of one-fourth of Wilma Buroker's estate. Ironically, Scott, the alleged shooter according to the Logan County Sheriff, who supposedly had taken his own life, was the beneficiary of another one-fourth of the estate.

With more than one-half million dollars at stake, one-half was going to a fifteen-year-old minor, Stacy, and the other half was going to Scott's estate, which would be administrated by his father, Steve Moody.

Because of the amount of money involved, Scott's estate would soon be attacked by two wrongful death claims. One claim would be filed by the Estate of Megan Karus, age nineteen. The other claim would be filed by the Estate of fourteen-year-old Paige Harshbarger, the child of divorced parents.

Chapter Ten

After reviewing the autopsy reports and examining the crime scene photographs, it looks to me like a professional hit.

– Retired F.B.I. Special Agent Tim Creedon

From the first time Stacy mentioned his name, John Martin became a person of interest to the detectives. Martin leased the property directly behind Sheri Kay's home, and he considered himself to be a close friend of the family. Even though Stacy told Detectives Stout and Brugler that Martin would never hurt her, he matched the description that Stacy had given Nikki. Detective Brugler contacted Martin and asked him to come in for an interview on Friday, June 3. Once there, Brugler explained to Martin that Stacy said the suspect looked like him, an older man, medium build with short gray hair.

Martin was told that the sheriff's office received information that Stacy called Martin the morning of the shootings. Martin was asked to tell his story from the beginning. He looked concerned. He took a deep breath, and then he began.

Martin explained that he was fueling up his tractor Sunday morning when he got a phone call. He couldn't make out who it was, so he got off his tractor to try and check the cell phone for the caller.

He explained to the detectives, "Little Stacy is the only one who calls me 'daddy.' I heard 'daddy' and I said, 'Stacy, I can't understand you.' Since the signal seemed weak, I told Stacy I would get with her later, explaining I had to get the crops in."

Martin continued, "Later on, Steve Wolfe called me asking if I heard that there was a shooting at the Shafer farm. My daughter Misti lives in one of the rental properties on the farm so I called her to see what was going on."

He reflected for a moment, "I didn't know what Stacy was trying to say to me. Like maybe help or something," he said.

Stout asked, "When did you get hold of Misti and what did she say?"

Martin explained that Misti didn't know anything. According to Martin, he told Misti about Wolfe's statement, that there was a shooting up at Sheri Kay's. Apparently, Misti then walked up the lane and saw all the cruisers.

When asked how long it had been after he had spoken to Stacy when Wolfe called him, Martin replied, "Probably about a half an hour."

Detective Brugler continued the questioning, "What time did you leave home to get fuel?"

Martin hesitated, but said, "I think it was around 10 till eight in the morning. That's when I went to the farm, but I couldn't get the tractor started."

"I tried to wake up my son, but he wanted to sleep in. So, I slid the fuel tank into the back of my pickup and went into town. I stopped at the neighbors to get some chickens, but I couldn't wake them either, so I headed into town to get fuel."

Detective Brugler explained to Martin that when Stacy was asked, who did this to you?, Stacy replied that it was "an older man with gray hair." The detectives asked her if she knew who it was. Stacy had explained to them that the man looked like John Martin.

Martin said, "No, I wouldn't hurt that little girl. The last time I was over there was on Friday. They had pups and I went over there to see them."

Martin said he later talked to Sheri Kay on Saturday, but they were headed to some graduation parties. When asked if he noticed if there were any problems, Martin said, "No."

But he did state that Sheri Kay mentioned something unusual Friday night.

"I know about the family history. When old lady Buroker died, there was a trust set up where money was supposed to go into an education fund. Sheri Kay talked about someone from the Attorney General's Office calling her regarding the fact that there wasn't any money in the fund. Sheri Kay told me she was getting a loan to put money into the account and pay the farm taxes."

———

Stout then asked, "Who owned a .22 caliber rifle?"

Martin looked down, thinking, "The only guns I know about were some guns Charlie Buck had gotten for Sheri Kay a long time ago. I think they were .357 magnum revolvers."

Because Martin had lived with Sheri Kay for more than three years, Brugler asked him if there was any possibility that his prints might have been on the gun that was used by Scott to shoot everyone.

Martin hesitated, looking dumbfounded, then said, "Not that I know of."

Detectives again went over a timeline with Martin as to when he left his house and where he went. He was asked, again, about the phone call he received from Stacy.

Martin said that he didn't know it was Stacy calling. He claimed he didn't recognize the number, even though it was Sheri Kay's phone number, someone he talked to frequently.

When Martin was asked about the time of the phone call from Stacy, he explained, "Misti checked the phone and she said it was 10:11 a.m."

Brugler leaned forward in his chair, "Tell us about the rifle Misti has."

By the look on Martin's face, he was surprised by the question. "I bought it off a friend several years ago, I think when Misti was fifteen or sixteen years old."

When asked if he knew of anyone who would do this to Sheri Kay, Martin expressed intense concern about Steve Wolfe. "Steve Wolfe was the reason I moved out of the house."

Then Martin went into detail as to why he suspected Wolfe. These may have been interesting speculations, but unfortunately his remarks were mysteriously deleted from the detective's report. Did the detectives think this was just rambling conversation by Martin to remove himself from suspicion?

The detectives later asked, "What do you think, could Scott possibly have done this?"

Martin said, "I really don't think so."

Martin then mentioned that he recently heard a rumor that Stacy and Scott had told a couple of kids that they would not be at graduation the next day.

"It was a rumor only. I don't remember who even told me."

————

The detectives explained to Martin that they needed to talk to Stacy in more detail "once she starts to come around." Asked if he would take a polygraph examination if needed, Martin hesitated, then said he would do anything to assist with the investigation.

But the detectives never asked Martin to take a polygraph examination. Had he taken one, his explanation about his activities that Sunday morning would have caused the needle to jump.

Martin knew what he had seen early Sunday morning, but he was afraid for his life to tell anyone. He saw a gray-haired man walking across the back of his farm, over to Sheri Kay's house, wearing only a blue tee-shirt that chilly morning.

Looking back, knowing what he now knew, Martin thought, "It was the 'fixer.' If he'd seen me that morning, I'm as good as dead."

————

Even after he heard Stacy's taped interview, Sheriff Henry continued to assert that Scott Moody, not some random stranger, had killed the family and their friends. "What drove this eighteen-year-old to lash out may never be known."

He grimly coordinated security for the multiple funerals.

More than one hundred people attended fourteen-year-old freshman Paige Harshbarger's funeral at the Rexer-Riggin-Madden Funeral Home in De Graff on Friday afternoon. Mourners drove past a sign in front of a nearby church that said: *We understand your sorrow and we share your grief.* The Riverside High School junior varsity softball team served as honorary pallbearers to honor Paige, their team's catcher, just after they collectively signed Get Well cards to send to Stacy, their team's pitcher.

————

The sheriff's office ordered the media to stay off the funeral home's private property for the duration of all the funerals and asked everyone to respect the wishes of the victims' families and stay out of the cemetery. "Hopefully, the news media considers what the victims are going through and stays out of the cemetery to let them grieve," said Colonel Keith LeVan, Sheriff Henry's top assistant. "This is devastating for the victims' families – to go through what they've gone through."

During and after the ceremony, two television crews reported coverage of the funerals from across the street from the funeral home in a space closed off with yellow "CAUTION" tape.

Riverside High School students attended services the next day for their classmate Megan Karus at the Gretna Brethren Church, with burial in the Huntsville cemetery with the same outpouring of grief amid national media interest.

The memorial for Scott, his mother Sheri Kay Shafer, and his grandparents, Gary Shafer and Sharyl Shafer, took place in a combined ceremony on Monday morning, June 6, in a packed chapel at the Rexer-Riggin-Madden Funeral Home with burial in the Greenwood-Union Cemetery.

Sheri Kay's uncle, Ron Shafer, who was next-of-kin for Sheri Kay and her parents, chose cremation for the bodies of his brother, sister-in-law and niece. Steve Moody would wrestle for years with guilt that Sheri Kay, the woman he once loved and the mother of his children, didn't have a grave. He couldn't change that decision, but he insisted on an open casket for his son Scott. Just inside the funeral home's doors stood a single rose in a vase surrounded by photos of the family. Four teenagers from Scott's high school wore purple jackets with emblems of Future Farmers of America. Friends came up to Steve after the service to express their condolences, slipping money to him to help pay for the expenses.

The community remained in shock as they grieved for Sharyl Shafer, a teacher who'd taught them in first grade; Gary Shafer, a farmer who'd helped countless neighbors; Sheri Kay Shafer, a single mother who had struggled to hold down a job, care for a farm, and raise a son and daughter; and children they'd watched grow up only to die as they were poised on the brink of adulthood.

Nobody in the county could focus on anything else.

Speculation abounded. A rural farming community, many of the mourners were hunters. They knew weapons and how loud a .22 sounded, the panic it generated at close range, and they understood the marksmanship required to make the close contact wounds that day. They had watched Scott grow up, had been proud of him judging FFA cattle showings, and admired him exhibiting animals he'd carefully raised.

No one had any answers.

The funeral director, responsible for embalming Scott's body, took Steve Moody aside to talk with him privately. "I've been doing this for years, and I've handled several suicides. Based on what I know – Scott using a rifle, the entry wound behind his ear – there's no way Scott could have shot himself."

Steve was stunned, but it wouldn't be the last time he would hear this, especially after the autopsy reports on all the victims were released later that afternoon.

The following Monday, passers-by would notice two flower bouquets resting against a telephone pole across the road from Gary and Sharyl Shafer's home. If they looked farther down the road, they would see two yellow cleaning service vans backed up to the side door of Sheri Kay's home.

––––––––

The Montgomery County Coroner's Office in Dayton released the preliminary autopsy results to the *Bellefontaine Examiner* on Monday morning, June 6. Rumors quickly began to spread when people read that Scott Moody shot himself twice in order to commit suicide.

Dr. Lee Lehman, a forensic pathologist with the coroner's office who conducted Scott's autopsy, noted two wounds: one below the left ear and another through the right side of the roof of his mouth. The first bullet lodged in Scott's sinuses, according to the report, and the second one went into the right frontal lobe of his brain. The first shot, below the left ear, was in close range, but not a contact wound. The second shot, through the right side of the roof of Scott's mouth, had an upward trajectory. Investigators concluded this second shot, the fatal shot, indicated that Scott was the shooter and had committed suicide. The sheriff's office theorized that Scott switched hands and changed his position to fire the second shot.

According to Sheriff Henry, "The first shot was not fatal because the .22 caliber semi-automatic rifle he used lacked adequate firepower."

The press quoted suicide experts saying that only rarely do people shoot themselves more than once in the head while committing suicide, but some have done that.

"There are people who are about to commit suicide, they flinch for one reason or another, the wound is not immediately incapacitating, and then they finish the job off," said Dr. Richard Callery, chief medical examiner for the state of Delaware in an article cited in the *Columbus Dispatch.*

But Dr. Callery didn't have all the evidence before him, and others suspected that his reasoning might apply to someone's use of a handgun, not a thirty-six-inch long rifle.

A deputy coroner for the Montgomery County Coroner's Office conducted the autopsies on the other five victims. In his findings, he noted that the grandfather, Gary Shafer, had suffered three shots in the neck behind his ear and that the grandmother, Sharyl Shafer, was shot once in the neck behind her ear and then shot once in her face.

The other three victims all were shot at close range, with the gun placed close to or against their skin, "probably sleeping at the time they were killed," said Sheriff Henry. The shooter shot Sheri Kay Shafer once in her left temple; Scott's girlfriend, Paige Harshbarger, was shot once in her left temple; and family friend Megan Karus was shot once in the right side of her neck, below her ear.

When the sheriff's office made its report public, including crime scene photographs, many reasoned that the placement of the shots behind the victims' ears at the temple, including the first shot to Scott, appeared professional, from someone who knew how to kill.

Speculation began to spread like wildfire.

Why didn't the victims in Sheri Kay's house wake up after the first shots?

How could Scott, who didn't like firearms, shoot so accurately?

Could someone unfamiliar with guns know to shoot behind the ear as the most effective place to kill someone?

What could have triggered the rage and cold-bloodedness in Scott in the minutes after Andrew Denny left Sheri Kay's house in his Dodge pickup truck?

Even if he had problems with his mother and grandparents, what would cause Scott to shoot his sister, girlfriend and classmate?

———

Waiting for Stacy to be released from the hospital, Steve and Audrey Moody would read through the newspaper articles, carefully examine the reports, rereading certain portions, jotting down questions. They would soon learn that there were no easy answers. Good friends would listen to their concerns, and some would volunteer their own thoughts. And one experienced police chief in another town in Logan County would be courageous enough to step forward and call Steve. He wanted to shed some light on the sheriff's incompetent investigation.

Chapter Eleven

I don't know what woke me up. It was dark, and a man was standing over me with a gun. An older man with short grey hair. He was wearing a blue shirt. I guess he had a medium build. I never saw him before. And then he shot me.

– Stacy Moody in an interview to Detective Jon Stout

Jon Stout always knew he wanted to be a cop, just like his father. Now, at age thirty-six, he'd risen to the rank of senior detective with the Logan County Sheriff's Office, a step up over his old man who still worked as a beat cop for the Bellefontaine Police Department. Stout enjoyed looking back at all the right tickets he'd punched to advance his career.

After graduating from Bellefontaine High School in 1987, Stout had worked a few crappy jobs as a laborer through a temporary employment service. He knew he'd never get anywhere on that path, so he put in his application with the Ohio Civil Service Commission to become a deputy with the Logan County Sheriff's Office and enrolled at Clark Technical College in Springfield, Ohio, to get an associate degree in criminal justice.

In January 1988, while still in school, the Logan County Sheriff's Office hired him as an auxiliary deputy. A year later, they promoted him to the position of corrections officer. The pay wasn't great – seven dollars an hour – but with patience he expected things would improve. After that stint, he did patrol duty on the road, a "road warrior," for eight years.

His big break came in 1997 with a promotion to temporary duty as a detective. He folded his police uniform, accepted the keys to an unmarked car he could take home at night, and enjoyed flexible hours, all at $13.60 an hour. Eight years later, he felt that he was finally receiving the respect he deserved.

And now, the Moody massacre.

As rumors spread throughout the community about Stacy's claim that her brother wasn't the one who shot her, and the unusual placement of the bodies and questions concerning the precision of the shots, Stout knew this investigation was getting out of control. This was especially so now that the crime scene photos went public and a police chief in another city publicly questioned the ineptitude of the investigation. Stout began to feel pressure to validate the sheriff's decision to close the case. But he hadn't been able to do much as long as Stacy remained in the hospital, insisting that a gray-haired stranger had shot her.

––––––

Stacy finally left the hospital twelve days after the shootings. Her throat still hurt, and she struggled to talk or swallow. She moved in with her father and the stepfamily she had rarely visited over the past several years. Now she walked into her new, makeshift bedroom off the dining room, the only room in the Moodys' two-story farmhouse that could handle the rented hospital equipment. Under strict orders to eat only soft foods lest she choke, Stacy had a feeding tube in her nose, she had to stay hooked to a machine that provided nourishment, and she had another machine to suction her mouth. In addition, Stacy had to wear a brace that covered her head and torso, which forced her to stare straight ahead.

A bullet exit wound on her right cheek still oozed pus and a shattered vertebra from the other gunshot required complicated arrangements when she needed to shift position. After the physicians concluded that she could handle the psychological trauma, her family slowly told her the details of the tragedy, the funerals of her mother, grandparents, brother and friends, and that the police had named her brother the killer.

It was inevitable. Within days, Steve Moody contacted Logan County Children Services and asked for help with Stacy's depression.

Sandy Berger got the assignment and drove to the home.

Sitting around Stacy's hospital bed, Audrey patiently explained to the caseworker, "Doctors told us that had one of the bullets struck her a mere fraction differently, either way, Stacy would have been paralyzed." As it is, according to Audrey, the bullet remained in her body. "To try removing it would be too dangerous for her."

The caseworker noted in her report that "Stacy was fully mobile but must take great care for a minimum of three months so as not to create greater injury, and risk paralysis." Berger continued. "Stacy sustained nerve damage in her neck, which makes it difficult for her to swallow and to talk loudly. Yet doctors affirmed that her condition would improve."

Audrey explained, "When we took Stacy to Wilson Memorial Hospital this morning, the doctor found a kink in Stacy's feeding tube, causing fluid to deposit in her lungs. The hospital staff removed the tube and put in another, which, thankfully, took care of the feeding problem."

During their session, Stacy reached out and held Sandy's hand while she told her that she didn't want to think about or talk about what happened, nor did she remember many of the details.

When Sandy asked Stacy whether she had trouble sleeping, Stacy replied that she hadn't slept well the night before but didn't know why.

Audrey said, "The last night Stacy was in the hospital, she had a nightmare about the shooting. I think she was anxious to leave the hospital and go home, but the hospital had been a place of safety for her. I think leaving there was taking away Stacy's sense of security."

Audrey quietly spoke with Stacy about needing to get some of her clothes from her mother's house and needing to purchase new underwear because Steve wouldn't permit Stacy to wear the thong panties her mother had allowed. Jokingly, Audrey assured Stacy that she wouldn't have to wear "granny panties" and that they'd find some way to compromise with her father.

As Stacy drifted off to sleep, Audrey and the caseworker went into the dining room where Steve joined them to talk. Audrey admitted she'd started having difficulty holding up, although she knew she had to. She now needed to take care of Stacy, Steve and her three boys. Both Audrey's and Steve's cell phones rang dozens of times during their meeting.

Steve came close to expressing open, raw emotion when he talked about the loss of his son and the two girls who had died, and then his ex-wife and in-laws. And Gary Shafer's brother, who had taken it upon himself to have Sheri Kay cremated, as well as Gary and Sharyl. Steve had assumed that Sheri Kay didn't have a will and told Gary's brother that he would assume responsibility for Sheri Kay's funeral arrangements. He stared at the table. "I once loved Sheri Kay, and she was still the mother of my children. I told Stacy that I would take care of her mother, but now I feel that I let her down."

They discussed how upset Stacy felt about her mother's cremation.

Steve went on and on, rambling on subjects from the mass funeral, his gratitude for the Future Farmers students who'd volunteered to milk the cows for a few weeks after the shootings, his new task as administrator of Scott's estate containing one-quarter of Wilma Buroker's still-tied-up-in-litigation holdings, his sorrow at the deaths of Megan Karus and Paige Harshbarger, the wrongful death lawsuits he faced from their families, and always, when his train of thought ended, gratitude that Stacy had survived.

The caseworker asked Audrey about her daughter, Nikki.

"She's not doing well, but she refuses to get professional counseling. Her boyfriend, Jeff, isn't doing very well, either," she replied, but continued that Jeff worked for Honda. They had given him some time off and referred him to a counselor.

They discussed possible psychologists for Stacy. The caseworker gave suggestions before she explained, "I was trained to do mental health counseling and have done it part time for a few years. I might be able to work with Stacy. You should talk about it with her. I'll also think about it and talk to you about it at our next visit."

Baffled by the upcoming challenges and unsure how to proceed, all at the table agreed on one thing: Stacy needed to face what really happened that day.

————

Now, seventeen days after the killings and in the comfort of her father's home, the detectives wanted to talk with Stacy once again. When the sheriff's office contacted the Moodys to set up another interview, Steve wanted first to check with Sandy

Berger, Stacy's counselor, and with Stacy to make sure she could handle yet another interview with the detectives.

At two o'clock in the afternoon on June 14, Detectives Stout and Brugler, along with Sandy Berger, arrived at the Moodys' home for their first interview with Stacy outside the hospital.

Gathered around the family dining room table, Stout allowed a minimal amount of small talk before he got straight to the point about the two scenarios that the detectives could see. "Either we have a killer on the loose or Scott did this."

Stacy opened her mouth to speak, but Stout interrupted her and said that all the evidence pointed to Scott.

A clock ticked in the background. No one said a word.

Detective Stout reviewed the evidence they had gathered to date. Now, in a soft, sympathetic voice, Stout said, "We need to get to the truth, Stacy. I believe you know what happened, and I need you to tell us what you know. Right now, we're looking for a gray-haired man."

Stacy stared at the table.

Stout became adamant, "You need to tell me the story one more time and then it's over, so long as you're telling me the truth."

Stacy tried to shift herself, but her neck brace prevented any movement. She forced herself into a position so her body could turn. Stacy threw another tissue onto the mound of white in the trash basket, glanced at the stack of Kleenex boxes her father had bought in bulk, and shifted her eyes from her father to her stepmother to the caseworker to Detective Stout to Detective Brugler, all staring at her in earnest.

She started to reply.

Stout told her to speak up. The dictation recorder, sitting in the middle of the dining room table, needed her statement.

In a hoarse whisper, Stacy said, "My dad told me yesterday you were coming out. I've thought a lot about this. The more I think about it, I don't remember seeing a gray-haired man. I remember seeing a dark figure, with a blue shirt on, with the gun shooting at me and I remember trying to get away. I don't remember seeing a face."

Steve's fists turned white. Audrey reached over to hold Stacy's hand. Everyone stayed silent.

"I remember getting up after that. I remember two shots after that. Then he shot me again. I don't really remember hearing any shots after that."

"You don't remember at all?"

"I don't remember," Stacy continued in her faint voice. "I remember getting up and going downstairs. I was falling everywhere. I remember sitting back down on a chair and going back to sleep for a little bit."

Stout sat back. "I don't want you to just say something to get me to stop talking to you. We need the truth."

She nodded. "I remember seeing Scott lying on his bed. I don't remember seeing him up moving around."

Stout changed the subject. "What's the deal with the bathroom? You already told us earlier that you were in the bathroom when Jeff and Nikki arrived."

"I don't remember being in the bathroom," said Stacy.

Stout thought for a moment, remembered the plan, sat up, and explained that he felt impressed with the details that Stacy could recall. He went over them again, this time stressing the bathroom. "Our concern is that Scott was up with you, after you were shot. Either he was in the bathroom with you or he helped you into your chair."

Stacy studied the detectives, befuddled.

Stout grew emphatic, "The worst thing you can do is hold something back. You will carry this inside you for the rest of your life. If there is something in there, you just need to get it out."

She said, "I remember getting up out of bed. I was having trouble going down the stairs. I fell when I was downstairs. I fell into the counter, knocking pictures over. I saw Megan lying there and figured she was just sleeping. I sat down in the chair and fell asleep."

Stout reviewed the details again.

Stacy nodded. Yes, he had the story right.

Stout asked, "How can you recall everything so clearly, but you can't remember this guy? That's why we're struggling with believing you didn't see the suspect."

Silence. Stacy began to cry.

Stout pressed forward, "It appears that you were up while the shooter was up. I promise we won't close this case until we know who the shooter is. If it was Scott, we need to know."

"I didn't see Scott."

"You didn't see a gray-haired man?"

Stacy looked at him, biting her lip. She replied, "I didn't see a gray-haired man." Stacy said she could only remember a dark figure, medium build.

Stout continued for the next forty-five minutes of the interview with questions about Stacy's relationship with Scott and Scott's relationship with his mother and grandparents.

"Me and Scott got along pretty good. We had our problems, like brothers and sisters. It was more my mom and him. Scott was excited because grandma, grandpa and my mom were looking at trucks for him. He was excited about graduation also."

"We're struggling to identify the gun Scott had," said Stout.

"Mom had a couple of shotguns. She kept one under her bed, the others were in the kitchen by the microwave." She thought for a moment before she stated that Dave Cusic, one of her mom's boyfriends, had one up at the house, too.

"I'm not sure whether he took it home or not. I think it was a .22. It was the gun he carried when he went hunting. He used it to shoot rabbits."

Stout and Brugler looked at each other. "We haven't heard that before."

The detectives moved to other subjects: the kids riding on the four-wheeler, the chores Scott performed when working with his grandparents, the loan for Scott's new truck. They covered a wide range of topics as Stacy calmed down. After her breathing returned to normal and her tears stopped, Stout directed the conversation back to early Sunday morning. "Stacy, we're looking for closure, and we're not closing the case until we are sure. Is there anything else you can recall since we've been talking?"

Stacy stared at the far wall, frowning.

"I really believe there is something else you want to tell us," said Stout.

Stacy said, "No. I'm just trying to think the morning through. I'm trying to remember if I heard anything. My alarm clock was going off. I remember turning my alarm clock off and going back to sleep. I don't know what woke me up. When I did wake up, he was standing in front of my window with a gun. I don't remember a face. I remember a dark figure. I remember the gun shot at me. Then I heard two more gun shots. Then he shot me again. I don't remember any shots after that."

Stout considered, "That makes sense. It appears everyone was tucked in when they were shot. Apparently, you were the only one awake. You saw everything except the shooter. You may be mentally blocking that out right now. We don't want you to say something except what you know for sure in your head."

"I remember saying, 'No! No! No!' to him and fighting," said Stacy as she demonstrated by holding her arms up. "I tried to roll out of the way."

Steve Moody scraped back his chair and strode to the window, his jaw working.

Stacy continued that she eventually got out of her bed in her still-dark bedroom with its white sheet hanging over the window to allow her the luxury of sleeping in on some mornings. She didn't know the time, but she left her bedroom and walked into her mom's.

"She was tucked in real well. It wasn't right. Normally, she's all over the place. It was weird seeing her like that, the blanket tucked under her chin, her hand resting gently across her chest.

"I went in and said 'Mom, wake up, wake up!' I was yelling at her and she wouldn't move and then I saw the blood coming out of her mouth."

Steve and Audrey could see that Stacy was tired, but the detectives continued with more questions about the milk money that her grandparents had agreed to give her mom, but didn't, and the arguments everyone would have, and what Scott's former girlfriend, Amanda, had to say about Scott.

As the conversation died down, Stout stopped speaking. The table stayed quiet. Then Stout's voice grew low, soft, as though from an eerie world. "I've been to your house. I know your mother. I know your grandparents. I know Scott."

Stacy drew back, surprised by Stout's comment.

Stout continued in a soothing voice, "I hope to have a special bond with you that will last both of our lifetimes."

After a long silence, Stout looked around the stunned table, coughed, and turned to Brugler to see if he had anything else.

Detective Brugler recovered and asked Stacy. "Let's talk about Dave Cusic growing marijuana at your mom's place."

Unexpectedly, Stout reached over to the center of the table and turned the dictation recorder off. Stacy's response went unrecorded.

Detective Brugler gaped at Stout. He was confused. So were Audrey and Steve.

Stout stood up, thanked the parents, and told them that the interview was over.

As Steve and Audrey walked the detectives to the door, Stout turned to Steve, "I feel like Stacy knows more than what she's saying."

Steve nodded his head.

"Steve, call me if she starts to open up. She may begin to open up after she starts therapy."

Steve pondered the question he had asked himself over and over: Why didn't Stacy seem more upset? He responded to Stout, "She's still holding something in."

Chapter Twelve

Stacy, if you change your story any more, it might be necessary for you to take a polygraph to get to the truth.

That won't be necessary. I've told you everything.

– Stacy Moody in her fifth interview to Detectives Stout and Brugler

Stout and Brugler returned to the sheriff's office, but Audrey phoned before they could finish writing up their report. "Stacy's broken down and she's crying. She wants you to come back." Stout and Brugler shook their heads in disbelief. This had happened faster than they'd expected.

As they drove back to start their fourth interview with Stacy, Stout pointed out that each time Stacy had given them her version of the story, the facts differed just a little bit. What would change this time?

Brugler sighed and shook his head.

When they entered the house, Audrey sat on the couch with her arms around a hysterical Stacy.

"What's going on? Are things coming back to you?"

"I'm starting to remember things," Stacy said. "I remember what seems like a flashback. Scott and Paige were arguing, and I could hear them. I don't remember walking around with him, but I do remember it was Scott. I remember waking up and seeing the gun."

"You saw Scott?"

Stacy broke down, crying harder.

Stout encouraged her, "Stacy, I know how good you'll feel when this is over and tell it once and for all."

Her tears diminished a little.

Stout continued, "Just start talking when you feel comfortable."

Stacy blew her nose, swallowed, and wiped her face. After a few easy questions, she began to reminisce about her grandparents. "Scott had a key to Grandma and Grandpa's house. Scott probably went down there with the four-wheeler. The four-wheeler is smaller and quieter than his truck.

"Grandma would come back to the house while Grandpa finished milking. Grandma normally started fixing breakfast. That is what they did when I was little. Grandpa would come back into the kitchen when he finished milking and would sit down and eat his breakfast."

Audrey kept her arm around Stacy's shoulder as she tried to take deep breaths. "Scott probably came in before they got back from the barn where they were milking and locked the house back up. There were places he could hide in the house. He probably came out and did it.

"If he shot them, he would have to have blood on his hands. Then he probably came back up to our house. I'm sure he probably shot me first because I don't remember hearing any other gun shots beforehand. He shot me and then I heard two other gun shots. Then he came back and shot me again."

"Did you know that it was Scott when you were shot the second time?"

"Yes," said Stacy.

"What color was Scott's shirt?"

"I don't remember."

"What happened next?"

"He probably went down and shot Megan."

Stout asked her if she knew this for a fact.

"No, after the second gun shot, I don't remember anything. I blacked out."

Stout paused, then pushed, "Did you see Scott awake, alive, or moving around any time after you were shot the second time?"

Stacy answered, "No."

Stout pressed the point. "The only person that can say Scott shot you for sure was *you*, Stacy. You saw him shoot you for sure?"

Stacy shook her head, yes.

"Did Scott say anything to you?"

Stacy hesitated, then said, "No."

"Was he in the bathroom with you?"

"I don't remember if he was or not," said Stacy.

"Did he help you into the chair?"

Again, she said, "No."

Stout kept on. "Tell me about the argument that Scott and Paige were having."

"It was in a flashback. Paige was telling Scott to put it down or something like that."

Stout nodded. "I need help with the flashback. I need to know if it's a reality or not, Stacy."

"I don't know. It could be. All I remember is Paige saying something like 'put it down' or something."

Brugler interrupted to clarify the matter. "Is it in your dream or is it real that you saw Scott shoot you?"

Stacy looked at both detectives. "I saw Scott shoot me."

Stout continued, "Is there anything else you want to add?"

Stacy started crying.

Stout, sounding empathetic, said, "Getting it off your chest will make you feel better."

Then Brugler asked, "When Scott shot you, did you realize it was him right away?"

Stacy shook her head, yes.

"He didn't say anything to you?"

Stacy looked away, tears streaming down her cheeks.

Audrey handed Stacy a new tissue and looked up at the detectives, pleading with her eyes. They ended the interview.

―――――

A week later, on June 21, the detectives returned for their fifth meeting with Stacy.

Audrey met Stout and Brugler at her front door. "Stacy hasn't been acting right since she talked with you last week."

They nodded grimly, entered the dining room, and sat down at the table across from Stacy. Still in her brace, she appeared more composed than when they saw her last.

"What's going on?" asked Stout.

Looking down at her lap, Stacy said, "I told you it was Scott, although I really didn't see him."

Confused, the detectives tried to engage Stacy, asking about events both before and after the shootings. She chatted easily about some things, but every time the conversation returned to Scott, Stacy got upset and didn't want to talk about him.

After the detectives pressed her, Stacy acknowledged that she saw Scott shoot her both the first and second times. "When I woke up, I saw Scott standing over me with a gun. Initially, I didn't realize who it was or what was going on. I thought it was some kind of a joke. I realized it was Scott, and then he shot me.

"Then he left my room and I heard two more shots. There was some separation between the two shots, as if he went from one room to another. A short time later he came back into my bedroom and shot me again. I think I passed out, but I'm not sure for how long."

Audrey held Stacy's hand as she choked down tears. "When I woke up, I walked downstairs, stumbling, and sat down in the recliner. At some point I looked beside the chair and saw Scott's leg kneeling beside me. He was wearing black wind pants."

Stacy had finished. She thought she had told her story for the last time.

Stout asked her if she'd told the truth or just said this to end the ordeal.

"This is the truth. I know Scott shot everyone. I saw him shoot me. I just don't want to believe it in my head."

Once again, Stout expressed skepticism. "Stacy, if you change your story any more, then it might be necessary for you to take a polygraph to get to the truth."

Stacy replied, "That won't be necessary. I've told you everything."

———

A polygraph wouldn't be necessary. Hypnosis would later reveal exactly what Stacy remembered, and who shot her.

Chapter Thirteen

"I don't want people to hate me for what happened," Stacy said about the upcoming school year. *"I don't want people to look at me differently, either. I just want people to treat me like a normal person."*

– Stacy Moody in her first interview to a newspaper reporter

Stacy gave her first interview to a staff writer from the *Bellefontaine Examiner* late Sunday afternoon, July 10, at the Moodys' quiet farmhouse in De Graff.

Gathered around a picnic table in the front yard, underneath an old oak tree, Stacy wore her neck brace that stretched down her torso. A small scar showed on her right cheek. But the quiet, unassuming farm girl tried to smile. The reporter had to strain to catch Stacy's soft words and wait through very long pauses in order for Stacy to catch her breath, but Stacy and her parents opened up as they answered the reporter's questions.

"The newspapers have been put away until she's ready," Audrey said. "As far as graphic articles, I haven't let her look at them . . . the media scares her."

Stacy chimed in. "I just take life day by day. My lifestyle has changed. My environment has changed." She paused for a moment. "I value life a lot more now, and I don't take things for granted anymore."

"She's taken it very well," Steve Moody said, looking at his daughter with affection. "She's a very strong girl."

The reporter asked how Steve was holding up.

He said that he had experienced mixed emotions after the shootings. "I was very sad and upset Scott and Stacy's whole family was gone, but I was glad I still had my little girl."

The Moodys reflected over the past several weeks about the outpouring of prayers, letters and cards, along with the support and donations that had allowed them to stop their regular lives and stay by Stacy's side while she remained in the hospital in Columbus. "There were so many places that put out donation jars," Steve said. "That helped us with hotel stays, food and gas. The community pulled together and helped us out a lot. Local churches helped with expenses and all their prayers helped."

Audrey estimated that Stacy had received more than 500 cards and letters from people all across the nation, often arriving at helpful times. In the depths of Stacy's depression, the pile of mail every day pulled her from her gloom. "The cards," Stacy said with a smile, "helped and we still receive some every few days."

Stacy said her stepmother had provided an incredible amount of support since the incident, and their relationship had grown stronger than ever before. "She was with me at the hospital the whole time," Stacy said, looking at Audrey with a smile.

"I had to keep everybody together," Audrey said. "I did my crying the morning it happened. After that, I just had to pull together and take care of my three boys, my husband, and Stacy, who needed one hundred percent of my attention for a while."

After a few more questions, Audrey went on. "The healing process has been in baby steps for Stacy," she said. "And there have been setbacks, but we are trying to move forward." With the estate tied up in probate court, money was tight, and they appreciated all the help they were getting.

"On the way home from the hospital, they told me what the community was doing and that lifted my spirits," Stacy said.

Could they give examples of the things people had done?

They offered so many that the reporter laughed. "Just a few, just to give the readers an idea. Name a business that helped."

During the weeks after the incident, Steve said that he, his sister, and his wife exceeded their cell phone minutes, racking up enormous bills. "I went 400 minutes over on my Nextel," he said. "They [Nextel] took those minutes off and put 200 on my next month's amount. They were fantastic."

The group that touched Audrey the most was Stacy's 4-H group, "Liberty Livestock," which had raised $335 from a car wash toward her medical expenses.

The reporter moved on to other topics. Stacy would turn sixteen on September 14. What did she want most?

Stacy beamed. A truck. Her mother had promised her a Ford pickup truck.

Steve and Audrey paled. The decades-long battle of Wilma Buroker's will in probate court had no resolution in sight. They had three other children, a mountain of hospital bills, and the sudden responsibility for Wilma's declining farm embroiled in debt and legal issues. Audrey hemmed and hawed before she gently pointed out that Sheri Kay had promised a vehicle; Steve and Audrey weren't able to do so.

Stacy stared in disbelief as tears started to well in her eyes.

The reporter tried to change the subject, asking Stacy about memories of her mother.

Stacy wiped her eyes and said that she had started to write a letter to her mother to help bring closure.

"I think it's doing a lot of good, helping her," Audrey said of the missive.

"When the letter is complete," Stacy replied, "I'm going to put it inside my mother's work boots and then bury the boots." Stacy explained how her mother had always said to "bury me with my work boots on."

After the reporter clicked off the recorder and thanked them, and Stacy returned to bed in exhaustion, Steve and Audrey discussed the interview. It seemed to have helped Stacy come to terms with her situation. Since she'd started getting better, boredom sometimes set in during the many long hours she now stayed awake in her rented hospital bed. Grief usually followed the boredom as Stacy's thoughts inevitably turned to her mother and her family and friends. They'd run out of ideas to help her.

When the emergency responders offered to host a reunion, the family thought it would be a great time to thank the many people whose quick actions had helped save Stacy's life. On July 7, personnel from Bellefontaine Fire Department's Riverside squad, the Logan County Sheriff's Office, and the MedFlight team from Columbus gathered with Stacy.

Emergency responders and medical professionals blinked back tears when they saw Stacy still alive. Several almost dropped their plates when they realized that she could walk. Stacy took a ride in a MedFlight helicopter over the Mad River Mountain ski resort, and then the flight personnel presented her with a tee-shirt to commemorate the trip. Her brothers bounced in excitement at the different uniforms, fire trucks, equipment, and especially at the helicopter.

That night, her siblings asked again about the upcoming Logan County Fair, which after Christmas and their birthdays was the most important celebration in their lives. It would start pretty soon. Could Stacy go on any of the rides?

Stacy had gone to the fair from the time she could walk and had a drawer full of ribbons to prove it. She loved to show livestock, go on the Ferris Wheel, eat carnival food, and spend time with friends and classmates, but she had made up her mind about this year's fair.

No way.

She would not go.

It meant making a public appearance.

"I don't want people just coming up to me and asking me questions and staring at me," she said, explaining that she didn't want to talk about the tragic incident she had survived just three months earlier. "But at the same time, I don't want people to be afraid to come up and talk to me."

After one friend after another begged her to go with them to the fair, Stacy relented. Yes, she'd attend, but she had one condition. She refused to exhibit livestock. Her father had entered her four dairy heifers, one dairy beef feeder, and two market lambs in the Junior Fair competition anyway. Stacy's stepbrothers, Steven, age twelve, Christopher, age ten, and Adam, age seven, could show them if she didn't change her mind.

According to Audrey, "She's had a lot of help from family and friends." She laughed. "Her brothers are on cloud nine about showing the cattle because they never have before. They're very excited."

After the Logan County Fair Board learned of Stacy's concerns, they did what they could to establish security and keep the media from intruding on what they hoped would be a normal event. It worked. Stacy had a fantastic time. Her friends all skipped the rides, too, or went while she did something else, and her brothers made no mistakes as they paraded the animals.

After the fair, an exhausted Stacy stayed in bed for days, but she insisted that the fun time had made everything worth it. Steve and Audrey agreed between themselves that Stacy had started to see a life for herself even through her new limitations. She couldn't play softball or do any of the heavy work involved in animal care, but her teammates and 4-H club friends kept her apprised of all the gossip and news.

As the summer moved on, the media continued to press for stories, pointing out that the whole state, and even the nation, cared about Stacy and wanted to know that she had started to return to normal life. The family thought about this, and then they agreed to another interview.

Once again, Stacy and her parents sat outside under a tree while the reporter set up, made some small talk, got everyone relaxed, adjusted the mike, and started in. The first few questions seemed easy. Then the reporter asked Stacy what she'd convey if she could say one thing to her family and the friends she lost that morning.

After a long silence, Stacy said, "I'd tell them all that I love them, and I'll be there, I'll see them when my time is done."

A few more questions.

Stacy believed a higher power had spared her for reasons she did not yet understand. The gunshots had severed a main artery to her brain, damaged her vocal cords, shattered a vertebra in her neck, and caused massive blood loss in the hours before she received medical attention. "I sat at the kitchen table and waited for them to get there," she said, explaining that she changed her shirt before help arrived. "I think God has a plan for me to do something,"

The reporter adjusted his diction equipment. Did Stacy know what?

Stacy explained she didn't know what plan, but she remained intent on figuring it out and fulfilling her purpose.

The reporter asked what she remembered of that day.

Audrey pointed out that Stacy had no recollection of many of the events of the tragedy or her hospital stay. Her family had decided not to attempt to explain things to her until she asked. When Stacy wanted to hear the details, they'd assume she felt strong enough to know them. They would tell her then. Not before.

"I don't remember hardly anything," Stacy said of her stay in the hospital. "I remember the last four days I was there, but other than that, it's just bits and pieces."

"I kept telling her she has to be strong and get through this," said Audrey. "I told her she has to carry on the family's memories, and she is the only one that can do this."

The reporter asked about the neck brace.

"I still have a chance of being paralyzed from the neck down," Stacy said. She had to wear this contraption for the next few months, but even after that the doctors had told her that she'd have to remain careful for the rest of her life. "If I get jerked the wrong way, I could become paralyzed."

Audrey answered the next few questions. Doctors had decided not to attempt to remove a bullet fragment still in Stacy's neck because it had lodged too close to her vertebrae and any surgery to take it out could result in paralysis. While in the hospital, Stacy had received feeding through a tube. Since her release, she'd had trouble swallowing. Someone had to watch her in case food lodged in her throat. "She has a very good chance of choking," Audrey said. "She has to take small bites and she can't eat alone."

Stacy so hoped she could act normal again and enjoy school. "I like to go to cow shows, play softball, and just hang out with friends," she said with a smile.

After a very long silence, the next question came about Stacy's future.

She replied, "I'm not sure what I want to do for a living after school. Maybe I'd like to be a photographer."

What about more immediate plans?

After graduating, Stacy said, she wanted to see the United States. "I'm planning on a road trip," she said. "I want to travel all over the United States."

Where did she see herself in ten years?

Stacy said that she hoped to have married and have two children. "I just want to live a happy, normal life."

"She's gone out a few times and had a lot of friends over since she got out of the hospital," Steve said. "She's enjoyed herself, too."

Her first chance to go out and spend time with her friends had come on July 2, when she went to see the Indian Lake fireworks show. Some of her best friends had helped her through this difficult time, Stacy said, by being there for her for certain events and helping her prepare her animals for the fair.

Stacy reflected with one final thought. "I don't want people to hate me for what happened," Stacy mentioned about concerns for the upcoming school year. "I don't want people to look at me differently either. I just want people to treat me like a normal person."

————

Stacy couldn't anticipate what would happen next, turning her world more upside down – if that were even possible – than anyone could ever imagine.

Chapter Fourteen

*After reviewing the crime scene photographs
and the sheriff's office investigative file, Murray
saw several problems. For starters, Scott's body
and the placement of the rifle. [Scott] was half
way down the bed with his knees bent and his
feet resting firmly on the floor. Above his head
were several blood streaks, as if the body had
been dragged from the pillow at the top of the
bed. Did he really shoot himself and then
reposition his body from the top of the bed to
where it was found, half way down the bed with
his feet on the floor?*

– Village of West Liberty, Ohio, Police Chief
Ron Murray, June 2005

As more and more information came to light, rumors
continued to spread throughout the community about
the hastily-closed investigation.

For one, Donna Smith and her husband, Roger, felt
indignant that the detectives seemed to ignore their story. They
lived on the other side of the county airport, directly across from
Gary and Sharyl Shafer's home. They had their own sorrow to
deal with, an unexpected family loss. Their extended family had
collected at Roger and Donna's house early Sunday morning
before church to discuss their mother's funeral arrangements.

The winds that morning, ten mile-per-hour breezes, flowed
from the Shafer farm, across the airport, and toward Roger and

Donna's home. Roger's brothers and sister arrived sometime around 6:30 in the morning. As they stood in the driveway in the chilly early morning dawn, they heard gunshots from the direction of the airport runway. Turning toward the runway, they heard more shots. After a little discussion, they concluded that hunters must have started early in the morning, maybe to get a jump on the upcoming deer season.

Once Roger and Donna heard on the news what had happened at the Shafer properties, they called the Logan County Sheriff's Office to report what they heard that morning. The detectives politely thanked them for their call, but never followed up. The Smiths heard nothing more from them.

––––––

Another local, Rita Price, also talked far and wide about concerns the detectives seemed to dismiss. She operated a local coffee shop and bakery. After twenty-seven years in business, she still got much of her business on Sunday mornings when all other restaurants stayed closed.

She knew all her customers' quirks and their family backgrounds. They talked with each other, just like you would at the beauty shop. That's what folks did when they came in for a cup of coffee and pastry and sat down for a half-hour or so.

Around 10:30 Sunday morning, the day of the shootings, a customer came in and asked if Rita knew why the police had blocked off State Route 47. Rita called home and told her husband, an avid law-and-order man, to turn on the police scanner to find out. Her husband put the telephone to the scanner, and Rita could hear the dispatcher say that officers were chasing a man across the road from the crime scene toward the county airport runway. Rita held up the phone so that other customers could hear the dispatcher. They looked at each other in confusion. What the heck had happened on State Route 47 by the airport?

Once the papers reported the shootings, Rita read every word. She kept looking for some mention of what she and others had heard that Sunday morning on her husband's police scanner about officers chasing a man over by the county airport. Rita and her friends continued to talk about what they had heard, and finally one of her customers decided to write a letter to the *Bellefontaine Examiner,* questioning the investigation.

For that customer's troubles, she received a message on her telephone answering machine, "You better keep your mouth shut!"

———

Steve and Audrey Moody followed all these stories and pondered them in the middle of the night when they couldn't sleep. They went back and forth on what it all meant. At times, they felt that they should ignore all the rumors and innuendo and assume that the detectives in the Logan County Sheriff's Office had come to the right conclusion, even if their work had flaws. Those of their friends who believed that Sheriff Henry had made the right decision gently pointed out the obvious: no other scenario seemed likely.

When faced with an event this horrific, of course the community would discuss it and second-guess the authorities. Good friends urged the Moodys to move on with their lives, put this behind them as best they could, and avoid thinking about all the speculation from people who knew nothing of police work or investigative procedures.

However, the Moodys couldn't ignore Police Chief Ron Murray.

The State of Ohio has three tiers of law enforcement: the state level, which includes the state highway patrol and the Ohio Bureau of Criminal Identification & Investigation (BCI); the county level with a sheriff's office; and the city/town level with local police offices and town constables. The officials in these three groups, especially at the county and city/town level, have equal authority and responsibility to investigate crime, but in different although sometimes overlapping jurisdictions. The entire state has the state highway patrol and each county has one sheriff, but within Ohio's eighty-eight counties each town or city has its own police force.

No one had more credible law enforcement experience in Logan County than Police Chief Ron Murray, responsible for public safety in the Village of West Liberty since 1977. Murray had spent his entire career working as a police officer. As a member of the Logan County Police Chiefs Association, the Ohio Association of Chiefs of Police, the National Police Chiefs Association, and the International Police Chiefs Association, he'd received numerous awards during his career, including the National Police Chiefs Honor Award for his work in West Liberty.

Murray was certified in every conceivable area of law enforcement: case management; advanced interviews and interrogations; hostage negotiations; undercover investigations; human relations and conflict management; investigations of bias/hate crimes; dealing with the suicidal; crime scene investigations; prescription drug investigations; investigations of physical and sexually abused children; traffic crash investigations; emergency response to terrorism and terrorist attacks; performance leadership; and a host of other specialty courses. When Murray had an opinion about law enforcement and investigations, everybody listened.

Ron Murray's son and Stacy Moody were friends at school. Audrey and Steve Moody knew Murray and his wife from school and church functions. When Ron Murray asked Steve Moody to stop by his office at his convenience, Steve assumed that Murray had reviewed the autopsy reports released the previous week as well as the investigative file provided to him by the Logan County Sheriff's Office and wanted to talk about it.

Chief Murray welcomed Steve and invited him into the department's large conference room. After some initial small talk about their families, Chief Murray told Steve that he wanted to be blunt.

Chief Murray wanted to point out several problems. For starters, Scott's body and the placement of the rifle seemed problematic. The photos revealed Scott on top of his bed, next to Paige Harshbarger, halfway down the bed with his knees bent and his feet resting on the floor. Above his head were several blood streaks, as if the body had been dragged from the pillow at the top of the bed. The top of the bed had spatters of blood in the location where Scott's head would have rested on his pillow when he slept.

Did he really shoot himself behind his ear, Murray wondered, and then reposition himself from the top of the bed, where the first bullet hit him, to where the investigators found him, halfway down the bed with both of his feet on the floor?

Murray surmised instead that someone shot Scott behind the ear, then dragged his body down the bed, planting his feet on the floor. He described the scenario: the first shot came as Scott lay on the bed in a sleeping position. The shooter then repositioned Scott, which required dragging him so that his feet hit the floor, and then shot him a second time. The first shot had probably killed Scott. Even if it hadn't, with that kind of a wound, could Scott have repositioned himself to the extent that he did on the bed?

Murray didn't think it likely and he'd grown troubled that investigators failed to comment on the unusual position of Scott's body, especially after they determined that the first shot didn't kill him. How in the world could Scott have moved himself halfway down the bed after the first shot?

Murray continued with his concerns and pointed to the position of Scott's arms. The photos showed Scott's right arm tucked against the side of his body with his thumb in the rifle's trigger guard. Murray could only come to one conclusion: it looked staged.

If Scott did indeed shoot himself a second time, his thumb would not have remained in the trigger guard. Rather, the recoil would have caused his right arm to fly away from the gun.

No involuntary reaction? No jerking from the fatal shot? How convenient to find Scott's thumb in the trigger guard with his right arm resting perfectly up against the side of his body. The position of his hand and arm seemed too perfect, even amateurish, as though from a movie director's point of view.

The rifle leaned up against Scott's right side, up over his chest and pointed toward his mouth. No recoil? No involuntarily jerk of the hand, allowing the rifle to come to rest at a more explainable position?

Murray told Steve, "It simply doesn't look right."

He also reviewed the weapon itself. According to Logan County Sheriff's Office investigators, Marlin Firearms Co., a subsidiary of Remington Arms, manufactured the gun. In proper working order, the Glenfield model 75C, .22 Long Rifle caliber semi-automatic rifle can hold fifteen unfired .22 Long Rifle cartridges. His detectives had measured the amount of weight necessary to pull the trigger: five and one-half pounds. Would Scott have had the physical capacity to fire the second shot?

The overall length of the Marlin rifle measured at approximately thirty-six and one-half inches, with a muzzle-to-trigger distance of approximately twenty-three inches. Murray re-examined his notes. According to Detective Stout and his team, Scott shot himself the first time in the back of his head, behind his left ear but not as a contact wound. Scott had no powder burn or singed hair where the bullet entered the back of his head. Therefore, the shot came from a rifle eight to twelve inches away from his head when fired.

Murray held up a yardstick behind his left ear. How could someone hold it at an angle – Murray thought about forty degrees – eight to twelve inches away from the back of his head and pull the trigger?

Murray had discussed the case with his deputies. They could not recreate the scenario with another .22 caliber rifle, approximately the same length, and doubted that Scott could have pulled this off.

Murray had more concerns. All of Murray's deputies concurred that Scott would have had to hold the barrel with his right hand, away from his head, and then pull the trigger with his left hand in a very awkward way to shoot himself behind the ear. However, the right-handed Scott had no burn marks on his right hand.

Also, the report noted that the casing from the last round did not fully eject from the rifle. The shooter had used the rifle ten or more times by that point, apparently without any failure. Why would a casing not properly eject after this last shot?

Murray suggested that someone else had placed a hand over the port, causing the casing not to fully eject.

Murray wanted to make Steve fully understand that he and his deputies had serious doubts. They did not believe that Scott was the shooter.

Marlin had sold the rifle to Gilbert Sporting Goods in Cincinnati in 1976. The store, which had gone out of business more than twenty years before the tragedy, sold the rifle in 1977 to Kevin Miller, age nineteen at the time, who lived in Bellefontaine. When questioned, Miller told Detective Bugler that he didn't have the weapon any longer; he thought he'd sold it to someone living on the west side of Bellefontaine sometime during the 1980s. He thought he might have traded it to someone for a crossbow, but to whom he couldn't remember.

The sheriff's office concluded that the rifle belonged to Gary Shafer and that Scott used it to shoot everyone.

A few questions to Ron Shafer, Gary's brother, brought a quick denial. He had never seen the rifle, and he knew exactly which rifles and handguns Gary owned. His brother had possessed only a few shotguns and handguns. Ron insisted that Gary would never have bought a used rifle.

Rumors exploded when the news leaked to the public. No one could say with any certainty where the rifle went after Miller purchased it in 1977. Some speculated that Detective Jon Stout's family gun shop in Bellefontaine, now out of business, but notorious for buying and selling weapons without maintaining the required paperwork, sold it. Speculation had it that guns placed in the evidence locker at the Logan County Sheriff's Office frequently went walking, often ending up for sale at the Stout family gun shop.

———

After Steve Moody got the picture, Murray decided to review the rest of his concerns. Together, they looked at more of the evidence.   The detectives found Scott wearing clean white socks. Why had he taken off his shoes? If he had walked around the house without shoes or boots on, how had his socks stayed so clean in a house with dirty floors?

Murray pointed to a photograph of Scott lying on top of his bed. The pair of jeans Scott wore while on the bed had no belt. A different pair of Scott's jeans lay on the floor with the belt in its loops.

Steve instantly recognized the issue for his skinny son. Scott never wore his jeans without a belt; they'd simply fall down because of Scott's slender waist and small frame. Why in the world would Scott put on another pair of pants without a belt? If he had worn the jeans on the floor with the belt on, why would he have taken them off and switched pants? The jeans with the belt had no bloodstains, so he couldn't have wanted to switch out of a desire for cleanliness.

The photos showed that Scott's room had clothes strewn all over the floor. His muddy boots lay next to wrinkled tee-shirts. Jeans that he probably wore, with a belt through the loops, lay on top of dirty clothes. The scene made no sense to Murray, nor to Steve.

Chief Murray grimly went to the next issue. The morning of the killings, the temperature stayed in the mid-40s and everybody else wore warm clothes. Why not Scott? If he'd switched clothes, what did he do with the bloody ones? With all the mud on Scott's boots, how could he not have tracked mud throughout the house?

Murray continued with the inconsistencies. Blood spattered the wall, next to where Paige lay. Whose blood? The Logan County Sheriff Office investigators never tested it, but recorded it as belonging to Paige.

That made no sense. Was Paige sitting up when she was shot? If so, then why had detectives found her lying down, facing the wall, but with a blanket tucked underneath her chin? Murray pointed out that the shot hit her behind her left ear, execution style, and from the placement he concluded that it came while she slept.

If Paige's blood hadn't spattered the wall, then Scott's blood did. That changed the scenario.

———

Murray looked at all the reports spread out over his large conference room table. He turned to the witnesses' statements. Murray picked up Andrew Denny's statement, then posed a question to Steve. "Andrew Denny says that when he left the house that morning there was a male sleeping on the sofa. Bret Davidson stated he slept on the sofa that night, but when he left the house that morning, saying goodbye to Sheri Kay, he clearly remembered seeing a big Dodge truck with distinctive smokestacks parked in the driveway. That truck belonged to Denny."

Murray paused, glancing at the statements. "Davidson said he looked at his cell phone to see the time when he woke up, and that he left the house around six that morning. Andrew Denny [the owner of the Dodge truck] said he left the house around seven."

Murray looked at Steve and said, "If Davidson wasn't sleeping on the sofa, who was lying there? Did Denny see someone else?"

Murray reviewed the timing, a critical issue since the murders seemed to have taken place immediately after Denny left.

Next, Murray moved in another direction. Several reports stated that the deputies found Gary and Sharyl's house locked and that they had to kick the door in to gain entrance. Other reports concurred that the Shafers had an obsession about locking their doors. How did the shooter get in and how did the door get locked when the shooter left?

Murray questioned the motive. "What could have set Scott off?" he asked Steve. "He apparently was sleeping when Davidson and Denny left. Why would he wake up suddenly and go on a shooting rampage? Everybody else was sleeping, so others in the house couldn't have set him off. And why would he go over to his grandparents' house first?

"Scott would have had to wake up, get dressed, walk over to his grandparents' house where they let him in, go into the basement to fetch the .22 rifle, shoot both of his grandparents while they were standing in their kitchen preparing breakfast – unusual head shots, behind the ears – lock their dog in one of the bedrooms at some point, return to his own home a quarter mile away, take off his sweatshirt, shirt, belt (or change jeans), and shoes, and then shoot everybody else."

According to Murray, it didn't add up.

Murray offered even more doubt.

Scott's close friends knew that he didn't like guns or care to shoot. To Murray, the shots behind the ear looked like professional hits. Even Scott's grandparents, Gary and Sharyl Shafer, were shot in the head behind their ears rather than in the body.

How could Scott have done that if he didn't know weapons well and while his grandparents stood and moved around?

Chief Murray knew that this was only the beginning. He was unsure whether he should share with Steve Moody at this time who he thought the killer could be and the motive for the shootings.

*Sharyl Shafer, Wilma Buroker
and Gary Shafer*

Scott Moody

Wilma Buroker home

Sheri Kay Shafer's home

*Misti Martin, Sheri Kay Shafer and Stacy
Moody, age 15*

Stacy Moody, age 14

Stacy in Showmanship trials, 2003

Megan Karus

Paige Harshbarger

Gary and Sharyl Shafer's home

Sheri Kay Shafer's kitchen

Entrance to Sheri Kay Shafer's home

Sheri Kay Shafer's bedroom

Entrance to Stacy's bedroom   *Stacy Moody's bedroom*

Scott Moody's bedroom

Sheri Kay Shafer's home

*Stacy Moody with members of the
Bellefontaine Fire Department*

Stacy with MedFlight team

Martha Winner and Stacy in her neck brace

Stacy Moody and her husband, Rick

Chapter Fifteen

I may be totally off the mark here, but that's the way I'm thinking. I'm taking it that you're thinking we're incompetent . . . that you don't believe the information we're giving you and you're going out and doing your own separate investigation.

– Detective Sargent Jeff Cooper, supervisor of the sheriff's office detectives, in a telephone conversation with Dr. Michael Failor, Logan County Coroner, June 2005

E ach of the eighty-eight counties in Ohio has a coroner, a licensed physician who serves a four-year elected term and works with, but not for, the sheriff's office and local police to perform autopsies or otherwise investigate questionable deaths. His duties are varied, but typically the coroner is responsible for maintaining the county morgue. When the identity of someone discovered dead is unknown, or the deceased person's relatives or other persons entitled to custody of the body are unknown or not present, the body is removed to the county morgue where it is held for identification and disposal. In addition, the coroner keeps a detailed record and fills in the cause of death on the death certificate in all cases coming under his jurisdiction.

Ohio law also requires that "when any person dies as a result of criminal or other violent means . . . by suicide, or in any suspicious or unusual manner . . . any member of an ambulance service, emergency squad, or law enforcement agency who obtains knowledge thereof arising from the person's duties shall immediately notify the office of the coroner of the known facts concerning the time, place, manner, and circumstances of the death."

It becomes incumbent, then, for the coroner to become involved with the investigation so that he can state the cause of death on the deceased's certificate of death.

On the day of the shootings, the dispatcher notified the Logan Country coroner, Dr. Michael Failor, of the tragedy, and he decided to send one of his assistants to the crime scene. Later that day, the detectives notified Dr. Failor that they had closed the case.

However, Dr. Failor, not the sheriff, had to sign Scott's death certificate as a suicide. As any coroner would, he had a professional responsibility to interview Stacy Moody, review the investigative material developed by the sheriff's office, and verify their conclusions about Scott's cause of death. Dr. Failor called the sheriff's office and left a message, asking for someone to call him about their investigation. A few days later, Detective Sargent Jeff Cooper, head of the department's detectives, returned his call.

According to the transcript obtained from the Logan County Sheriff's Office, the following telephone conversation took place between Dr. Failor and Sgt. Cooper:

Dr. Failor: I was wondering if I could come out and – if there's a tape, listen to the tape, or if it's an interview, listen to the New Directions interview, the one with Cheryl Garland-Briggs [director; local counseling service].

Sgt. Cooper: Why?

Dr. Failor: Because it would help me in my investigation. The reason why would be, it would be added weight to the suicide thing. Also, did you ask the counselor, Cheryl, why she waited two weeks to share her findings?

Sgt. Cooper: Well, the thing with her is, number one, her stuff is confidential. But she waived the confidentiality because in her mind the person who came and talked with her, Sheri [Kay], is dead. Okay. But I don't know why she waited eight days.

Dr. Failor: Uh-huh.

Sgt. Cooper: What the situation is, doctor . . . The thing that's come into my mind is, you're not believing what we're telling you. The way I'm taking it is – what you're saying is – 'I want to listen to this lady because I don't believe you talked to her.'

Dr. Failor: No, that's not . . .

Sgt. Cooper: That's the way I'm taking it.

Dr. Failor: No, no . . .

Sgt. Cooper: Because every time we go talk to somebody and tell you what has happened, well – you want to interview them.

Dr. Failor: Well, what I wanted to do is come out and listen to the tape and see what the counselor says regarding her meeting with Sheri Kay and her concerns about Scott. And then I really need to be independent enough – not to be suspicious of anybody doing a bad job or anything else. When this is all over, people are going to come to me and say – well, we still don't believe that it was a suicide and that the sheriff announced too early, and then it seems it is covered up and stuff.

Sgt. Cooper: Well, wait a minute . . . your job is to determine the cause of death. And in this case, it's your assistant on duty that morning, Dr. Davis, it's his job to determine the cause of death.

Dr. Failor: Well, we're working together on this.

Sgt. Cooper: I'm just telling you my opinion. In my opinion, that is what I'm getting out of this. You don't believe what we tell you, and you're the first coroner that's ever had questions about what we tell you as far as the information that we have. Why do you need to go and get it yourself?

Dr. Failor: I think it's my duty . . .

Sgt. Cooper: Well, I'll tell you what, doctor. We've got the information here and I will let you look and listen to anything you want when the sheriff tells me to do that. And until then, I'm not going to release anything. Do you understand?

———

Dr. Failor: I talked to Jon Stout earlier and that's why I was calling. I think you're misinterpreting my motives.

Sgt. Cooper: I may be. I may be totally off the mark here, but that's the way I'm thinking. I'm taking it that you're thinking we're incompetent . . . that you don't believe the information we're giving you and you're going out and doing your own separate investigation. For instance, you bring in the picture of the older gray-haired EMT member that was working on Stacy, wanting to know his name.

Dr. Failor: Well, see . . .

Sgt. Cooper: That's what I mean. With you running around and doing a separate investigation.

————

Dr. Failor: Okay. So, Jon Stout did most of the interviews. I called him this morning, but he wouldn't talk to me about the interviews. That's why I'm calling you. I'm interested in his interview with Amanda Arthur [Scott's previous girlfriend]. I wasn't aware, again, that she had been interviewed. And that sounds like it was a really good interview for the evidence of suicide. I also need to go see Stacy with the EMT member and with Jon Stout.

Sgt. Cooper: What?

Dr. Failor: There would be three of us there, probably. I hope the lawyer isn't there. The last time the lawyer was there, he screwed everything up. I don't really want to talk to him. Anyway, I'd probably like to go back and talk to Stacy again and what I wanted to ask her would be about the meeting her mom had with the counselor and whether what I heard is right, that the boy – her brother, beat her up and her mother up, and whether that's true or not. Is Stacy trying to cover for Scott more than she should? I could get a feel for how she reacts.

Sgt. Cooper: You're asking a lot. What else?

Dr. Failor: Well, I really need to meet with Cheryl from New Directions to find out if she knows where the .22 shotgun came from and whether there is anything else that would be important for me to know before we decided that this was a suicide or murder.

Sgt. Cooper: Okay. This is what I'm talking about. If we talked to Amanda Arthur and the counselor and now you want to talk to them. Why do we do it? So why don't you just go do it? It just gets back to like I say. The way it appears to me, you know, we go interview these people and you hear about it and so forth and then you want to go in and interview them.

Dr. Failor: No, no, that's not my intent. But actually, there's nothing wrong with me re-interviewing people or even checking out the quality . . .

Sgt. Cooper: Then why do we even do it? We'll just let you do it.

Dr. Failor: No, no, I don't want to change the way anybody works.

Sgt. Cooper: Well, if you don't believe in what we're doing, why are we wasting our time doing it?

Dr. Failor: It's not that I don't believe it. It's just that I need to . . . to do some things myself, just to run point checks to make sure that when we call it a suicide, it's a suicide.

Sgt. Cooper: Like I said, just as soon as I talk to the sheriff and he tells me to release this to you, I will do that.

Dr. Failor: Okay.

Sgt. Cooper: And that's my next step. And I will tell him you're requesting this stuff. If he tells me to do it, then I will give you a call right back and say, hey, here's the material – here you go.

Dr. Failor: What if he tells you not to do it?

Sgt. Cooper: Then I won't do it.

Dr. Failor: Okay. Then what do you think I should do?

Sgt. Cooper: Well, that's your problem.

Dr. Failor: Okay. Anyway, I decided . . . I just wanted to do my job well. I'm going to do it well, and if I make people mad at me I don't like it, but that's the way it goes. I'm not stirring up trouble, I'm not necessarily a supporter or an antagonist of anybody. I'm just trying to do a good job.

Sgt. Cooper: And I'm going to make this point to you. That's why we didn't want you going down to Columbus to see Stacy. The reason for that is because two interviews were already done on the basis to hit Stacy on the conflicts from what she's telling us and what the evidence shows us. And that's why we didn't want you doing that, and you went ahead and did it anyway. And when you go down there and do that, and she gets a case of the "whatever" or, you know, something that Jon [Stout] had set up and to have her later on in an interview – that gets messed up and that screws up what we're trying to accomplish. If we stopped to tell everybody what we were doing on an investigation, it would take us three years to get it done.

————

Dr. Failor: We're just trying to do a good job, not to dispute anybody's finding or make trouble. We just want to have this, so it's done, and we can look ourselves in the mirror and talk to other people and say, yeah, it wasn't just the sheriff's opinion, it was the coroner who had to decide whether it was a suicide and we didn't just know . . .

Sgt. Cooper: It wasn't just the sheriff's opinion. It was BCI's [Ohio Bureau of Criminal Identification & Investigation], it was the pathologist down in Montgomery County. You're exactly right.

Dr. Failor: That would be ideal. That would be perfect.

Sgt. Cooper: And that's what we've been doing. I will go talk to the sheriff . . .

Dr. Failor: I haven't heard anything from BCI, either. See, I don't hear these things.

Sgt. Cooper: And there again. What, we're lying to you?

Dr. Failor: No, no . . . I haven't heard from them. I can't know what they say if I haven't heard from them.

Sgt. Cooper: Well, we're telling you that. We've said that repeatedly. We said that in the two meetings we had out here. Now, if you choose not to believe that then you're saying that we're liars.

Dr. Failor: No, I think what's happening . . .

Sgt. Cooper: And that's what irritates me. When it gets down to it, that's what irritates me, Dr. Failor. And when you say I need to hear this because I need to hear it, you're saying I'm a liar. That would be like me questioning everything you do as a medical doctor.

Dr. Failor: Yeah.

Sgt. Cooper: You see what I'm saying? When you're doing that, that's what you're doing. You're calling me a liar.

Dr. Failor: No, I'm not.

Sgt. Cooper: That's exactly what you're doing. And that's why . . . and that's why I'm peeved. And so as long as I'm in charge of this investigation, I'm not going to release anything until the sheriff tells me to.

———

Sgt. Cooper: I'm saying that what you're doing is . . . how we're perceiving it. How I'm perceiving it when I tell you something. And I'm telling you that I interviewed this lady [Cheryl Garland-Briggs] and she said ninety days prior to the graduation date that she was visited by Sheri Kay Shafer and Sheri Kay Shafer told her that she had been beaten . . . and the family had been beaten by Scott, and domestic violence issues are there, and she was in fear that he was going, that Scott was going to kill them.

Dr. Failor: Did she say that?

Sgt. Cooper: That's what she told me.

Dr. Failor: Did she say that Stacy was beaten also?

Sgt. Cooper: She said the family – domestic violence. So, I'm assuming Stacy.

Dr. Failor: Yeah, I'd heard Stacy was beaten, too. Yeah, I would like to confirm that myself.

Sgt. Cooper: And there you go again. That's exactly what I mean. That would be like you telling me he died of a heart attack. Okay, so I'm going to see other people to find out how many say it was a heart attack? You see what I'm saying?

Sgt. Cooper hung up the phone. He was tired of these conversations with Dr. Failor, always insinuating that he was lying. He was tired of being second-guessed, especially by someone he thought was incompetent in his work, always interfering with police investigations. This time, Failor better not screw up this investigation. Maybe he should send someone out to talk with him.

He had heard subtle hints from deputies when he put up his first flyer for the benefit he wanted to sponsor for Stacy, but Richards just shrugged it off. Why should he reconsider the idea? But the rumors within the community were growing stranger and stranger. When Robbie Richards, who owned Vicario's Pizza in Bellefontaine and routinely put the local high school sports team photos in his windows or placed a jar on the counter to help those in need or donated pizzas for community events, decided to sponsor a benefit for Stacy Moody to help her family's expenses, his nightmare began. The Logan County deputies that frequented his shop for take-out pizza and soft drinks dropped subtle hints that maybe he should reconsider the idea. Richards ignored the advice, but the warnings and rumors continued, escalating in seriousness.

Like many in the community, Richards couldn't see Scott Moody as the shooter. He thought the whole investigation was a set-up, and he happily told his customers his opinion, regardless of whether the Bellefontaine police and Logan County deputies heard him or not.

The benefit itself raised a significant amount of money and went off quite well, but Richards started to get harassed. He grew concerned, and he couldn't understand the harassment. It was escalating, and Richards was becoming paranoid, literally terrified.

Finally, in early November 2005, one of the sheriff's detectives, Frenchie Robinson, followed Richards as he left his pizza store to drive to a local club. Richards tried not to think too much about it until hours later when he looked out the bar window and saw Detective Robinson still sitting in his car, watching the door.

Richards called one of his closest friends and told her the situation. He speculated that it had something to do with Stacy

Moody and her family and the benefit he'd sponsored for them. He felt certain that the Moody boy hadn't shot anyone. Now he suspected that the detectives would kill him because they thought he knew too much. On the phone, he wept out of fear. Richards went so far as to ask his friend to look after his children if something should happen to him.

Richards then made a second phone call. He decided to call the sheriff's office, asking to speak to a supervisor in the detective's department. What did he have to lose? He wanted to complain about Frenchie Robinson, the detective waiting outside the bar. "Please call him off!" he pleaded.

Surprisingly, it worked.

A few minutes later, Richards looked outside the bar window and saw the detective drive off. Now consumed with terror, the next morning Richards drove to Dayton to retain legal counsel to defend him in case he got arrested for some unknown reason, or worse – in case he needed an attorney to handle his own estate.

A few weeks later, Detective Frenchie Robinson with the Logan County Sheriff's Office tendered his letter of resignation, supposedly due to his involvement with drugs.

Some speculated that the reason given for Robinson's resignation was a smokescreen, and that seniors in the department had real concern - and worry - that Robinson had loose lips. He might end up talking about things that were no one's business unless they worked for the Logan County Sheriff.

Chapter Sixteen

Stacy noticed handcuffs down by the seat buckle.
She picked them up and began looking at them.
She was putting them back when Stout told her to
give them to him. Stout took the handcuffs from
Stacy, then handcuffed her left wrist to the
steering wheel. Stacy told Stout that they hurt
and to take them off.

– Stacy Moody, being interviewed by attorneys
from the Ohio Attorney General's Office

D etective Jon Stout was tired of the rumors. It had been
two and one-half months since the massacre and town
people would not leave it alone. Stacy Moody had to
think that Scott did it, so why wouldn't she say so? Stout was
going to finally take care of it and bring these rumors to rest.

Jon Stout suggested to Steve and Audrey Moody that he
should take Stacy to lunch so that she would understand that the
police were her friends. It was Stout's pretext that she would
eventually open up to him and tell him what he wanted to hear.
Steve and Audrey Moody liked his idea; they thought it made
sense. Stout intended to befriend Stacy, gain her trust, and help
her confront her memories of the terrible day when her brother
shot her. It seemed like a reasonable plan to all of them.

The Moodys thought about Stout's successful track record in
solving so many cases, the trust that Sheriff Henry placed in his
star detective, Stout's rapid rise in the ranks, his years of
experience interviewing people, and his certainty that he'd

already solved the case and just needed Stacy to admit what she already knew. They knew that he, not his first wife, had primary custody of his three children. They knew his sister, who worked for the prosecutor's office. They felt safe trusting him. As the senior detective on the case and the one who'd investigated this tragedy from the very beginning, he knew the facts of the case better than anyone.

All the therapists in their community, no matter how strong their credentials, would find Stacy's situation out of their depth. The Logan County Children's Services caseworker had driven over with the detectives, which validated that Stout had the trust of Children's Services. Unlike local counselors, Detective Stout had seen violence again and again, including the images that haunted Stacy's nightmares.

Who could help Stacy better than Stout? Certainly not Audrey and Steve. Overwhelmed by their grief, monumental financial challenges, a legal mess that had gone on for over a decade, a farm in need of extensive upkeep, and a badly injured teenager they no longer knew that well, not to mention their own three boys and their own farm and the many things they put on hold in order to deal with the crisis, they clutched at the lifeline Stout offered. From their perspective, Stacy had problems even before the tragedy had occurred. The psychological baggage of lying about the shooter would only add to her troubles. She needed help and she needed it now.

When Detective Stout offered a way to help Stacy face her trauma, Steve and Audrey Moody said yes.

———

Stout arranged to pick up Stacy on Wednesday, August 17, for lunch. He arrived that day at the Moody home around noon in his unmarked vehicle and explained that he was on duty. He suggested that he take Stacy over to Indian Lake, a ten-minute drive, and buy her a fast-food lunch somewhere. Stacy and Stout got into his county car and left.

Stacy had other ideas. She wanted a nice lunch, maybe one at Red Lobster in Lima, thirty miles away.

Stout initially said no to Stacy's request. "I can't be gone that long," he said. "I'm still on duty."

But Stout changed his mind and radioed the dispatcher, saying he had a follow-up case in Lima and wouldn't return for the afternoon.

Stacy told her parents that Stout paid for the meal with some type of credit card, and the tab came in around $25. Stacy seemed pleased. She "had gotten into Stout's wallet pretty good."

After their lunch in Lima, Stout took Stacy cruising past several drug dealers' homes located in the seedier neighborhoods in Bellefontaine and Logan County. According to Stacy, Stout wanted to show off his "sheriff powers," explaining that he knew where all the crooks lived.

After more than three hours, Stout finally took Stacy home. According to Stacy, nothing weird took place and she enjoyed herself.

Stout's version differed slightly. He told others that fifteen-year-old Stacy kept staring at him with "love eyes" and, after he asked her several times what she had on her mind, Stacy told him that she loves "giving head," suggesting – at least in Stout's mind – that she wouldn't mind performing oral sex on him.

When questioned later by a social worker assigned to her case, Stacy said this whole conversation centered on Stout repeatedly asking her what she liked doing in sports. Somewhat exasperated, Stacy finally answered Stout with a smart, sassy remark saying that she liked having oral sex, or as her friends would say, "giving head."

Stacy admitted that after she said this Stout smiled and showed surprise. She realized that maybe she shouldn't have said what she did, and she quickly changed the subject. Neither said anything further along those lines.

———————

Several weeks later, on September 7, Stout and his partner, Mike Brugler, stopped by the Moodys and Stout asked Stacy when they would have lunch again.

Stacy, feeling somewhat intimidated and impressed by their presence, just smiled. A few days later, Stout came to Riverside High School around 12:30 p.m. one day while on duty, again in his unmarked cruiser, and invited her to lunch.

This time they went through McDonald's drive-thru and then drove out to Indian Lake – a ten-minute drive away – to have lunch. After they parked, Stacy noticed another man parked in the same area.

Stout slyly commented with a sexual innuendo, "I'll bet we just ruined what he was doing."

Stacy then noticed handcuffs down by the seat buckle. She picked them up and began studying them.

"Do you like those?" said Stout. "Give them to me."

Stout took the handcuffs from Stacy, reached over and grabbed her arm, then handcuffed her left wrist to the steering wheel.

"Ouch! They hurt," exclaimed Stacy. "Please take them off."

Stout, with a wolfish grin, complied and unfastened the cuffs.

"Want to drive?" he said.

Stacy said no, but after he asked her several more times,

Stacy finally said, "Okay."

A little reluctant because at fifteen years old she didn't have a valid driver's license, she put a hand on the wheel. At Stout's insistence, Stacy then moved over and sat on Stout's lap and began steering his unmarked police car as they drove through the parking lot and finally out onto the highway.

(Stacy would later remark to her friends that she could feel Stout's erection as she sat on his lap; he was getting a "boner.")

Stacy finally got off his lap and moved back over to the passenger side of the car. She watched Stout adjust his clothes and laughed. The two of them started flirting with each other, back and forth – sexual comments – until Stacy finally asked him what his wife would say if she knew what they were doing.

"It's simple," Stout replied. "My wife would never know."

Stout began teasing Stacy. "I've got naked pictures of you from the hospital and I'm keeping them in my desk drawer. Because you're so hot, I sometimes show them to other detectives."

Stacy grew angry until Stout confessed, "I'm only kidding. I don't have any naked pictures of you."

The conversation continued along the same lines. Stout wanted to see those "pretty things," referring to Stacy's breasts.

At first, Stacy said no. But Stacy was enjoying the attention. It had been a rough year and she was never sure of what people thought of her. Stacy lifted her shirt and showed him her bra.

Stout reached over and rubbed her breasts for a moment, saying, "Oh yeah, these are nice." He then slipped his hands inside her bra, cupping her breasts.

Before anything further happened, Stout's cell phone rang. Audrey was calling to explain that he had to get Stacy home because her tutor had arrived. According to Stacy, Stout "raced her home" and dropped her off. Nothing else took place at that time, and Stacy freely admitted that she didn't feel upset over what had happened.

————

Their third private time together took place on September 13. Stout contacted Audrey and Steve Moody and explained his plan to pick Stacy up from school and take her to lunch. This would give him an opportunity to talk to Stacy, maybe allowing her a chance to open up a little more so that she might talk about the shootings and what she remembered.

Audrey and Steve Moody, unaware of the conversations and events that had taken place between Stacy and Stout, easily gave their consent. They were impressed that Detective Stout, showing his obvious concern, would want to take the time to try and help Stacy.

Again, Stout came to Stacy's school in his unmarked vehicle while on duty to pick her up to take her to lunch. Stout had a surprise for her when Stacy got into his car. He had a birthday card for her – "Happy 16th" – where he wrote a special note inside. Stout told her that he planned to take her to a special meeting at the "general's" offices in Dayton. Stacy had no idea what he meant, but she had a tutoring session that afternoon and said she couldn't stay away that long. Not surprisingly, a few minutes later he received a phone call stating that the meeting location had changed to the sheriff's office, so he could take her to lunch after all.

Once more they headed to Indian Lake and purchased fast food from Burger King. They took their food to another rest area to park and watch the boaters out on the lake.

A lady in a boat went by and Stout said, "Look at her, she's really fat. She has one boob in front of the boat and another boob in the back of the boat."

They both laughed.

While sitting there, Stout reached over and took out his handcuffs. Stacy gave him a look of surprise. Without asking, this time he handcuffed Stacy's left wrist to the steering wheel and her right wrist to her seatbelt latch. Stacy smiled, even though she was incredibly nervous.

Stout then moved over and put his head on her shoulder and started rubbing Stacy's breasts, over her shirt.

"I'm a little scared to be handcuffed," Stacy whispered. "What if somebody sees us?"

Stout said, mockingly, "I've never done this before. I won't go any further than you want me to."

Stacy enjoyed his touch, believing him, thinking that maybe this was okay.

She finally asked Stout to uncuff her, which he reluctantly did. They kidded around with each other, and then Stout said, "Here, climb over and sit on my lap."

Once she was on his lap, Stout kissed her.

Stacy raised an eye in surprise. "Dude, you have a wife!"

"She'll never find out," he said.

The two of them started making out, hands going everywhere. Stacy felt comfortable with Stout, freely admitting that she was not forced to do anything she didn't want to do. She enjoyed the attention.

Stout just smiled to himself, the rumors were true. He could put another notch on his belt.

Another car pulled into the rest area and, after adjusting their clothes, Stout took Stacy home.

———

Stacy was thrilled when the community organized a benefit "poker run" on her behalf. Participants, usually riding motorcycles, had to visit five to seven checkpoints in the area, drawing a playing card at each one, with the object to have the best poker hand at the end of the run. Winning was purely a matter of chance, but the event could raise hundreds of dollars for a worthy cause and everyone could get together afterwards to celebrate the event over a few beers.

To Stacy's surprise, Stout won one-half of the 50/50 drawing. But instead of giving the money back to Stacy's family as a donation as most people would choose to do, Stout elected to keep all the money and supposedly gave it to his wife.

When Stacy shamed him, Stout ended up giving her $100.

"See, I'm a good cop," he said with a smile.

With Audrey and Steve Moody's full approval, Stacy and Detective Stout spoke frequently on the phone. He was also talking to her parents, telling them that he felt he was making head way with Stacy's well-being.

During one call, Stacy expressed an interest in photography and police work. The next time they spoke, Stout suggested to Stacy that she should go on a stakeout with him. Stout told her to tell her parents that Mike Brugler, his partner, would be along too, so that everything would seem on the up and up.

On Friday night, September 30, Stout pulled his unmarked vehicle up to the Moodys' house around 11:00 that night to pick up Stacy. He brought with him some baby spoons from Sheri Kay's house. The sheriff's office had received them from a woman who had bought them at an auction of Stacy's family's belongings. The woman thought Stacy might want to have them since they had belonged to Stacy and her brother Scott.

Stout, of course, was no fool. He thought this gesture would make him look good in Audrey's and Steve's eyes.

Stout explained to Audrey and Steve that the sheriff's office was going to stake out a tractor factory plant that evening where it was rumored that tractors were being stolen during the shift change, sometime around midnight. He and Brugler were going to be the main detectives. According to Stout, as soon as they left they were going to pick up Detective Brugler.

Brugler knew nothing about any planned stakeout.

While at the Moodys' home, Audrey briefly told Stout about Bill Sadler, Steve's sister's boyfriend. Audrey had an unusual request. "Would you check him out? I saw him grab Stacy's butt at her birthday party."

Stout tried to hide his amusement by looking down at his shoes. He smiled and said that he'd check him out. Knowing what he had planned tonight, someone grabbing Stacy's butt should be the least of their concerns.

––––––––

Stout and Stacy said their goodbyes and left to drive toward Bellefontaine, cruising around various neighborhoods. Stout seemed excited while driving Stacy by the "pink house," one of Bellefontaine's notorious drug havens. They also drove past Stout's house and by his new rental property, then headed over to the offices of Logan County Children's Services. At about 11:30 p.m., Stout parked his car in the agency's parking lot.

"Why are we parking here?" Stacy said, surprised.

Stout replied, "Nobody ever looks around here."

Stout gave her a wolfish look and then reclined his seat all the way back.

Stacy whispered, "Okay, put your gun belt out of the way because I'm not coming over there to sit on your lap until you do."

He unstrapped his belt with his service revolver and put it on the floor in front of his seat. Stacy shimmied over next to him, climbed up on his lap facing him, and began kissing him full on the mouth. Stout clumsily began to fondle Stacy's breasts while bragging about his tattoos.

"I don't believe you have tattoos," Stacy cooed, because I'm sure they're not permissible."

Stout unbuttoned his shirt and slid it off. Stacy first examined his chest, then peeked at his back.

"The large tattoo on my back almost caused my second divorce," he laughed.

Stacy took off her shirt but decided to keep her bra on. After a few moments of kissing, touching and grabbing, he unhooked her bra and she then gyrated out of her jeans and thong underwear.

Stout still had on his pants, so Stacy confidently bent down to undo his pants with her teeth.

Stout thought to himself, "This little freshman is a hot one."

"You don't have to do anything," he assured her, hoping otherwise. "Just climb up on my chest and sit on my face. I just want to give you a little lick."

At first, Stacy demurred. "I don't think so."

But within moments, she worked up the courage to do as he asked. Stout began performing oral sex on her, his pants still on but unzipped. After Stout enjoyed her for a little bit, Stacy slid back down on his lap and reached into his pants to pull out his penis. She helped Stout remove his pants and sat on him naked, rubbing back and forth, teasing him.

"We better stop," she said as she tried to slow down, "because I don't want to get pregnant."

"Don't worry," Stout gasped, "I'm unhooked."

Stacy knew what "unhooked" meant, farm slang for having

had a vasectomy.

―――――

Stacy eventually slid over to the passenger side.

Stout tried to calm his breathing, saying, "Are you done already? Did you climax?"

"Yes," Stacy said.

He reached over, felt her wetness, and smiled.

After a few moments, Stout told her, "I'm going to get dressed and go pee."

Stacy put her bra and top back on but left her pants off. When Stout got out of the car to relieve himself, Stacy jumped over to the driver's side, turned on the car, locked the doors, and drove it forward as though driving away.

She meant it as a joke; after what they had just done, she just wanted to play with his mind.

Stout hurried back to the car, pulling up his zipper. Stacy said she planned to drive, so Stout shrugged and got into the passenger's seat, moving Stacy's pants out of the way.

They then left the parking lot with Stacy behind the wheel, heading for the streets of Bellefontaine. They kissed some more, then Stout finally took Stacy home around 2:00 in the morning.

Stacy went straight to bed, telling no one what had happened. She knew she had been a willing participant but hoped no one would question her about what had taken place, especially since they never went to any stakeout with Detective Brugler.

―――――

The following week, Audrey called Stout and asked if he might come over and try talking with Stacy one more time about that dreadful morning. To Audrey's and Steve's eyes, she finally seemed emotionally ready to face the tragedy. They felt grateful to Stout for befriending Stacy and helping her deal with the reality of that awful experience. They thought of Stout as a godsend who had contributed to Stacy's well-being.

After an exchange of niceties with the Moodys, Stout suggested that Stacy ride with him over to De Graff where he needed to get gas. They could talk along the way.

After filling up his car at a local station, they drove down State Route 235. Stout slowed the car down and then pulled off the road onto a long, narrow lane with an abandoned farmhouse at the end. He finally came to a stop at the end of the lane.

Stout began, "You know, I would lie to you if it would get you to sit on my lap."

Stacy, giggling, obeyed and climbed up onto his lap.

Stout paused, looking her in the eyes, then said, "We need to finally get this out in the open and bring some closure to the shooting. The sooner you agree that your brother was the shooter, the more we can sit here and play around. You need to stop the 'what ifs.'"

Stacy, ever compliant, looked at Stout and told him softly that her brother had done the shooting.

As soon as she said it, Stout reached over and began kissing her and rubbing her breasts. Stacy slid off his lap and reached down to unfasten his pants.

After several minutes of playtime, Stout pulled up his underwear and pants and took a disheveled-looking Stacy home.

————

Late one dreary Monday afternoon in October the phone rang at the Moodys' house. Audrey heard Stacy pick up, but her nurturing instinct told her to listen in. Gingerly lifting the receiver of the family's land line to her ear, she froze as Stout told Stacy that his wife was planning to go out of town for the weekend and that she could come over and spend the night at his house. Stacy remarked that her parents would never let her do that.

Stout interrupted, telling her to lie to her parents and say that she was going to spend the night at a friend's house, maybe Krissy's.

Audrey, shocked, quietly put down the phone.

What in the world was going on? Was this Jon Stout, the Logan County Sheriff's Office star-performing detective, the lead investigator for the gruesome Moody killings? The one she trusted with her stepdaughter?

Was Stacy, who just celebrated her 16th birthday, having sex with a thirty-something-year-old married man?

Oh my god, she needed to talk with Steve right away. They needed outside help. Everything she had heard about the Logan County Sheriff's Office must be true. The place was absolutely corrupt.

Audrey started making telephone calls. Maybe the one suggestion she and Steve eventually received was the best: the agency with the necessary resources to fight police corruption in Logan County was the Ohio Attorney General's Office located in Columbus.

Chapter Seventeen

If this employee [Stout] was found guilty and charged with dishonesty, isn't it possible that he would have made dishonest statements in the past against citizens in court cases in order to achieve a conviction for the prosecution?

– Letter published in the *Bellefontaine Examiner*, December 5, 2005, by Elizabeth Miller, a local resident

On November 4, 2005, Logan County Children's Services filed a complaint with the Logan County Sheriff's Office against one of the department's senior detectives, Jon Stout, based on allegations that he had sexual contact with a minor. On November 8, 2005, Sheriff Henry placed Stout on administrative leave (suspended with pay) until an investigation reviewed the charges.

Initially, Sheriff Henry wouldn't release Stout's name to the public, but he did confirm to a news reporter that an investigation had begun. Sheriff Henry admitted that he hadn't read the report from Children's Services and had decided to simply let the investigation take its course.

Privately, Sheriff Henry knew that this was bound to happen. Within the department, a standing joke to new road warriors went: "If you wanted to get a quick, satisfying blow job, go troll the high school's parking lot for the young and dumb ones." All it took was an accusation that you knew about their drug use along with a promise that you wouldn't tell the school and their parents in exchange for a "personal counseling session." Sheriff Henry had expected better of Stout than that.

With the Logan County Prosecutor at his side, Sheriff Henry decided to hold a press conference to try and quell the barrage of questions assaulting his office. "Any kind of accusation makes you sick, to think it may be true," the sheriff said. "But I deal with these things as straight up as I can, and I will have no control over it. It will be investigated the same as any other charge.

"The Buckeye State Sheriff's Association, which assigns detectives from across the state to investigate crimes within other departments, sent an investigator to Bellefontaine last week to conduct interviews," Sheriff Henry said.

Logan County Prosecutor Gerald Heaton, who according to procedures would have to recuse himself from the case because Stout's sister worked as a secretary in his office, commented that "once that internal investigation is complete, a prosecutor from outside Logan County will decide whether charges are warranted."

On Tuesday, November 29, the Logan County Sheriff's Office conducted an administrative hearing regarding the allegations against Stout. An internal affairs officer presented the sheriff's case against Stout. Stout, without the benefit of counsel, had two local deputies appear on his behalf. The hearing went quickly and ended with a decision that Stout, a sixteen-year-employee, had violated departmental policy regarding conduct and behavior. According to the department's records, this employee's dismissal also included charges of dishonesty and insubordination as outlined by the Ohio Administrative Code.

Sheriff Henry offered nothing further and answered all questions with the statement that he wanted to protect the integrity of the criminal investigation. The sheriff had never wanted to make the decision to fire his top detective. He said, "Mr. Stout has many commendations in his personnel file and he has worked doggedly on many cases.

"This is going to leave a big hole in the department," Sheriff Henry said. "Jon solved a lot of cases. He was instrumental in a lot of cases, here and outside the county. He was instrumental in a lot of drug cases."

However, when the hearing officer recommended dismissal, Sheriff Henry had no other choice but to end Stout's career as a peace officer in Logan County. He hoped this would conclude the issue. It didn't. The State of Ohio got involved.

————

The Ohio Attorney General's Office assigned Scott Longo, an attorney with the Child and Elder Protection Section, as special prosecutor in the case with the job to determine if Stout had done anything criminal. If Longo filed charges after reviewing the case, a report of his findings would go to a Logan County Grand Jury.

Logan County residents shook their heads. They'd had an unusual year of police misconduct. Another detective and the county dog warden had both tested positive for marijuana use and resigned. In late summer, Stout's former partner, Larry Garwood – serving as a detective with Stout – was found guilty of three misdemeanor charges for taking a fully automatic machine gun from the sheriff's office property room and shooting up camper trailers on a neighbor's property in 2004. In the beginning of November, a county deputy working as a jailer lost his job for abusing his position. And now Stout.

"I'll be glad to see 2005 come to an end," Sheriff Henry said. "It's been a rough year for us."

Elizabeth Miller, a Bellefontaine resident, decided to sum it up in a letter published in "The Forum" section of the *Bellefontaine Examiner*:

> *"While it is disturbing to learn that your tax dollars are being used to pay officers' wages who are supposed to be upholding the law and now many are guilty of criminal activities, it is even more disturbing to realize that their criminal activities have been covered up and smoothed over by their superiors and co-workers.*
>
> *"No ordinary individual would have been shown the leniency and clemency that these criminals who wear the badge that we are supposed to 'bow' to have been shown by their superiors and the court system. Truly this tells us there is a different code of judgment for them and the rest of society.*
>
> *"I'm very certain that had I trespassed on another's property, shot up their campers with a machine gun, slashed their tires and stolen items from them, that I would have received more than a fifteen-day suspended jail sentence and a $500 fine. I also believe that the missteps made early in the investigation of this officer [Larry Garwood] who committed these crimes were deliberate as was the reluctance of those in authority to act on the victim's complaints against Larry Garwood, forcing the victim to hire an attorney to defend his property and rights against this aggressor.*

"Not only are these officers often protected by the legal system, but they are also allowed to resign and be awarded a job with another police department, again on taxpayers' money. I shudder to think that all those American soldiers in Iraq are dying for this kind of democracy.

"In addition to Mr. Garwood, two more who are drug users are allowed to resign by Sheriff Henry for so-called 'extenuating' circumstances. Would that be so that they can continue to abuse our tax dollars by drawing a pension? They should have been hung out to dry like any ordinary citizen would have been in a private- sector job.

"Sheriff Henry's statement that he instituted random drug testing a year ago when he could no longer look a person in the eye and say we have a drug free workplace indicates they were using drugs all along – and wasn't the random drug testing actually a requirement of a new insurance [policy] that county employees were switched to?

"Now, we have one of the elites charged with sexual contact with a teenage girl, dishonesty, and insubordination and fired only after administrative hearings. Sheriff Henry's statement that the firing was not a decision he wanted to make sends the message that he would have preferred the actions of this employee [Stout] be swept under the rug also.

*"If this employee was found guilty and
charged with dishonesty, isn't it possible that
he would have made dishonest statements in
the past against citizens in court cases to
achieve a conviction for the prosecution?*

*"How does this happen that so many in law
enforcement commit such criminal acts except
that there is an unwritten rule that they will
receive immunity to punishment that ordinary
citizens would have to endure.*

*"The leader of the pack has either had his
head buried in the sand or has chosen to
whitewash all of the misconduct. Therefore, he
should probably resign and allow someone
who can exert proper authority and
leadership."*

———

In late December 2005, the Ohio Bureau of Criminal Identification and Investigation (BCI) issued their report on their DNA investigation of the Moody massacre. To some it was thought to be inconclusive, but local police authorities continued to say that Scott Moody shot six people before killing himself.

Many area residents, however, continued to doubt that he was the triggerman. It was still hard to fathom why a young man with his life ahead of him would cross over into the abyss of murder and suicide, not to mention shooting himself twice. Someone else must have committed the murders, many believed, and this new report did nothing to answer their lingering doubts.

The sheriff's office continued to assert they'd made the right decision to close the Scott Moody case as a murder/suicide. Nothing in their voluminous case file, aside from the sole survivor's early statement, pointed to any other possibility. Instead, the evidence strongly supported a theory that Scott, who had grown despondent and talked of suicide, carried out the Memorial Day weekend shootings. Stacy had originally stated that she saw a grey-haired man the morning of the shootings. But Stacy later had recanted her statement after working closely with Detective Jon Stout.

The same Jon Stout now disgraced for sexual impropriety toward her.

Sheriff Henry had hoped that public opinion would change after the state crime lab released their findings. He felt certain it would vindicate his decision to close the case.

———

BCI technicians had tested DNA collected from the trigger, stock and barrel of the gun in Scott Moody's hand. The DNA included blood and human tissue taken from the muzzle and barrel.

According to the state crime lab, DNA tests linked the blood and body tissue found on the murder weapon solely to Scott. Scott alone had gunshot residue on his hand. The report estimated the chances of the blood and tissue belonging to someone other than Scott as one in 26.34 quadrillion.

So what, thought other professionals. What did that prove, especially if someone else had shot Scott the first time in the back of his head and then had placed the weapon in Scott's mouth and placed his thumb on the trigger and fired the second shot after Scott was dead? Of course, Scott would have gunshot residue on his hand, and any blood and body tissue found on the .22 caliber rifle would be Scott's.

But if this weapon had been used to kill five other people, why was there was no evidence of blood or body tissue from the other bodies that had been shot? Had the rifle been wiped clean before the second shot, supposedly killing Scott?

The incident reports completed by deputies, including Stout, all stated the same theme – Scott was lying on a bed with the gun next to his chest and stomach and with his right thumb in the trigger guard. The muzzle of the gun was near his head.

What the reports didn't say was that the scene looked staged, the rifle carefully laid next to Scott's side with the barrel pointing toward his head as if someone had laid the rifle there after firing the second shot.

————

The state crime lab report brought a host of follow-up opinions and arguments.

Ken Betz, who had headed up the Miami Valley Regional Crime Laboratory for thirty-five years, pointed out the significance of the presence of blood and tissue on a gun, particularly on the barrel and muzzle. "Crime scene investigators typically do not find a victim's DNA on a firearm used in murder cases unless the victim was shot at a very close range," he said. "However, technicians often find blood and tissue on guns used in suicide."

Sheri Kay Shafer, Megan Karus and Paige Harshbarger had all been shot at close range, behind the ear. No explanation was given for these facts, nor was one given for the possibility that the rifle had been wiped clean after Scott was shot the first time, behind the ear and at close range.

Dr. Lee Lehman, who conducted the autopsies on Scott and the other victims, said it is rare to find a gunshot wound inside a murder victim's mouth although he commonly saw those wounds in suicides. According to Dr. Lehman's findings, "Scott sustained two gunshot wounds – one that traveled from below the jaw and upward into his sinus cavity and the other one inside the mouth into the brain. Both wounds had evidence of contact burns from the muzzle blast," he said.

Other experts disagreed. Some thought the shot below the jaw appeared subjective; the photographs of Scott clearly show the first contact wound behind his left ear, above the jawbone. This first contact shot might have traveled into Scott's sinus cavity, but its upward movement was only a few degrees, not the implication left by Dr. Lehman that the rifle was held under Scott's chin before it was fired.

It was confusing. Dr. Lehman's nebulous statement that "the autopsy findings are consistent with a ruling that Scott shot the victims before killing himself" befuddled other experts. How in the world would an autopsy conducted on other victims reveal Scott as the shooter? Wouldn't that be convenient in homicide investigations if cadavers could simply talk, telling authorities who shot them?

A second series of tests found gunshot residue on Scott. But experts argued that no one should use such tests as the sole basis for determining what happened in a shooting. Those tests simply provide more pieces of the puzzle.

"There are two types of residual tests," Mr. Betz said. "One test looks for chemicals found in primers used in centerfire bullets, while the other looks for particles discharged from a rimfire round such as the .22 caliber rounds used in the Moody/Shafer shootings.

"It is possible for a person to shoot a gun and have no residuals found on the person," he said. "Some firearms, depending on condition and type, discharge almost no residual, and residual can easily be washed off. A revolver with an open breach will discharge more residual than a semi-automatic or bolt-action firearm."

When asked, Mr. Betz explained, "It is hard to plant gunshot residue on a person. And the type of residual you would get from a .22 caliber rimfire embeds itself into the skin."

Cleon C. Mauer, a self-employed firearm specialist from Bracey, Virginia, who had worked in crime labs in three states since 1963, reviewed the state crime lab residue tests at the request of the *Bellefontaine Examiner.*

"They're not saying he fired a firearm, but it (the residue) is there," Mr. Mauer said. "A '22' does not produce much gunshot residue. You're more apt to find it from a revolver. When you come on a crime scene, you're trying to put together the pieces of a puzzle," he said. "You're looking for what is consistent and what isn't consistent."

He concluded that inconsistencies lead investigators to search in other directions.

Although many believe that suicides rarely happen by someone shooting themselves twice, both Mr. Mauer and Mr. Betz said it is possible. "I have had cases where an individual has shot himself three times in the head," Mr. Mauer said. "It is possible, but it's not common."

"We see at least one case a year," Mr. Betz said.

———

But all these analyses ignored the fact that in this case Scott Moody used a rifle, not a handgun, at an almost impossible angle for a person to have shot himself behind the ear. The experts offered no cases where someone had committed suicide with shots in the head – twice – with a rifle.

In the middle of the swirl of opinions, Logan County Sheriff Michael Henry said that he had hoped laboratory results would have ended speculation on what happened on May 29, 2005. It didn't.

But Sheriff Henry remained adamant. "This is consistent with what we were seeing all along," he said. "We deal with facts. These are the facts. And we've had four investigators from the Ohio Attorney General's Office investigating this."

He said detectives made an early decision to call in state investigators instead of relying solely on themselves or neighboring agencies. "It was important to preserve the integrity of the investigation," he said.

Unfortunately, he failed to mention several things. He didn't explain that the crime scene had been tampered with, that some of his own detective reports had been fabricated, and that meaningful evidence existed that had not been pursued. Apparently, the lone survivor's statement of seeing an older, gray-haired man wearing a blue shirt point a gun at her, and then shoot her – twice – was of no importance, even though others had suspicions of who that person might have been.

Chapter Eighteen

The sheriff's office has been dealing with the Moody/Shafer problems for a long time. Since the beginning of my employment, I've been dealing with these people for domestic violence, for sexual misconduct, for accused molestation, vandalism, pretty much anything you can imagine. All of the detectives, including myself, was [sic] warned – be very, very careful with these people.

– Detective Jon Stout testifying before the Logan County Grand Jury, January 25, 2006

Months of investigation by special prosecutors assigned by the Attorney General's Office to review the Stacy Moody sexual molestation complaint finally led to the empanelment of a Logan County Grand Jury. Detective Stout's actions with a then fifteen-year-old minor were serious felony offenses.

On a cold January morning in 2006, the members of the Grand Jury took their seats in the historic Logan County Courthouse to continue listening to the evidence presented by the prosecutors concerning Stout's case.

"For the record," said Prosecutor Scott Longo, addressing the members of the Grand Jury, "we are going to have Jon Stout testify before you. I'm going to read him his rights; explain to him, you know, what he can and can't do as far as asking questions of a lawyer. But before we bring him in, I wanted to put on the record that yesterday afternoon we played for the Grand Jury the videotape up to the point that it completed Detective Jon Stout's statement, which he gave on November 9, 2005.

"This morning we played the audiotape or the audio portion of the interview of Mike Brugler, Stout's partner. And all of this was done without the stenographer or the court reporter in the Grand Jury room. All right."

———

Jon Stout was brought into the courtroom and sworn in by the court reporter. His testimony before the Logan County Grand Jury that morning would be revealing.

"Why don't you have a seat," said the prosecutor to Stout. "And if you would, tell us your name for the record."

"My name is Jon Charles Stout."

"And, Mr. Stout, you – you're here voluntarily; is that correct?"

"I'm here to tell my story to these folks, yes."

"Are you aware you are the subject of this investigation?"

"Yes, sir."

"And last week I spoke with a Greg Lewis, who I believe at least at this point in time was your attorney; is that correct?"

"Greg Lewis is my attorney. He's not able to be in here, so there's no sense in him coming up from Columbus, wasting his time."

"I'm going to read you your rights – which I'm obligated to do since you're the subject of this investigation – and go over a couple of ground rules with you and then I have some questions for you.

"Let me start, and I'll give you an opportunity to say something," said Longo.

"Okay, sir."

"I know that you know what your rights are. I'm assuming that since you've been a detective for a number of years you've probably read the rights to a number of people, but I'm still obligated to make sure you understand these things.

"You have the right to remain silent, and you have a Fifth Amendment right and U.S. Constitutional right to not incriminate yourself, not to testify – be compelled to testify before the Grand Jury; are you aware of that?"

"Yes, sir."

"It's my understanding that you want to waive that right and testify before the Grand Jury; is that correct?"

"Yes, sir."

"If at any time during this Grand Jury proceeding while you're in this room you decide you don't want to answer any of my questions, or for that matter, any of the questions asked by members of the Grand Jury, you can refuse to answer those questions at any time. Are you aware of that?"

"Yes, sir, I am."

"You have a right to have an attorney present – not in the Grand Jury hearing room, but outside – that you can consult with, and it's my understanding from what you've said that Mr. Lewis, since he could not be in this hearing room for your testimony, is not here so he's not outside."

"That is correct."

"It doesn't mean that – if you want to consult with your attorney, you could stop answering questions, could leave the room, either by telephone or some other way and get hold of Mr. Lewis to seek counsel for a specific question, and then, if you choose to, come back into the Grand Jury [room] and answer that question or address the Grand Jury. Do you understand that?"

"Yes, sir, I do."

"Do you at this point knowingly, intelligently, and voluntarily waive the rights that I've explained to you, and are you willing to go forward with my questions?"

"If you give me the opportunity to speak, I will do that, yes, sir."

"I'll give you an opportunity to speak as well."

"Uh-huh."

"So, are you going to waive your rights at this point in time?"

"Yes, sir."

———

"I know you made a statement on November 9 to Detective Consolo. [Deputy Sheriff Consolo from Sandusky County was assigned by the Ohio Attorney General's Office to investigate Stout's case.] It was tape-recorded. And then I think the last ten or eleven minutes was just the audiotape because the tape had run out. This Grand Jury has had the opportunity to view that and listen to that tape, so they've heard your statement. I have some specific questions for you. Is it your interest at this point in time to make a statement?"

"Yes, sir."

"I'll go ahead and let you do that. I may have questions and I may follow up. The Grand Jury has been instructed that it is permissible to ask questions as well with the same rules that apply, that you don't have to answer if you don't want to. Do you understand that?"

"Yes, sir," said Stout. "All I'd like to do is make a statement. I put together what I feel is important. If I can just have an open floor to do so, I would appreciate that, and then I'm open for any questions that you or you folks on the Grand Jury have. I'll try to get through this as quickly as I can.

"For starters, I would like to introduce myself again. My name is Jon Charles Stout. I'm a former detective with the Logan County Sheriff's Office. If I go too fast, let me know. I served seventeen years with the sheriff's office. I was hired when I was eighteen years old. I was, I would say, recently terminated due to this situation."

Stout continued, "I was never, ever accused of or put in a position for misconduct, that being sexual misconduct."

Stout made the right decision when he decided to clarify the "sexual" part of misconduct; he had faced allegations of misusing his office the year before when officers discovered stolen property at his home. And maybe he should have thought twice before stating he had never received an accusation of sexual misconduct. The prosecutor had already talked to two high school girls who admitted that Stout had caught them with drugs, but that he offered to overlook the facts in their cases in return for sexual favors.

Most of the girls at Riverside High School knew about Stout and the perverted road warriors that worked for the sheriff's office, but in the classic response of molestation victims they felt too afraid to tell. Stout seemed proud to explain that as a divorced man and now remarried to another woman, he continued raising the three children he'd had with his first wife.

"I'm the custodial parent," he explained. But he didn't explain why he was raising them "on his own" without any involvement by his former wife. He also testified that he assisted in raising his current wife's daughter, age fifteen at the time they married, the captain of the Bellefontaine High School cheerleading squad.

In Stout's way of thinking, he'd established his bona fides as a decent family man.

"The sheriff's office has been dealing with the Moody/Shafer problems for a long time. Since the beginning of my employment," Stout said, "I've been dealing with these people for domestic violence, for sexual misconduct, for accused molestation, vandalism, pretty much anything you can imagine."

According to Stout, "All of the detectives, including myself, was [sic] warned immediately as soon as this happened – where all of the homicides took place – be very, very careful with these people. You know the problems we've had. We were warned. I ended up kind of being the liaison officer for the Moody family/Shafer family throughout this investigation.

"They clearly were not fond of the sheriff's office," said Stout, "but I established a rapport with them, and they decided to use me as their contact through the sheriff's office throughout this entire incident. I was the one that conducted all of the interviews. I usually get stuck becoming involved in high profile cases.

"Let me give you an example," Stout exclaimed. "Jason Sutherly was one of the people I interviewed. He reports he leaves the house around 3:30 in the morning on the 29th, the morning of the homicide. He tells me he had sex and slept with the mother, Sheri Kay. He's a twenty-five-year-old male, and Sheri Kay Shafer is Stacy's mother.

"During the interview, he tells me that the reason he originally had involvement with the family is that he wanted to have sex with Stacy, and she was fifteen. And he says Sheri Kay, which is mom, now wants to be careful regarding their relationship so that Stacy doesn't find out and get mad."

Stout continued, "Sutherly also states that Stacy dates a lot of men. He makes reference to her mom taking her to Pennsylvania to spend a weekend with her boyfriend, which would be another adult male. Remember, Stacy is fifteen.

During my interview with him, Sutherly talked about how drunk Stacy is the night of the homicide, talked about the guy she slept with in her bed the same night."

Stout paused, glancing at his notes. "The same day I interview another guy by the name of Andrew Denny, which [sic] is nineteen years old. He says he received a phone call from Stacy around midnight on the day of the homicide. She was drunk and wanting him to come over from Cable, Ohio, for a party. When he arrived, they immediately went to bed together. After they had sex, he said they went to sleep in the same bed all night. Again, Stacy was fifteen years of age; Denny was nineteen. He states to me that's the second time he's been at the home."

Stout shifted gears, now wanting to talk about his interviews with Stacy. "My first interview was on June 1 in Columbus. Actually, it was set up for the following morning at 10:00, but Audrey Moody, being stepmom – and I may refer to her as mother because that's what Stacy Moody calls her now. Mom says Stacy is starting to talk, that was around 8:00 at night.

"Like I said, I was supposed to be in Columbus at the hospital the following morning. At 8:00 that night, Audrey calls my cell phone; Stacy's starting to talk, can you guys get here immediately? So, we leave our families and head for Columbus and the hospital.

"Detective Brugler and I went to the hospital right away that evening and spoke with her. Stacy gave a very detailed statement about the events. One of the first things she said was about a suspect being a gray-haired man, medium build, although she really couldn't see his face. This will be the first story she tells.

"On June 2, the following day, Detective Brugler and I return again to the hospital, giving Stacy some time to think, maybe get into more details. Stacy acted very sedated, although she added to the story by saying the suspect was holding a rifle having a flowered gun stock and giving a more detailed statement about the suspect. She actually gave us a name, which was one of the men that Sheri Kay Moody lived with over the years. She said he looked like him, a guy by the name of John Martin – yeah, John Martin. What he was wearing, the gun stock having a large barrel. This will be her second story.

"Before we talked to her any further, we decided to wait until she got home from the hospital. In the hospital, it was just too difficult to talk with her. There were nurses. It's a – I'm not sure what level intensive care or what it was, a trauma center. It was very difficult to talk to her. So, in talking to the mother and father, it was decided, let's wait until she comes home when she's ready to talk. We want to get the real story and do this just one time and be done with it.

"So, on June 14, Detective Brugler, Sandy Parker [Logan County Children's Services caseworker] and I went to the home to obtain a detailed interview. Stacy then recanted her first two statements, telling us in great detail about everything but the shooter's face. She didn't see Scott Moody, her brother, do anything. Again, this is the third story that she's changed on the third time I've talked to her.

"After we finished the interview and returned to the sheriff's office, approximately one hour later we were requested to come back to the home. Now Stacy gave us a detailed statement regarding her brother and the second time he shot her. So now she's telling me it's her brother. This is the first time that she says that. This is the fourth – fourth story that I've gotten from her. Every time the story changes somewhat.

"On June 21, Detective Brugler and I were again called to the Moody residence by Audrey Moody, advising us that Stacy needs to talk – she hasn't been right since the last interview.

Stacy told us that it really was Scott – it was Scott, so we wouldn't have to talk about it anymore. Again, changing the story slightly. This will be the fifth time.

"Approximately two hours after talking with Stacy, she changed her mind again. She saw – now she's saying she saw Scott shoot her twice. First time she said it was Scott once, and now she's saying she saw him shoot her twice. She heard Scott's girlfriend say, 'No, please, no,' then she heard a shot. She also saw Scott downstairs when he knelt down beside her at the chair. This is the most detail she's given in all of her statements. Sixth story she's changed on us.

———

Stout paused, looked at the members of the Grand Jury. "Over the next three months, I deal with calls every week from stepmom or Stacy asking me to come to an appreciation gathering, to call her, to take a helicopter ride, family wants me to come to Stacy's 16th birthday party, pay to take me out to lunch to show appreciation. I was asked by Stacy to go to her homecoming football game to watch her be an assistant attendant when she was elected.

"Mom calls weekly, asks me to assist family, problems with reference to the homicide. I'm asked to go to the residence where the homicide took place to gather some belongings. I'm asked to go to the homicide location so that Stacy can walk through it. I'm asked to pick Stacy up at school to speak with her about a person that they're accusing of touching her inappropriately.

"I'm asked to pick up Stacy at school and take her to the sheriff's office to sell magazines, so she can get a homecoming dress. On September 15, Steve Moody calls me and wants me to stop by and speak with Stacy. I went over on the 16th. The

Moody family had just given a TV press conference regarding the sheriff's office messing up the investigation, saying that they were too quick to announce that Scott Moody was the suspect. They gave Channel 2 a written press release, bashing the sheriff's office.

"When I got there, Stacy told me she had a lot of questions, and she stated she didn't see Scott shoot her. The parents asked me to speak with Stacy one-on-one, thinking that this might help with some of the confusion. Again, Stacy stated she didn't see Scott shoot her. This is the seventh story she's given me now where she's changed it.

"Stacy asked several crazy questions. I advised her that maybe it would be best if I set her up with a polygraph. Stacy then stated, 'I did see Scott shoot me although it's hard to accept.' This is the last and final story that she's given me; eighth story she's given me where she's changed her mind eight times about what happened and added to or taken away from the story every time she talked to me."

Stout looked down at his lap, referring to his notes. "This was a note that I had written for my attorney. It sounds inappropriate, but I guess I'll read it. I think you'll get the drift.

"I wrote, 'Stacy is a pathological liar that knows exactly what happened that night – she knows exactly what happened that night and she still hasn't told the truth.'

"Other points of interest that I wrote: Sheri Kay Shafer accused Steve Moody of molesting Scott and Stacy when going through the divorce.

"Steve Moody wasn't sure the father of Scott Moody might have been Sheri Kay's dad, the grandfather. We had to do a DNA test to decide.

"With the sex drive Stacy Moody appears to have at a young age, I would guess maybe Steve Moody may have molested her.

"Also, Audrey Moody accused Bill Sadler, Stacy's physical therapist, of being too friendly with her. I was number three.

"I was the third person to be accused of touching her inappropriately."

"Let me explain," said Stout. "Stacy Moody's best friend is Krissy Dorsey. Her parents are Tom and Lori Dorsey that work at the Logan County Sheriff's Office. Stacy's not been allowed to have contact with her since this incident came out but [Krissy] has come forward at the sheriff's office to say that she knows of all her [Stacy's] sexual partners and I've never been mentioned. She wants to talk to Stacy, but she's not been permitted to do so. Stacy's been removed from the school district and, apparently, she's not been permitted to have contact, as far as I know, with anyone.

"There are five incidents which I'm being accused of – by the investigator. These five incidents are supposedly dates I had with Stacy. The first time that I – I wish I had the dates for you folks, I just don't. I was asked by Stacy's family to – she wanted to take me out to lunch. She had, let's say, been harassing me pretty good. The helicopter incident I made reference to earlier, she says in front of everyone, 'I want Mr. Stout or Jon to do this helicopter ride with me.'

"She also called me and told me that she had – she said, she's starting to remember things and that there's another dead body back in the woods along the fence line, and it's in a truck. It's hard to hear her because of what was going on with her voice. I'm under the impression now that's been resolved, but it's still very difficult to understand her at times.

"So, I'm basically freaking out, thinking 'Oh, god, there's a seventh dead body' and I'm ready to call in people and start trying to find this person knowing that we don't have anybody missing.

"She starts laughing. She said, 'I'm just kidding, just a joke.' She just referred to it as yanking my chain.

"Stacy said, 'I owe you lunch. I'm going to take you out to lunch.' This is with her parents involved. So, a date was set up to go out to lunch. I picked her up – I can't tell you really what time it was. Probably 12:00 or 1:00 or 11:00, somewhere in the afternoon for lunch. I suggested McDonald's or Wendy's or Burger King at the Lake.

"She absolutely carried on that that was not going to happen, and we were going to go out to eat somewhere nice, referring to Columbus, Springfield or Lima. Which I was actually against, but I unfortunately said, 'Yes, I'll do that,' as long as her parents were okay with it. Which they were.

"So, we went to Red Lobster in Lima even though I told her I can't afford Red Lobster.

"Stacy replied, 'I've got money Mom and Dad don't know about, just tell them you paid, whatever.'

"So, we went to Red Lobster and – and I brought her home. Her dad joked with me about 'the next time you asked her out some place nice to eat like that, I want to go with you because I want a good steak.' It was a joke. That was the first incident where we were one-on-one."

———

"Second incident, stepmom calls and says she wanted me to talk to Stacy, she was concerned about Stacy's physical therapist, Bill Sadler. He was too 'hands-on' with Stacy, maybe touching her. She wanted me to pick her up at school, if I'm not mistaken, and talk to her about it.

"So, those arrangements were made. I picked her up at school one day and ran her up to the Lake this time. We grabbed some lunch at this time because the reason Stacy goes to school half a day, she has problems eating and she's afraid she's going to choke at school, so she doesn't want to eat lunch at school.

"So, she ate lunch. And that takes her forever to eat a four-piece Chicken McNuggets meal and a set of French fries because of her throat. We sat there, finished eating, probably drove around. I spoke to her about Bill Sadler. She said that he touched her and that he kind of puts his hands in places he shouldn't when he's hugging her, but she's going to make sure nothing goes on there.

"The third incident they called me – one of them called me and wanted me to take Stacy to the sheriff's office to sell magazines. She was elected junior attendant and wanted to know if I'd pick her up and take her in to sell some magazines at the sheriff's office so that she could get a dress for free, apparently. So, I did. I got her lunch, and then I took her in the sheriff's office and we sold a half dozen magazines, I guess.

"The next one I've already kind of went over. The fourth one was the news release. I was called by the parents to come over and talk to Stacy. What they did was they let her see all the newspaper articles and all of the letters, and she really hadn't seen any of that, which brought up a lot of questions and confusion. I think this was September 16.

"Whenever the new press release was given to Dayton Daily, Channel 2, that would have been, I want to say, the day after or maybe two days after that. So whatever date that is, you can coincide with when I was over there. Stacy had told me that 'Mom keeps saying' – mom, meaning Audrey Moody – 'keeps saying these things to me making me think it's not true that my brother did this.'

"The truth of the matter is, they didn't want the brother to be the one that did it. That would cause all kinds of family financial problems if Scott was the shooter.

"I think Steve Moody may have thought Stacy was involved in it. He spoke to me about it saying, 'Jon, I'm scared a little bit for my kids here. What if Stacy is involved? She's not showing any emotion. She's not been upset, and she's not crying. I'm a little nervous about this.' I said, I really need to talk to her one-on-one, so I can get this out of her, find out what's going on."

"That's what we did. We decided to leave, to take a drive away from everybody. After a few minutes of driving, I drove down a dirt lane and parked the car. We sat and talked. Actually, I had to go to two different places. First place was State Route 24, which is an intersection outside of De Graff. Two different people pulled up, asking if everything was okay? This was interrupting my train of thought, so I went down the road further and pulled in a farm lane.

"And she came forward and said, 'My brother's the shooter. I just saw him do it. Everything I've told you is correct, I just don't want to accept it. Mom keeps saying things, making me think that maybe I'm making this up. That's what they want me to think.'

"I hit her with a polygraph, and she said, 'No,' she didn't want to do that. She said, 'I just want to tell you the story.'"

Stout hesitated, "I'm almost done. One thing I guess I want to get across to you folks is, these people were calling me. These people were very persistent with me. I know phone records were pulled. Any time you check a phone record with these people, they've called me from somewhere, either from a cell phone or home phone. I've either immediately answered or called back. I didn't call these folks. I didn't request any of this. This was all done by them."

Attorney Longo looked at the members of the Grand Jury. "Let's take a fifteen-minute break," he said. "We've got a lot more ground to cover."

Chapter Nineteen

I'm a born and raised country fart, you know. At home, it's nothing for me to open the back door and go pee instead of going to the bathroom, just being the way I am.

– Detective Jon Stout testifying before the Logan County Grand Jury, January 25, 2006

Prosecutor Scott Longo looked around the Grand Jury room. He had everyone's attention. He asked Stout, "Shortly after Stacy got home from the hospital – they had removed her feeding tubes – the parents were very, very concerned about food basically causing her to choke and maybe not being able to breathe, is that right?"

"That is correct."

"In fact, it's true, isn't it, that Audrey and Steve Moody, on several occasions when you would have contact with them, told you about their concern . . . if you're going to go to lunch, you've got to be very careful and very patient because she has to eat very slowly. She could choke, and they didn't want to lose her because of some food that got stuck in her windpipe and causing her not to be able to breathe."

Stout responded, "I was told she had problems eating and I already addressed that when we would stop to eat; we wouldn't be out cruising while she's sitting there chewing on a French fry. That is correct."

232 ROB ST. CLAIR

"Would you agree that Audrey and Steve were very concerned about this medical issue? It's – it's getting better, but she still has to be careful?"

"I wouldn't agree that they were concerned with me," Stout said. "They're the ones that wanted me to take her out. That's why I was placed on the school roster – at the school as one of the people to pick her up. I was told by Audrey that in case they can't pick her up, they wanted me to pick her up because I knew her medical issues and so on."

Longo continued, "They trusted you as far as dealing with her ability to swallow, eat. If there was an issue or problem – you would be able to get her some assistance; is that accurate?"

"I know how to deal with CPR, yeah."

"Okay. Stacy told Detective Consolo [Longo's investigator] and referenced it in her statement that she made a comment that I think was – by everyone's ability to characterize it – was an inappropriate comment to you the first time you went to lunch with her, the one at Red Lobster?"

"Correct."

"She made a comment about liking to give oral sex. She may have used the word liking to 'give head' or something like that."

"Correct."

"And she described your reaction as being kind of – it was very clear to her that you felt surprised with what she had said, and she just kind of got an odd feeling from you. And she indicated that she meant it to be kind of a joke, very inappropriate, but that you had a big smile on your face, the kind of reaction that made her think maybe that wasn't the right thing to say. Would you agree with that?"

"I would agree with that. She liked to joke."

"Would you agree that that was an inappropriate comment for a fifteen-year-old to make to a thirty-six-year-old detective?"

"Yes."

"Okay. Now, your partner, Mike Brugler, in his statement to Detective Consolo, he says that Stacy was very 'touchy-feely' – and that doesn't necessarily mean when he was alone with her because he says he wasn't alone with her – but like bumping hips – never with him, but with you, fooling around in that way. Would you agree with that?"

"She liked to poke you in the chest and she'd give you a bump and – that is correct."

"Bill Sadler was somebody that Audrey had some concerns with that might be getting a little bit 'touchy-feely' with Stacy."

"Correct."

"All right. Did you ever have an opportunity to talk to Bill Sadler about maybe acting inappropriately in front of or toward Stacy?"

"I know what kind of man Bill Sadler is, and I informed Audrey . . ."

"What do you mean by that?"

"He's an odd man. I can see him doing this. And I informed Audrey, now it's probably best to just keep them away from one another."

"When Audrey is talking to you about what she believes to be inappropriate conduct between Bill Sadler toward Stacy, wasn't that after your trip to the Red Lobster?"

"It was – I think it was the second – yes."

"As a matter of fact, I think you just testified that you picked her up to talk to her about Bill Sadler the time you picked her up at school and went to McDonald's."

"Uh-huh."

"All right. Now, according to your statement, she had made a fairly inappropriate comment to you about liking to do oral sex; she's bumping around, touching – you know – poking, however you want to describe it. Did you tell Audrey, her mom, that Stacy's – maybe she's acting a little bit beyond her years? Did you ever say anything to Audrey about that?"

Stout said, "Audrey and Steve were not involved with Stacy until the incident on the 29th. Stacy was just starting – the way I was told, was just starting to go back over there. Stacy did not care for Audrey. She made that clear to me multiple times.

"I did not divulge to Audrey that her stepdaughter touches too much, and she talks too much. Audrey made reference that Stacy seems to have a liking for adults."

"All right. But you didn't tell Audrey or Steve about the comment in the car?"

"No."

"And you didn't, as a detective who had just been alone with a fifteen-year-old who says she likes to 'give head,' didn't say, 'Know what, I'm never going to be alone with this girl because she may be trouble,' did you?"

"I deal with people like that on a weekly basis."

"But you didn't stop being around her alone?"

"No, I did not."

"All right," said Longo. "You describe in your statement an incident when she comes out after school with a 'Hooter' shirt on that had been turned inside out because it was an inappropriate shirt for school, and she takes off her shirt in front of you – she has a bra on – and turns it back right side out. And you described that as being completely out of line; a bra's a bra, and a swimming suit's a swimming suit, and that's inappropriate behavior. Is that a fair characterization that you made?"

"I was shocked when she did that."

"You didn't tell Audrey. You didn't tell her that she had done that either, had you?"

"That is correct."

Longo looked at his notes. "You carry your – at the time while you were a detective, you carried a Nextel cell phone; is that correct?"

"Yes, sir."

"And is it also correct that you used that Nextel to connect to people within your department?"

"Whomever. Whoever has a Nextel, yes."

"But you didn't use the radio in your car on a regular basis to check in and out of your department with what you were doing; is that fair to say?"

"I use the radio very, very little."

"Okay. On the date that you went to the Red Lobster, you indicated in your statement that you didn't radio in to tell them what you were doing or where you were going, but you did use your Nextel phone to let them know you were going to Lima, didn't you?"

Stout had a firm response, "That's what the detective [Consolo] tried to say to me, but I don't recall calling anyone and saying that I was going to Lima. I'm the second in the division, myself and a supervisor at the sheriff's office. Detective Jeff Cooper is the only one above me. If I recall correctly, on that date he was off. So, he tried to say I radioed on the radio some ridiculous thing – I don't remember what it was. It was kind of comical to me."

"Are you telling the Grand Jury that when you were a detective with the sheriff's department, you determined how long you worked, what you worked – was entirely up to you?"

"No, I'm not saying that at all. As a detective we're very free with our time. We've got to put in forty – we usually put in sixty hours a week, so our supervisor's very open with us about the time we work and what we do. We've got open reins on what we do."

Longo paused for a moment, then said, "One thing you didn't talk about at all is the 30th of September, and that would be the stakeout where you and Stacy were going to go look at people that might be stealing tractors from the store up at Lakeview."

"Okay. I apologize. I might not have discussed that."

"Do you want to talk about that one?"

"Sure."

"Whose idea was it to go on a stakeout?"

"Well, that's something I had planned."

"With Stacy?"

"No."

"What do you mean? Whose idea was it to go on the stakeout and have Stacy go with you?"

"Stacy."

"Okay. You had already set up this stakeout?"

"Yes, sir. Yes."

"At the hardware store, where they sold tractors?"

"Right."

"Because of some problems with people stealing things during a shift change or something."

"Correct."

"And it was unclear from your statement on whether or not you went up there or not. Is it your testimony here today that you did go up there?"

"Yes."

"That particular night, did you spend any time watching the tractors?"

"I was up there. The information I received was individuals were stealing tractors, typically on Friday and Saturday nights at shift change, which would be around midnight. That was the information I received. I was up there – I'm going to say it very loosely – it could have been an hour, could have been two hours.

I'm going to say an hour at this point in time because I just don't remember exactly how long we set up there."

"You and Stacy?"

"Correct."

"Now, we know that you – and I'm assuming that attempting to get Stacy to be able to go with, you told her parents that your partner, Mike [Brugler], was going to be there, which was a lie."

Stout grew adamant. "At Stacy's request. She called on Friday evening and said she was bored, which was common for these people. 'We're all sitting here bored, there's nothing to do, what are you doing?' Oh, nothing, I'm going to be going to work in a little bit.

"She previously spoke to her parents in my presence about wanting to come out and see what we do at night. She asked me what I was doing. I told her I was going to be on a stakeout. She asked if anybody else was going to be there, and I said no. She said, 'Well, they won't let me do that.' That was the end of it.

"A couple of hours later I get a phone call from Audrey. 'Stacy's wanting to come out and ride with you tonight, are you okay with that?' That's fine. We have people ride with us all the time. I don't mind, especially when it's something boring like that when you're sitting there staring at a building for however long. So, Audrey says, 'Stacy said that several of you guys are going to be out together.' That kind of threw me for a loop, just like the oral sex comment. I made a poor decision and said, 'Yeah, there will be others out there.' And I shouldn't have said that."

Longo said, "You don't recall telling Audrey and Steve that, hey, we've got to get going, we've got to go pick up Mike? You don't remember saying that?"

"No, no."

"So, if they testified to that, then they're mistaken or perhaps just lying?"

"I don't recall saying anything like that, and I would say at this point I wouldn't believe anything they said, so . . ."

"You're before a Grand Jury, admitting to at least going along with a lie."

"Uh-huh."

"And you're telling the Grand Jury that you wouldn't believe anything the Moodys would say, but aren't you in fact telling them that you were part of this lie?"

"I am sitting here today with you folks on my own free will. I'm trying to be open and honest with you. This is not common for a person to be sitting in this position, being accused of something, but I want to tell you people what happened. I am telling you that I went along with that and I should not have. It was wrong."

———

Longo decided to change the subject, "Now, you – you have custody of three boys or two boys?"

"I have three children, ages fourteen, twelve, and seven; the seven-year-old being a female."

"And you are the custodial parent?"

"I am the custodial parent."

"You and your wife live together with these three kids?"

"Yes, sir."

"You work forty – get paid for forty hours, work about sixty, and you seem to be spending an inordinate amount of time dealing with the Moody family because of this murder/suicide and trying to get this big case resolved; is that fair to say?"

"Yes."

Longo looked at his notes, "How long did you spend driving around on the 30th of September with Stacy before you took her home?"

"I picked her up – I think I arrived at her house around 10:00 p.m. I stayed there with them and talked with them for probably fifteen minutes. Seems like the boys were there. So, we left somewhere around quarter after, so – I say that loosely, and as I told the investigator, I do this so much that . . ."

"Do what so much?"

"I'm out at night so much doing casework like this, I think I took her home between 1:00 and 2:00 in the morning. I'm not going to say that it was 1:00 or 2:00. It was somewhere in that area."

"That's fine."

"I'm just trying to be honest."

"It's my understanding that during that night you – did you say that you were at the Lakeview Hardware, but you were also driving around to show her maybe some of the not-so-nice parts of Logan County in the Bellefontaine area; is that right?"

"That is correct."

"Drive by your house?"

"Correct."

"Clearly, the stakeout part of the night was over with and you spent three – two to three hours just cruising around."

"No. If I say I was up at the Lake for an hour – well, yeah, I guess you're right. If I was out from 10:00 to 2:00, it would be two to three hours, that would be correct."

"Going here and there, maybe stopping by Children's Services' parking lot to take a leak?"

"That is correct."

"Now, I'm not that familiar with Logan County, but I'm somewhat familiar with where the sheriff's office is, which is probably not too far around the corner from Logan County Children's Services."

"Uh-huh."

"I mean, you were doing official work, a stakeout, you had a ride-along with you. Did you think of just stopping at the sheriff's office and, you know, taking care of it there?"

Stout replied, "No. I mean, I could have, yes, I could have, but I didn't. I'm a – I don't know how to say this appropriately. I'm a born and raised country fart, you know. At home, it's nothing for me to open the back door and go pee instead of going to the bathroom, just being the way I am. I believe I told the investigator that I was going through the parking lot and making reference to what the buildings were, and I stopped and got out and peed. I also believe I told him that I walked over to the bushes and did so."

Stout continued, "He's telling me that the incident that I'm being accused of was that evening in the parking lot. I find it odd if I just performed oral on her and digital penetration, inserting my finger in her vagina, without being rude, why did I go walk around the corner and take a leak versus apparently, I was just naked with her, why not just pee right there? Sure, I told the investigator that I walked around the building.

"The other problem I have is apparently I performed oral sex on her, which I don't do to my wife – either of my wives. If you confront my ex-wife or my current wife, I don't perform oral sex on them. But I didn't refuse to perform oral sex on her, and so it's 'all for her, none for me.' I guess, without being rude, I find that very odd."

"Okay. You've said that Stacy's called you when she is bored, and she would talk to you for hours, right?"

"Forever, yes."

"She would talk to you sometimes for hours, at least an hour or longer."

"The longest I can recall her talking and actually make

reference to it she would call me and – it was for an hour – and just carry on about how she hated living, hated living with her stepmother, she hated her, just on and on and on and . . ."

"Would you say that she was able to talk to you? That she was opening up to you? She felt comfortable around you?"

"Yeah. That was my goal."

"All right. When you would go to lunch, you'd pick her up from school, but you didn't go in and sign her out, she was actually gone for the day; is that right?"

"Yeah. That was set up through the stepmom. We'd go somewhere where we could sit, and she could eat."

"And you – you told Detective Consolo that after you would eat, you would then drive around for a while, sometimes as much as a couple of hours."

"No. I – well, I better be careful what I say. As I said, it would take her sometimes an hour to eat a four-piece Chicken McNuggets meal and fries. I may be wrong about that. It would take her sometimes up to an hour to do just that. I – I would take her out, driving her around – she was interested in what I did - showing her, and . . ."

"You're saying that after that hour you'd spend perhaps another hour or more just driving around Logan County with this fifteen-year-old or sixteen-year-old girl, depending on when she turned sixteen?"

Stout grew tense. "Your job and my job are two different jobs. My job may consist of driving around Logan County for eight hours and not talking to a soul, or my job may be working in Logan County for twelve hours interviewing people. So, part of my job is to drive around and . . ."

"So, you were just going about your regular job and you just happened to have a fifteen or sixteen-year-old girl with you to ride along during those times."

"Uh-huh. It was usually arranged with her mother."

———

"Who is Detective Cooper?" asked Longo.

"He's my supervisor."

"And is Detective Cooper the person who told you when this all came out to not have any contact with anybody associated with this case?"

"I understand what you're saying here. When the incident came out about the news release, Detective Cooper blew a gasket because the Moodys bashed us. They really did bash the sheriff's office for not doing a proper investigation. It looks like there's some mass murderer out there. So that does sting a little bit. He blew up. 'Do not have any contact with the Moodys, hell with the Moodys, stay away from them.' Another day later . . ."

Longo interrupted, "I'm talking – let's focus on one day. I'm thinking about the day this comes out that there's an allegation against Detective Stout with the Logan County Sheriff's Department, and you were instructed by a superior to not have any contact with anybody associated with this case. Do you recall that?"

"Yes."

"After that – when was that? Do you know?"

"I was terminated November 29. I think I'm going to say, very loosely, November 4. November 7, maybe. So that was when Detective Cooper came to me and said, 'Stay away from these people, don't contact them, don't have . . .'"

"And isn't it true that he told you not to talk to anybody at all about this investigation, including your partner, Mike?"

"No."

"You weren't told not to talk to any of the witnesses involved in this case, including your partner?"

"No. I was to stay away from the Moody family and not to have any contact with them. That's what my orders were."

"You talked to your partner on the 6th, which was a Sunday. And again, you talked to him again on the 10th of November, the day after you were interviewed by Detective Consolo. Do you recall those two conversations?"

"I'm not going to say that didn't happen. Mike Brugler, which is the person I worked with at the sheriff's office as detective, was very upset and very concerned. He was scared. He was new – I mean, he was a new guy as far as detective. I remember him coming out to the house one day, nervous and upset."

"He described you as being nervous and upset."

"Well, I've never been put on administrative leave before, so . . ."

"He also said that you were interested in – you were apologizing to him because you used his name when you lied and told the parents that he was coming with you on a stakeout, but that he wasn't going to be there."

"I – I would apologize to him for even this going on at all, yes, that's very possible."

———

"All right," said Longo, holding up a birthday card. "Tell us what this is."

Stout read the card. "'Happy birthday, 16. Have a wonderful birthday. You deserve it. You're an incredible person, and you will be – will be in a special spot in my heart for – friends forever. You are a friendly person and will be in a special part in my heart. Friends forever.'

"I told her that the first time I ever interviewed her," said Stout.

"I realize this is a photocopy, not an original, but that's your handwriting; you wrote that?"

"I did."

"You gave this to her at or near her birthday, is that right?"

"It would have been whenever one of the times her mom – it would have either been when she asked me to talk to her about Bill Sadler or it would have been when they wanted me to take her to our office so that she could sell magazines."

"Close to but after?"

"Her mom made reference that she was having a birthday party, and – actually having two birthday parties, one of them for a bunch of kids, and asked me if I would be the chaperone and stand there while these kids were having a party somewhere. And I said, not really, don't want to get in the middle of that.

"And then they wanted me to come over to a family birthday party. Again, these people are calling me and wanting me to be involved in all these things, and I said, no, and I didn't do it. So, sometime after her birthday I gave that to her."

Prosecutor Longo paused for a moment, referring to his notes. He then glanced over at his co-counsel, looking for an indication as to whether his team might have any additional questions. Receiving a negative response, he continued.

"All right. Ladies and gentlemen, those are all the questions that I have at this point. Do any of you have any questions for Mr. Stout?"

One of the jurors spoke up. "Yes, I do."

"Sure," said Stout.

"I'm having trouble understanding why you kept being alone with this girl, knowing she's promiscuous and a known liar. Why would you continue to put yourself in that position? I know in my position, I would never do that."

"Okay. I deal with people every single day. As an officer, I was in this position every single day. If you listened to the interview, I had a goal here. I knew there was more to this story than what I'm being told. This case was closed. It was closed ten days after it happened, but I really wanted Stacy to open up to me and tell me what happened that day. And that's the – the aggressive nature of myself."

Stout looked at the jurors, then continued. "If anyone knows anything about me, I'm an extremely aggressive officer. I love to get the truth out of people. That's what I do. And I – I deal with crack addicts, female prostitutes on a weekly basis that are offering these same things that she said. I can handle it.

"She made reference to offering to give me a 'blow job.' I wrote it off as was noted, okay, whatever, and kept on driving. Wasn't interested. I have prostitutes doing the same thing, too. Whether you folks recognize that in Logan County or not, there's multiple prostitutes offering oral sex to us, myself weekly. Roll off it. You don't do it. I can handle it."

Another juror commented, "I deal with kids on a daily basis. I don't put myself in that position."

"I bet if you thought about it," said Stout, "you would."

"No, no," said the juror.

Longo then said to Stout, "You came in here with excerpts of supplements that you did because as a detective you're trained to document everything, isn't that right? But you didn't supplement what Stacy told you during these lunches, and the hours in the car, and the stakeout, you didn't supplement your case file with those comments, did you?"

"I don't supplement anything that I talk about with people in the car. I supplement casework that I'm doing and not general conversations. I don't record general conversations. Ever."

"So, is it a general conversation that you're after when you were going on these lunches and the stakeout, or were you after the goal, and that was to find out what the truth was, was it a homicide or was it a suicide?"

"My goal was to get her to tell me what happened that day, yes."

"You think Stacy has it out for you?" said Longo.

"I've got a couple different ideas as to why this happened to me."

"If you're interested in sharing them, we're interested in listening."

Chapter Twenty

I have my concerns that if that family [Moodys] was paid the right amount of money that they would go forward and do this to me because Joe Rosebrook is doing ten years in prison for wanting to have a man killed and several other things. He made it very clear he's spent $150,000 on this private investigator to see that that's done.

– Detective Jon Stout testifying before the Logan County Grand Jury, January 25, 2006

T he Grand Jury members returned from their break and took their seats. Regardless of the prosecutor's instructions, they had talked amongst themselves, asking each other questions, commenting on Stout's testimony. In a small community like Bellefontaine, whether people like it or not, everyone knows everyone else's business.

Most of the members of the Grand Jury knew the Stout family. Jon Stout's father worked as a beat cop for the Bellefontaine Police Department and his sister worked as a secretary at the Logan County Prosecutor's Office. At one time or another, most of the men who had business downtown had visited Stout's Gun Shop, rumored to traffic in stolen guns.

They also knew some of those who died that day. One had a daughter on Stacy's softball team. Stacy's grandmother had taught several of them to read and write in first grade. Few believed that Scott Moody had shot his family and friends. Now, as a group, they felt disgust listening to Stout's testimony, the way he'd violated the trust put in him, and his behavior toward a young, fifteen-year-old girl, a shooting victim who had just lost almost all the members of her family. What excuse could Stout offer for his behavior?

———

Stout took the stand, glanced at his notes, and then responded to Prosecutor Longo's question to proceed.

"Okay. I worked a – these are just thoughts. I don't know if these are correct or not, to be straight up with you folks as far as that goes. I had worked a very large case in Logan County, that being the Rosebrook case, Joe Rosebrook. It was my case. This was in the paper, 'chop shop king.' This thing was extremely high profile. This man's got a very large, very, very large amount of money.

"Approximately two years ago, he'd had a private investigator from Columbus investigating me – working me, watching my every move every single day – I'm sorry, watching my every move. I shouldn't say every single day. That's exaggerating. Sometimes I feel that way – he was putting stories out on the street that I'm involved with theft, I'm involved with all kinds of sexual issues, I'm involved with dealing, I've got all kinds of stolen property."

Prosecutor Longo interrupted, "Do you know the name of the investigator?"

"Yes. Gary Phillips. Which I would be willing to bet is part of this case, which is what I'm getting to."

"Okay," said Longo. "Please continue."

"I have – I had an informant in prison with Mr. Rosebrook watching him, because Rosebrook made a hit out on me:

$20,000 if you run me over while I'm on my motorcycle, another $5,000 if my kid's on there, too.

"So, obviously, I want to keep close dibs on this man and know what his moves are.

"I've got an informant in prison doing that now. I can't talk to that informant, so I have to do it through another man. If the inmate was calling me directly, that would be a problem obviously. This is all recorded. I can get access to this.

"Two weeks prior to me being confronted on this Friday, the informant called my other informant on the street and said 'something's going on with Jon Stout. Joe Rosebrook's extremely excited. He's got him. He's finally going to get him.' I've got hours of documented conversations from Joe Rosebrook and Ann Rosebrook, his wife, saying they are going to get me. It's going to happen. They've tried and paid people to set me up already."

Longo asked, "Do you think that Stacy Moody is a tool of this guy?"

"I don't know. Stacy Moody was really excited after this – after these homicides took place that she was going to be a millionaire, one of the big shots because she would tell others, 'We're going to be millionaires, I'm going to get the whole estate, there's no one else left, I get all of the estate.'

"But this family soon realized that if Scott Moody was the shooter, they're not going to be millionaires.

"This is a million-dollar property out on 47. It's a thousand acres, but they're not going to be seeing that. That's going to these other two families of victims that were killed. And that's why the family became upset with the fact that Stacy had said that Scott did it. They didn't like that. And they were trying to influence her – and she discussed that with me – to convince me that Scott was not the shooter."

Stout looked around the room and continued. "I have my concerns that if that family was paid the right amount of money, they would go forward and do this to me because Joe Rosebrook is doing ten years in prison for wanting to have a man killed and several other things.

"He made it very clear he's spent $150,000 on this private investigator to see that that's done. Gary Phillips, I'm being told, is investigating this matter for the Moodys, and the Moodys are being paid by the Rosebrooks. That bothers me. Gary Phillips is from Columbus. He should have nothing to do with the case that I'm involved with unless it's to set me up."

"I'm from Columbus," responded Longo.

"I appreciate your humor, but Gary Phillips is a private investigator from Columbus. I don't know how you'd even get hold of him – hire him to come and do a job for you. I find it very peculiar that he is working with the Moody family on some matters."

"How do you know he's working with the Moody family on it?" asked Longo.

"I received phone calls with reference to that. If I'm wrong, I'm wrong."

"You're talking about – I can appreciate your concern." Longo continued, "But you're talking about somebody that's watching over you and keeping track of your daily movements, and – or maybe not every day, and you come before this Grand Jury, you say you know this investigator from Columbus is working with the Moody family.

"I find that a little bit odd that you would know that much about what the Moody family is doing, but you're saying somebody's looking over your shoulder telling you. It seems like somebody is looking over their shoulder telling you what's going on there."

Stout said, "An informant. I'm watching Mr. Rosebrook's moves. And I'm still currently doing that, and that is what I'm being told. And, again, I'm telling you this only from what I'm being told. I was told both that he was hired on prior to this being divulged and I was told he was brought in afterwards to assist in burying me. And he truly has tried to do so.

"So, what I just said to you are two different scenarios in my mind. If I'm discredited by the Moody family – I bet if I asked Stacy Moody today, did you see Scott Moody shoot you, she would tell me no, and she told me about five times or more that he did."

———

"But isn't it true that if Scott Moody's the shooter," said Longo, "this case not only is closed now, but it was closed a few days after the shootings took place? If Scott Moody's not the shooter, then you open a can of worms and there's someone out there that did this, maybe it's a gray-haired guy with a blue shirt, and that could cause the detectives at the sheriff's department problems because they closed it too soon. I mean, that could cause problems for a lot of people."

"Correct. Yes."

"All right."

"Yeah, I'm open with that. She told me Scott did it. But if they discredit me, and now they're – these two other families that are suing because their children were killed are going to be going after Scott's estate only because the person that lived on the estate's the one that did it.

"Audrey is the one I've dealt with ninety percent of the time because Steve's very quiet. It's kind of reverse roles, I guess. She's the more outspoken; he's the more quiet. She was upset that Stacy said it was Scott."

Longo said, "But she was the one that was calling you, saying Stacy seems to be opening up."

"Correct."

"Stacy wants to talk."

"Yes, yes."

"You think if she had a problem with Stacy saying Scott did it that she might stop calling the detectives investigating it, let me . . ."

"Who would know what Stacy was going to say because she was opening up? That was – I didn't know what she was going to say, nor did Audrey."

Another juror had a question. "This is kind of a multiple – pooled question. Did I hear you correctly that Stacy shared with you that because of the murders and whatnot that she was going to be a millionaire?"

"Uh-huh."

"Okay. Do you remember when she said that to you?"

"The whole time."

"When you say the whole time, I mean . . ."

"From the time . . ."

"If you were a detective, it should be documented somewhere that she said that."

Stout was annoyed. "What does that have to do with the case?"

"Well, you – I just want to know when she said that we are going to be millionaires because then as you were just recently talking now, I'm – did you know? Was it just your – one of your assumptions or whatnot, now we've got the Rosebrooks tied in with the Moodys?"

"There's two different things I was trying to get out to you folks, to try and explain to you what's in my mind as to why this would be happening to me," said Stout.

The juror looked confused, "Okay."

"Stacy and her dad and Audrey all talked about how this was a million-dollar property. As a matter of fact, her dad was – I mean, he talked pretty rudely about [Sheri] Kay in front of Stacy, and it was an uncomfortable thing.

"He made reference, you know, well, Steve Moody said, 'You're going through a divorce, Jon, and you always wish your wife gets – ex-wife gets run over by a semi. All of the pain would go away. We've all said that, haven't we, Jon?' Okay. No. But they talked openly in front of Stacy poorly about [Sheri] Kay."

———

Another juror commented: "Okay. Can I ask you another question?"

"Yeah, ask me as much as you want."

"When you were with the Moodys and/or with Stacy, did you discuss the Rosebrooks?"

"I could have, yes. That's – that was a very key part of my life."

"Are you able to tell us who told you this connection with the Rosebrooks and – or what they have out with your informant or – or the . . ."

"I – I only restrain from saying to you who that person was because there's already been one man's life put at risk. Joe was charged with it. Joe was setting – charged with setting up a murder-for-hire that I worked. I almost had him for a murder-for-hire against myself, but I wasn't able to pull it off. I am afraid that if I bring that name into this, there's a third murder-for-hire."

"Okay," said the juror. "Well, if you have these assumptions that – you know, which you've just explained, would you not go to your superior and, you know, maybe I shouldn't be the detective on this case, let me back off because I've got these thoughts?"

"What assumptions?"

"With the Moodys connecting with the Rosebrooks," said the juror.

"No. No. I was gone from the sheriff's office when I learned about this."

"Okay."

"Yeah, I was – I was terminated – well, let me back up. Before this came out, I was informed by the informant that Joe's very excited, he's got me, this is going to be good. Didn't have anything to do with the Moodys, okay? That's all the informant said, Joe Rosebrook is very excited. He's got me. I didn't realize it was going to be for this. You understand that?"

Stout looked around the room, but he couldn't read the jurors.

"Joe Rosebrook's been – he's planted stolen property on my property, they – they have done – they've had people call in bogus crap about me – and I apologize for saying crap, but it is very frustrating. They've tried for two years to put something on me. Nothing – I've got to work all my cases no matter what Joe Rosebrook's doing. When the informant called two weeks prior to this coming out and said, 'Joe Rosebrook said to me he's got Jon,' it wasn't in reference to the Moodys, it's just 'He's got Jon, he's excited, he's got something on Jon.'"

"Okay," acknowledged the juror.

"It wasn't until after I'm fired I'm thinking, god, was this it? You know, this is – this is when I get another phone call about Gary Phillips – from my informant in prison. Gary Phillips is working with the Moodys. He is being paid by Jeff Rosebrook, which is Joe Rosebrook's brother, who is a millionaire, owned

HBD in Bellefontaine here. Jeff is paying Gary Phillips to work the Moody case."

"Okay."

"I'm just being told that. I'm not telling you folks I know that, I'm just being told that."

Another juror spoke up, "I have a question. If you knew a private investigator was following you, hired by the Rosebrooks, did it – you didn't think about being alone with Stacy, that may be a tool?"

"No."

"I guess . . ."

"I deal – you got to understand."

"I know," said the juror. "You deal with . . ."

"There's more criminals in Logan County than we all care to realize, believe me."

"I guess if I knew someone was watching my every move," said the juror, "I wouldn't put myself with a promiscuous fifteen, sixteen-year-old."

———

Stout shook his head, showing signs of contempt. "I'm in a position where I've got riders with me every day, female and male, adult and juvenile. And let me back that up saying that differently. Not every day. Commonly. And so, no, if you sit back here in hindsight and say, you know what, maybe it wasn't too smart.

"It's kind of like the old story, you arrest 10,000 people and you quit patting them down after 8,000, you just kind of get lax, you don't worry about that stuff. I wasn't thinking. This family is calling me almost daily. I wasn't thinking this was going to come up and be an issue. I really wasn't."

A question from another juror: "I guess my other question is – I wrote this down at the beginning – what do the Moodys have to gain? If what Stacy's saying is not true, what do they have to gain? What are you thinking?"

"There's two different things. They're getting money from the Rosebrooks. Obviously, there's been $20,000 – and this is almost – I mean, I was so close to having this thing locked up, the informant got scared and decided not to do it. There was $20,000 plus another $5,000 if one of my kids is set up. And that's documented. That's all documented in records. It's not – I'm not making this up.

"So, what would they – these are people that you folks in here know. Take Rosebrook, there's all kinds of rumors about how much money is being hidden by this man and what he's done all his life. What would they be willing to pay someone to set me up? And, yeah, there's a lot to gain. Obviously, the Moodys were excited about this so-called million dollars.

"Now, if they discredit me and say I was being sexually involved with Stacy and that's why she is saying the things that she was saying, I've now been discredited and now they can take away that Scott Moody was not the shooter, which will assist them in getting their inheritance that they feel is coming to them out on 47."

The prosecutor interrupted, "Is it your position that if Scott Moody is not the shooter then somehow his estate is not liable at all?"

"I think it's a lot less liable," said Stout. "That's how I feel. I think that if I'm done wrong on a property by a property owner that I'm going to be – I mean, I'm not a suing type of person, but that's a common person's mind in today's game. Obviously, everybody knows to sue. And I fully expect to get sued out of this and lose everything, and my insurance isn't going to cover that. So, I disagree with that."

A juror spoke up: "I have a question. I saw in the newspaper that the State Route 47 houses – there where the shootings happened – that both of those farms were auctioned off. Is that true?"

Jurors looked at each other, one of them saying, "They're sold."

"I don't know," said Stout.

"She's going to be able to get the money," said a juror.

"No, that's locked up in a trust until it's all done," replied Stout.

"Mr. Stout," said a juror. "The problem I'm having is, okay, you know there's a probability of it coming out. But instead of keeping your partner with you, you take this sixteen-year-old child on a stakeout . . ."

"When I was with Stacy, it was just the two of us. Mike wasn't there. We had a pretty tough summer. With this case here, there's a couple other cases that we had – as I said, we were working sixty hours plus a week sometimes. So, you're talking summertime, which is when everybody takes vacation, this family calling me when I was on vacation by cell. Unfortunately – and I don't know about you folks, but my job vacations are kind of comical unless you're actually gone. Just didn't really happen."

"Right," said a juror.

"So, I was – Mike would be off for a week and then I'd – we kind of worked it that way so people would be covered – and then I would be there a week. There could be a month we might not even see each other."

Another juror, "There wouldn't be any other officers you could have grabbed at the time, knowing you would be with a minor and knowing this girl has done things that really aren't respectable to you?"

"In hindsight, you are correct. I could have thought about this differently. Again, I'm in this situation a lot."

"I know it's probably," said a juror, ". . . probably it's because you were in this business so long that you became lax."

———

Stout felt lucky, a sympathetic juror. "Oh, yeah. Definitely lax. Just like the pat down deal. I'm probably one of the biggest offenders arresting a guy that's got crack and everything else – what we primarily work is the higher cases – and not being real – say, hey, get in the front seat, we're going to jail. That's the way it goes. That's sad. That's why I see officers in the news getting killed because I'm one of those guys. I think I can whip the world's butt and I don't think anybody is ever going to come down on me like this. So, I'm lax, yes."

"Right," said Mr. Sympathetic Juror.

Another juror, "I have a question. Do you carry handcuffs in your vehicle?"

"I carry probably four sets of handcuffs in my vehicle."

"Okay," said the juror, "Did you ever put handcuffs on Stacy Moody?"

"She pulled out handcuffs – let me back that up. She was trying to handcuff me one day. Actually, it was when we just – she was just finishing eating. And as I say, she's touchy, like poke at you, always goofing around and stuff. She – right on the passenger side – I should say it this way.

"On the passenger side of the car was one of my sets of handcuffs. She's got them right where she is sitting. She pulled them out. And there's a center console or a center little divider in the – you guys saw the pictures of.

"To me, coming at me, trying to put handcuffs on me. I tell

her, 'You better stop doing that. You're going to get yourself – you don't know how to . . .' and joking, horse-playing around. I took the handcuff and handcuffed her left arm to the steering wheel. 'And now who's handcuffed?' A joke, screwing around."

Another juror asked, "So why would you joke and screw around? That just freaks me out that . . . that a fifteen-year or sixteen-year-old's in a car and you are – a detective in our sheriff's department is horsing around with handcuffs. I think those handcuffs are for if you're going to arrest somebody, a criminal, and you stick them in your back seat."

"Well, that's – you and I live in a different life. Those handcuffs are horsed around with constantly. Constantly. My kids got handcuffs on them more than they don't."

One of the jurors interrupted, "So, that justifies that you can horse around with her and she can sit here and tell us that, yes, and he handcuffed me to the steering wheel?"

"Well, I don't see anything out of line with that. She grabbed the set of handcuffs and tried to handcuff me, and I took the set of handcuffs and I handcuffed her arm to the steering wheel, horsing around. I don't see any issues with that myself."

———

Stout pressed forward. "I'm sitting here telling you folks the truth. I can sit and say, nope, I'm sorry, but I didn't handcuff this girl, it didn't happen, but it did. She was horsing around. She is – she is a tease. Do you find it sick that someone calls and says, 'Hi, there's another dead body?' You know what I mean? That's her. That's Stacy Moody. She's a – she's ornery and that's how she acted."

"I don't know," said a juror. "If I felt uncomfortable with this girl early on, is there someone else you could have referred her to, like Children's Services, and say listen?"

"Referred – I'm sorry, go ahead."

"With you being alone with her and the comments that she – you know, the sexual comments she made, I would hope you would be uncomfortable with that."

"I deal with that daily," said Stout. "I roll off it. I can handle her making those kinds of remarks. This is a fifteen-year-old that sleeps with adults. She grew up – she was with a nineteen-year-old the night of the homicides. Her mother had sex with a twenty-five-year-old – that she's been with. She's spent the weekend in Pennsylvania with another adult. Those are things I learned just from the homicide, not from her.

"This is not – we're sitting here – this is a sixteen-year-old girl that parties almost weekly, and evidently – or instead of saying every weekend – quite often and was with sexual male partners, adult partners."

Another juror commented: "You being an adult and knowing some of this information, were you tempted . . ."

Stout interrupted, "I'm not interested in being with her."

"Well, that's beside the point. I still feel you put yourself in a bad position."

"You're right."

"If you were uncomfortable, why couldn't you say, 'Listen, Stacy, I don't really want to do this anymore. I'll set you up with someone at Children's Services where you can become comfortable' – because it's apparent she likes older men."

"Uh-huh."

"And, you know," continued the juror, "this – I know personally I wouldn't put myself in that situation. And I have a daughter that's going to be fourteen, fifteen years old, and I sure would not let her go out with some man on a stakeout at 10:00, 11:00 at night."

"And your daughter and Stacy Moody are two different people."

"I'm sure they are."

"It's about two different people," said Stout. "And I'm glad to say that probably . . . I don't know you as a father. This girl grew up as a fourteen, fifteen-year-old partying and having sexual relations with adults. She's not like your daughter, okay? I was – I can handle these comments. I'm a jokester, too."

Prosecutor Longo could tell that the jurors were starting to feel uncomfortable. He knew that specific sexual details were about to come out. It was time to call a recess, let tempers cool.

Chapter Twenty-one

I talk – you know, talk smack, and we're all a bunch of guys and we talk smack, but I don't recall Mike saying to me have you, you know, done that to her [Stacy] yet. I guess I should be careful because I'm not here to tell lies. If he was in a joking manner somewhere, spouting off, saying something like that, that could have been said, but I don't recall that.

– Detective Jon Stout testifying before the Logan County Grand Jury, January 25, 2006

Prosecutor Longo waited until everyone had taken their seats. He thanked the jurors for their patience, telling them that they should be wrapping things up soon. "Let's continue with your questions," he said.

"I have a question," said a juror to Stout. "How do you know that Stacy was sexually active? Were there tests stating that she was a virgin or whatnot? Do you know that? Did she tell you that she was a virgin, or did she tell you that she was actually sexually active?"

Stout replied, "I can't say to you that I have – I can't prove that she's had sex with anybody. I just know that her best friend, her best friend for several years, being Krissy Dorsey, was open about saying that she knew Stacy was lying about this because Stacy had told her about all of her sexual partners. Krissy says Stacy's been sexually active since she was twelve."

"In the first part of your statement, you said Stacy was drunk at the time of the party when the shooting started."

"Correct."

"Was there . . ."

Stout interrupted, "Stacy said she was drunk the night of the shooting. As a matter of fact, that reminds me. Stacy stated there was [sic] condoms in her bedroom and she wasn't really sure if she had intercourse. She asked me what [Andrew] Denny said, if they had had intercourse. I wasn't looking for condoms at that homicide. I told her I can check photographs to see if there was [sic] condoms up there found. And I told her that Andrew Denny said that they had slept together, had sex, and then she passed out."

"So, did you even – when you said that you were going to look and see if there were condoms in the picture and stuff, were there?"

Stout looked bored, "In all honesty, I never looked for – I didn't really care. It didn't have anything to do with what I was there for."

"Okay," said the juror. "Do you recall a conversation with you and your partner about having your partner asking you if you fucked her yet? Can you tell us what that was all about?"

"If I fucked her yet?"

The prosecutor decided to step in. "Do you recall your partner asking you kind of out of the blue, referencing Stacy, 'So, did you fuck her yet?' Do you recall that?"

"No, no, I don't."

"Does it sound like your partner Mike saying that?" asked Longo.

"Mike's not a – no, it really isn't – to use the terminology, did you – well, I don't even like to say it, honestly. I don't recall that conversation."

A juror said, "You don't?"

"Yeah."

"You know, then why would he say something like that?" asked the juror.

"Unless he's spouting off about something, joking around. Mike knows me well enough to know that I wouldn't do that; it's not me."

"So, you're saying that's out of character?"

"To have sex with a minor?"

"No. Just the statement."

"Yes, I believe it is," said Stout. "I talk – you know, talk smack, and we're all a bunch of guys and we talk smack, but I don't recall Mike saying to me, 'have you' - you know – 'done that to her yet.' I guess I should be careful because I'm not here to tell lies. If he was in a joking manner somewhere, spouting off, saying something like that, that could have been said, but I don't recall that."

A juror asked, "When you would go to lunch, why would you – why did you feel you had to drive around and park at the islands? Why didn't you just sit in McDonald's parking lot and eat?"

"I eat lunch – that's something that we do. If we ever go parking somewhere, that's a good place to sit and you can do anything, just watch the boats."

"On the island?"

"I mean, I can't believe that you folks haven't went back and sat on the island and just watched things going on."

"Not with a fifteen-year-old girl," said a juror.

"Well, that's – you're not in my same position," replied Stout.

————

"If Stacy is lying about all of the sexual contact she testified about," asked another juror, "why wouldn't she have made it bigger, said you actually raped her? What did she have to gain with just what she said? Why didn't she, you know, say you actually raped her?"

"If I would have raped her, there would have had – there would be evidence to show that."

"But it's two months later," responded the juror.

"You're right. I can't answer why Stacy would do anything she does."

The prosecutor asked, "Do you investigate sexual assaults?"

"You know I investigate sexual assaults."

"Then you should know," continued the prosecutor, "if in fact what you're saying is true and you have a sexually active fifteen or sixteen-year-old, the fact that another man may have had sex with her, there would be no proof of that.

"In fact," continued Longo, "you probably also know that you could have a four-year-old child, sexually penetrated, vaginally penetrated, and chances of having physical evidence from that is almost nonexistent in a four-year-old."

"I disagree with that."

"Well, you'd be wrong," said the prosecutor.

"I may be wrong."

Longo stared in disbelief at Stout. "I know you're wrong. You're telling me, you're telling this Grand Jury that this sexually active girl who sleeps around with everyone, if you had sex with her, if you, the detective, had sex with her then everybody would know because of what? What would be the evidence showing that you had sex with her?"

Stout hesitated, "That's the – I don't know – I cannot answer why Stacy did what she did or said what she said. I find it peculiar that she said that I performed oral sex on her not knowing what I do in my own bedroom, and that's one thing that I do not do – and there's two wives out there – one ex-wife and my wife that will tell you that. I don't perform oral. The other thing I find peculiar is that I digitally penetrated her while I'm performing this oral, according to what I'm being told, and I was satisfied with that.

"I am an adult, a male, a person that likes to be sexually gratified also, but this time I'm okay with performing oral on her but I'm not okay with her performing on me, and that's why we shut it off? But I'm also too embarrassed to let her see my penis, so I have to go around the corner to go pee, so she won't see? That's where her story, I feel, falls apart."

A juror asked, "That's my question. Why didn't she – if she's lying, why didn't she say more?"

"Well, maybe it makes her feel dirty that she had sex with an adult, I don't know, or with myself," said Stout. "I can't answer why she shut the story down at that point in time. I find that one of the peculiar things. I'm surprised I'm also not being accused of forcibly raping her. I'm glad, but I find that also odd."

"You were told by Detective Consolo that Stacy has no hard feelings against you," said the prosecutor.

"That is correct."

"She didn't come forward to tell on you."

"I feel the driving force of this is her stepmother. The other thing . . ."

"If you overheard a conversation with your daughter," said Longo, "and you decided to tell somebody that might be able to do something, would you consider yourself to be the driving force?"

"I would . . ."

"If you made the report to Children's Services or the detective bureau that somebody might be doing something to your daughter?"

"Any mother who took the initiative to listen to telephone

calls between whomever and confront her daughter, then I would consider the mother the driving force of this. This phone call, just like when Detective Consolo – now, I don't know whether there is a phone call recorded between Stacy and anyone, but if you listen to the tape, I immediately confronted him with what he said.

"'Now that I' – he said, 'now that I've heard your voice, I can say that I heard a recorded conversation between you and Stacy' with me inviting her over to my home. I called him basically a liar immediately because that . . .'"

"Because you knew that conversation wasn't recorded?"

"No, there is no way, because that phone call never happened."

"And after this conversation took place, Stacy still wasn't upset with you?"

"I haven't talked to Stacy. I – I have no idea what her – I have not talked to Stacy since prior to this coming out."

"All right. I have no . . ."

"But the problem I've got is," continued Stout, "if he had a recorded conversation with which – how do I know what's recorded at the Moody house and what's not? I know they recorded conversations back in the day. That's something [Sheri] Kay and Steve did back and forth, they did back and forth nonstop because she was always bringing in tapes – listen to what Steve is saying."

"Listen to what he was saying?"

"When Steve and [Sheri] Kay were in that divorce, a pretty ugly divorce, they kept recording each other, accusing each other of all kinds of misconduct."

"That would have been years ago," said Longo.

"I don't know when they got divorced."

"He's got three boys now."

"Ten years. And it's not going to change. So, when he [Consolo] said to me that 'now that I've heard your voice and I can say that I've heard you on a tape-recorded conversation wanting her to come over to your house,' I pretty much called him a liar because there was no possible way that there's evidence of that. There is no possible way that happened, and I don't know – I – I'm either calling his bluff or I'm not."

"It's true after he said that, you knew it wasn't recorded?" said Longo.

"How would I know? How would I ever know whether this is recorded or not?"

––––––––

"Would you agree with me that Stacy was fond of you?"

"Yes."

"She wanted to spend time with you?" Longo continued, "She'd call you and talk for hours, you'd go driving around the nicer parts of Logan County, she wanted to be around you. Wouldn't you agree with that?"

"You're stretching it."

"Okay. Wouldn't you agree that she was fond of you?"

"I already answered that, yes."

"All right. Now, she's a fifteen, sixteen-year-old girl that's kind of got a thing for this detective that's spending time with her. You write little cards to her, you draw a little picture, you call her, and you attend a dance with her, all these things you did you know you've done them, you've admitted them even to me – listen to my question.

"She's got a thing for you. She's confronted on November 2nd by her dad and her stepmom that they overheard a – that Audrey overheard a conversation between you and her, and you're telling me that she – who doesn't have a beef with you at all because she likes you – didn't get hold of you and tell you, hey, they're saying that they recorded it but I know there's no recording, nothing at all?"

Stout replied, "I'm telling you as God as [sic] my witness that I was told on Friday – let me – on Tuesday this came out; on Friday it was brought to my attention that Stacy wanted to talk to me. I was told on Tuesday that Stacy wanted to talk to me, okay. Are you listening to me?" demanded Stout.

With a look of disbelief, Longo replied, "I'm listening."

"And I said, 'Well, what's going on? What do you need? Is there some problem at home, something's happened at home?' Apparently, she needs to talk to me. Okay. I'll shoot over there and find out what's going on. 'You better not do that,' she says. 'They're upset with you. I'm not allowed to see her no more,' blah, blah, blah. Okay. That's fine. I tell her if she wants to get ahold of me, she knows how to do it.

"And that was – I never had contact with her – I can't tell you when was the last contact. It was prior to that Tuesday."

Stout tried to calm down but decided to just plow on. "Once Krissy Dorsey told me Stacy had problems at home, she wanted to move out, she did not want to be around these people anymore. They're crazy, she needed to see me immediately, that was – I never talked to her from that point forward, and that's the truth.

"I have no way of knowing whether that conversation that they claim was recorded, whether any conversations I had with her, her mom, or dad were ever recorded. There's no possible way of me knowing whether it was recorded, okay? This is not CSI. I don't know.

"The other thing I guess that bothers me is why isn't there any evidence of me and Stacy having all these sexual relations in my car? My car was processed. You folks saw the evidence.

If there's excretions coming from her, they should be on the seat, or on that back rest, or in the back seat, or on the floor somewhere. And I'm being advised through my attorney that no evidence was ever found."

———

Prosecutor Longo turned to one of the jurors: "Another question?"

"On one of the occasions," said the juror, "I think you were with her five different times."

"There was [sic] five instances," said Stout.

"That she was in your car."

"That she was with me one-on-one."

"Okay," said the juror. "Any of those times did she ever climb from her passenger seat and sit on your lap in the driver's seat?"

"No. And I appreciate you saying that. That reminds me of a couple more things. I don't care what she says, Stacy has never been on my lap in my car. Stacy has never driven my car, which Detective Consolo tried to convince me he had a written statement – if you guys heard it – saying that she pulled out of the Children's Services' parking lot driving my vehicle, which is absurd. She's never drove my car or sat on my lap while in my vehicle.

"Detective Consolo also referred to me making a comment as to saying I had a 'boner.' I haven't used the term 'boner' since I was in middle school as far as I can recall, nor would anyone thirty-six years or twenty-six years old use the term 'boner.'"

"But a sixteen-year-old would say that," commented a juror.

"Right. A sixteen-year-old."

"You may not say the word," continued the juror, "but anytime that you were with her, did you ever have an erection?"

"No. No. No. I was – apparently my thoughts and her thoughts were two different things. I recognize that she's fond – I'm not sitting here trying to deny – if you think about every part of this story that I've told you, it's the same thing she's saying other than she's throwing in this sexual contact at Children's Services. That is absolutely not true."

A few moments of silence passed, the jurors looking at each other.

"Any other questions?" asked Longo.

Another juror spoke up, "I have one. This is bothering me. I guess as a taxpayer and a citizen of Logan County, why would our sheriff's department, no matter how high up the rank you are, ever let anybody – let any officer of any rank take just anybody off the street and let them ride around with them in their car and also leave the county and not let them know where you're at and what you're doing? I have a problem with that."

"Okay," said Stout. "Let me explain. As a perk for being a detective, working seventeen years and being paid eighteen dollars an hour, which I feel is pretty poor being in a position that I'm in – maybe it was fair twenty years ago; I don't know – for seventeen years I've been risking my life and being paid eighteen dollars an hour for working forty hours a week, with no overtime.

"My Nextel phone never stops ringing. I'm not ever – I was never off work. It just didn't happen, okay? A sixty-hour week was very common, and I was paid for forty. Time off just wasn't – I mean, I pretty much lived through the sheriff's office.

"As a perk, we were permitted to drive a vehicle. It changed sometimes. Sometimes we could drive within the State of Ohio, sometimes it was within a five-county radius, sometimes it was within a two-county radius, you know. It changed many times.

"As to when I left the sheriff's office, we were permitted so many gallons of gas a week and then we – as a detective you have to drive – your car is your personal vehicle also – and then we had to put gas in after that. And which I commonly did. It was just a perk that the sheriff's office had.

"If you go out to the Logan County Sheriff's Office right now, there's probably somebody riding with an officer out there, especially in the evenings. That was the big time if you want to come out and see what's going on in the county, that's a big thing. It's very common."

A juror spoke up, "I have an eleven-year-old daughter. I can say, 'Hey, you want to see what the sheriff does at night?' If so, then I can impress her to the point where she may or may not want to do these things that are in her teenage world, I can go out there and put her in a vehicle with you and say now, 'Go, have a good time?'"

"No, sir. Not an eleven-year-old. Not an eleven-year-old."

"But a fifteen-year-old can."

"That's with the parent's consent."

———

The prosecutor drew everybody's attention, "Are we close to wrapping up? I don't want to stop questioning, but . . ."

The Grand Jury foreman replied: "Yeah, we're stopped."

"All right."

"I'm sorry, folks," said Stout. "I don't control what goes on at the sheriff's office in that manner. It's – it's just what happens. Are you about done, sir?"

"I am," commented the prosecutor.

But another juror spoke up, "You made a comment – on your taped testimony there, you made the comment that [Sheriff] Mike Henry didn't know half of what was going on. Can you explain that?"

"Yeah. I think Mike Henry does an outstanding job as sheriff. We have a job to get done. We've got – and I refer to the crack – I say, 'crack heads,' that's probably inappropriate, but crack addicts, dealers. 'Go out there and get these guys off the street and do your job.'

"He doesn't know how we do our job, he just knows that it gets done. As long as it gets done, he's happy as long as it's being done appropriately. That would be the type of comment he would make. How can one man know everything that 120 officers and employees are doing?"

"Does anybody report to Mike or . . ." said a juror. "Do you tell Jeff Cooper and then Jeff reports to him, or who's the person directly under Mike that should know like the day-to-day operations?"

"They do know the day-to-day operations, but right down to the specifics, nitty-gritty, who was arrested for DWI and who got picked up for this and that, they don't know all that. There's no way to keep up with that. They've got their own responsibilities to deal with as I have my own responsibilities, and that's what they do. I don't know how else to answer that."

"Was there another question?" asked the prosecutor. "I think maybe Mr. Stout had something he wanted to end with, which is perfectly fine. Are we finished with questions? Mr. Stout, did you say – I don't know, I kind of got the impression you wanted to say something."

"First of all," said Stout, "I'd like to thank the prosecutor for giving me an opportunity to speak. You could have been rude and said, 'No, you're going to answer our questions.' I do want to tell you I sincerely appreciate that, appreciate you folks' questions.

"I guess I've always said that we as law enforcement live in a whole different world than those people outside of it, and I truly feel that way. Not better than, but different. And it's a messed up world. I'm here to tell you folks that I maybe in hindsight made one or two poor decisions. Are those decisions criminal? I don't feel so.

"All I ask from you folks is, in your decision-making as to what you're going to do – I guess you could say with my future – these charges shouldn't be brought against me. Really, look at the law and know that I've always tried to do the right thing. That's all I have to say, and I appreciate your time."

"All right. Thank you, sir," said the prosecutor.

Stout got up from his chair, looked at each of the jurors, trying to make eye contact, then turned and defiantly walked out of the courtroom. He glanced over his shoulder, taking a sigh of relief. "Thank goodness," he said to himself, "they didn't ask me about the "fixer."

———

Prosecutor Longo looked over at his staff. They were all shaking their heads in disbelief. What a performance, what a pack of lies, especially by someone with his experience with the sheriff's office. No wonder there were so many rumors of corruption in Logan County. If Stout was typical of the department's detectives, and maybe even typical of the rest of the sheriff's office, how bad could it be? How high up did the corruption go?

Now Longo better understood what his chief investigator, Detective Consolo, had told him. "It will be a long day in hell before I ever return to Logan County. I don't need to have my tires slashed again."

And what in the world is this Rosebrook thing all about? Was Stout using this as an excuse? Unbelievable.

Chapter Twenty-two

*Our analysis of the facts has revealed very
serious charges against a man who apparently
took advantage of his role in a position of trust
and influence. This case illustrates that no one
is above the law.*

– Ohio Attorney General Jim Petro, press
release issued January 26, 2006

A ttorney Scott Longo couldn't believe it. It was one of the
worst performances by any witness he had ever observed
in presenting cases to grand juries. He had just watched
a Logan County deputy sheriff – a detective no less – commit
perjury – numerous times – in one of the most disgraceful
presentations to a grand jury he had ever seen. Stout had lied
numerous times, all the while displaying a cocky, "good old
boy" attitude. What a liar. What a bullshit artist. Stout
epitomized the typical macho cop who was above the law, and
who would say anything to save himself. The members of the
Grand Jury sat there, bewildered and disgusted. This was the
most senior detective in their sheriff's department.

Longo handed each of the members of the Grand Jury a copy
of the indictment he had prepared the previous week. He took
the time to read to them each count and explain its meaning. No
one had any questions. He turned to Scott Wears, the Grand
Jury foreman, and asked him to sign his name on the second
page.

At 3:00 p.m. on Wednesday afternoon, January 25, 2006, the
Clerk of Court of the Logan County Court of Common Pleas
accepted for filing the indictment for public indecency,

endangering children, interference with custody, contributing to unruliness or delinquency of a minor, and sexual battery (two counts) against Jon C. Stout. Stamped in and properly recorded, Case No. CR 06-01-0018 was assigned to Judge Mark S. O'Connor, the Court's senior justice.

The jurors of the Grand Jury of the State of Ohio, within and for the body of Logan County, on their oaths, in the name of and by the authority of the State of Ohio, do find and present that:

COUNT I.

John C. Stout, on or about the 30th day of September, 2005, at the County of Logan aforesaid, recklessly and under circumstances that his conduct would likely be viewed by as an affront to others who are in his physical proximity and who were not members of his household, did expose his private parts and/or engage in sexual conduct, in violation of Revised Code §2907.09(A)(1) and (A)(2), Public Indecency, a misdemeanor of the fourth degree.

COUNT II.

Jon C. Stout, between the dates of August 17, 2005, and October 31, 2005, at the County of Logan aforesaid, did, as a guardian, custodian, or person having custody or control, or person in *loco parentis* of a child under the age of eighteen, to wit: date of birth 09/14/89, created a substantial risk to the health or safety to the child under the age of eighteen years of age or a mentally or physically handicapped child under the age of twenty-one years of age by violation of a duty of care, protection, or support, in violation of Ohio Revised Code §2919.22(A), Endangering Children, a misdemeanor of the first degree.

COUNT III.

Jon C. Stout, on or about the 31st day of October, 2005, at the County of Logan aforesaid, did, knowing he was without privilege to do so or being reckless in that regard, entice a child under the age of eighteen, to wit: date of birth 09/14/89, from the parents of the child in violation of Ohio Revised Code §2919.23(A), Interference with Custody, a misdemeanor of the first degree.

COUNT IV.

Jon C. Stout, on or about the 31st day of October, 2005, in the County of Logan aforesaid, did aid, abet, induce, cause, encourage, or contribute to a child or a ward of the Juvenile Court in becoming an unruly child, as defined in §2151.022 of the Ohio Revised Code, or a delinquent child, as defined in §2152.02(F) of the Ohio Revised Code, to wit: a child date of birth 09/14/89, in violation of §2919.24(A)(1), Contributing to Unruliness or Delinquency of a Child, a misdemeanor of the first degree.

COUNT V.

Jon C. Stout, on or about the 30th day of September, 2005, at the County of Logan aforesaid, did engage in sexual conduct with another, not his spouse, when the offender was the person in *loco parentis*, guardian, or custodian of the child, to wit: cunnilingus with a child, date of birth 09/14/89, in violation of Ohio Revised Code §2907.03(A)(5), Sexual Battery, a felony of the third degree.

COUNT VI.

Jon C. Stout, on or about the 30th day of September, 2005, at the County of Logan aforesaid, did engage in sexual conduct with another, not his spouse, when the offender was the person in *loco parentis*, guardian, or custodian of the child, to wit: digital penetration with a child, date of birth 09/14/89, in violation of Ohio Revised Code §2907.03(A)(5), Sexual Battery, a felony of the third degree.

contrary to the form of the Statute in such case made and provided, and against the peace and dignity of the State of Ohio.

As the afternoon wore on, Joel Mast with the *Bellefontaine Examiner* waited patiently in the hallway outside of the clerk's office, expecting an indictment. His headline the next day - "Former sheriff's detective indicted" - rocked the community. Television, radio, and newspapers across the state covered the story, each leading with Ohio Attorney General Jim Petro's press release.

"Our analysis of the facts has revealed very serious charges against a man who apparently took advantage of his role in a position of trust and influence," Petro said. "This case illustrates that no one is above the law."

Two days later, on Friday, January 27, 2005, Stout and his Columbus attorney re-entered the courtroom that Stout had testified in so many times as a witness for the prosecution. They moved through the courtroom that always smelled of the fear and despair from a thousand faces hoping for or dreading justice, to the long defendant's table. Stout sat down beside his attorney and hunched forward. He didn't need to look around to see the court recorder or the bailiff or the row after row of reporters seated behind him or the television cameras in the two back corners of the room.

When the bailiff announced, "All rise," Stout stood up and adjusted his tie. Logan County Common Pleas Judge Mark S. O'Connor entered the courtroom, avoiding eye contact with anyone in it, and climbed to the bench, the sleeves of his black robe billowing.

"Be seated."

The judge opened a court file, shuffled through it, and reviewed a summary of the investigation conducted by an investigator with the Buckeye State Sheriff's Association and now prosecuted by a special prosecutor with the Ohio Attorney General's Child and Elder Protection Section.

The Logan County Sheriff's Office had fired Stout last November for violating departmental policy regarding conduct and behavior, for dishonesty, and for insubordination as outlined by the Ohio Administrative Code. Judge O'Connor glanced around the room. Both Sheriff Henry and Logan County Prosecutor Heaton and their staffs had carefully distanced themselves from the state's investigation early on, but through the grapevine the judge knew that Stout continued to have connections to the sheriff's department, and his sister Jan worked as a secretary in the prosecutor's office.

With all that going on, Judge O'Connor pondered the appeal that Stout had filed with the State Personnel Board of Review to get his job back. How could he think that might happen if this court found him guilty?

The judge adjusted his glasses to study the charges against Jon Stout. Under state sentencing guidelines, a third-degree felony sexual battery could carry up to five years in prison for each charge. The guidelines did not, however, make a prison term mandatory. He flipped to the next page. The next scheduled hearing would take place on February 27. In today's hearing, Judge O'Connor needed only to establish Jon Stout's plea to the charges.

"Not guilty," responded Stout's attorney, "to all charges."

The judge had expected that. He listened as the attorneys droned on, each arguing for or against bail, and at what amount. After each side presented their argument, the judge shifted in his chair, adjusted his glasses, and read from a paper. Glancing at the crowd where Stout's wife sat two rows behind her husband, the judge announced his decision. He pointed out that Stout was married, owned property in the community, and did not represent a flight risk. In the silence, the judge mandated a recognizance bond. Stout could remain free, out of jail, upon his promise that he would appear in court for all scheduled hearings.

"So ordered," as the judge slammed his gavel.

———

It was obvious to everyone, from the corner drugstore counter clerk to the city hall maintenance man, from the dairy farmer out on State Route 42 to the local bank teller. Stout was a liar. If he'd been lying about his behavior with Stacy Moody, a young fifteen-year-old shooting victim, someone who had suffered through one of the worst tragedies the community had ever witnessed, did he also lie about the results of the Moody/Shafer investigation?

No one believed that Scott Moody was the shooter. Jon Stout's indictment simply added fuel to the fire. Had Stout been lying all along about the shootings? Was he simply parroting Sheriff Henry's refrain, "Let's close this case?"

Was it possible that someone else was involved in the shootings? It was an idea that had been festering in the community for months. If so, it was not something unheard of in this small farming community with so many unsolved murders in its past.

Chapter Twenty-three

"Anyone who goes to court against me is a dead SOB," Rosebrook said, but he still denied any connection to the bombing. "Ray Payne made a lot of people mad. There were a lot of people that could have done that to him." But Payne blamed only one person: Joe Rosebrook. The explosion delayed the trial. Guards stood outside of Payne's hospital room as prosecutors waited to see whether he would survive.

– From a jailhouse interview with convicted felon Joe Rosebrook

Shortly after Stout's indictment, Joe Rosebrook, age fifty, sat on his bunk in his prison cell at the Lebanon Correctional Institution outside Cincinnati reading his mail. One of his friends had sent him a recent edition of the *Bellefontaine Examiner.* He loved the headline.

Detective Jon Stout, that no-good son of a bitch, had finally gotten in trouble. Maybe he'd get sentenced to Lebanon.

Rosebrook hated Stout, the detective responsible for his ten-year sentence for conspiracy to commit aggravated murder, receive stolen property, obstruct justice, and conceal or alter a motor vehicle's identity. Rosebrook's sentence had started in April 2005, just one month before the Moody massacre, and now he couldn't wait to see what that child molester Stout would receive as his sentence for fondling Stacy Moody, a fifteen-year-old school girl.

Recently, Stout had made a big deal out of the fact that Rosebrook wanted to kill him. Well, maybe he did. Stout kept portraying himself as a good cop and above reproach, that anything against him only came as he tried to do his job and put the crooks in jail. Joe Rosebrook had another side of the story to tell.

According to the *Columbus Dispatch,* Logan County Sheriff Henry had accused Rosebrook of running a multimillion-dollar vehicle "chop shop" out of his sprawling, seventy-five-acre property in the northern part of the county. Inside a large pole barn, he'd rebuilt cars with stolen parts and swapped legal identification numbers to make it all look legitimate when the car eventually went up for sale and needed a title.

But while under house arrest, Rosebrook had paid Dan Ott $2,000 – and provided him a photo, an address and a promise of another $13,000 – to kill a fellow, the town scum, known locally as the sheriff's department's "fixer." Rosebrook knew for sure that the "fixer" worked closely with Jon Stout.

In a jailhouse interview after he pleaded guilty to the charges, Rosebrook said he eventually called off the hit. "My family was being threatened and I thought they were in danger," he said. "It was a stupid mistake. I didn't want to go through with it."

In another sting operation, law enforcement caught up with Dan Ott and indicted him for stealing Chevrolet Corvettes in Ohio and Pennsylvania for chop shops. According to an FBI affidavit, Ott told agents that he had stolen more than one hundred of the sports cars, receiving $1,200 per Corvette from people like Joe Rosebrook, who broke them down for parts.

Everyone seemed to know Joe Rosebrook. For two decades, Rosebrook ran a multimillion-dollar chop shop in Ohio's northwestern Logan and Union counties. Car thieves fanned out across the state to feed his operation, stealing from private garages and dealerships and even taking cars off the streets. In recent years, he had expanded to eBay, shipping thousands of dollars' worth of car parts as far away as Hawaii, Washington and Canada – all under the noses of the police.

The sheriff's office first caught wind of Rosebrook, a high school dropout and father of three, about twenty-five years earlier, listing him as a suspect in several unsolved thefts, mostly of junk auto parts from inside barns. Then in October 1983, deputies caught his buddy Payne with stolen goods. Payne ended up talking to the police. He told them that he and Rosebrook had broken into a rural Union County barn and had stolen an engine, a table saw, and rolls of insulation. He admitted to other thefts as well. Based on Payne's admissions, Logan County detectives suspected Rosebrook of arson, likely for insurance fraud. With that, a flurry of investigations followed.

Prosecutors finally charged Payne and Rosebrook with theft and breaking and entering. Payne took a deal. Rosebrook refused; he wanted a trial. With opening statements set for June 13, 1984, and Payne set to testify against his buddy, on June 11 Payne climbed into the 1980 Ford in his driveway and turned the key. The van exploded. Payne lost his right foot and part of an arm. FBI agents found traces of dynamite under the van. Officials suspected Rosebrook, though proof never surfaced.

"Anyone who goes to court against me is a dead SOB," Rosebrook once said, but he denied any connection to the bombing. "Ray Payne had made a lot of people mad," Rosebrook said later. "There were a lot of people that could have done that to him."

But Payne blamed only one person: Joe Rosebrook.

———

Detective Jon Stout said it really didn't matter who wired that van. The message seemed clear: "You don't talk about Joe Rosebrook."

Payne still doesn't, except to say that he no longer blames Rosebrook. "What's done is done," he said in a later interview to a reporter. "It's something I'd rather not talk about."

Few witnesses would talk. "When we got close to solving something connected to Rosebrook, we'd hear the same thing over and over again: 'I'm better off alive in jail than out here and dead,'" Stout said. "It was scary, the influence he had."

Over the years, Sheriff Henry came to know about Rosebrook – his cunning and the loyalty of his relatives and buddies. "He was like Robin Hood," said Jeff Cooper, chief of the Logan County Sheriff's Office detectives' department. "If someone needed a vehicle part, he had it. If someone needed a certain car model, he got it for them. If they needed money, they'd ask Joe."

Sheriff Henry credits his detectives for sticking to the case. Driven in their pursuit, they often worked the case on their own time despite Rosebrook's threats against them and their families and despite Gary Phillips, the private investigator Rosebrook hired to tail them.

Sheriff Henry tried during his entire eighteen-year career as sheriff to coax state and federal authorities to help crack the Rosebrook case. "No one was ever interested," he said. "I think they thought we were overestimating what this guy was doing. Now they know."

Finally, in 2002, Logan County Prosecutor Gerald Heaton decided that the evidence pointed to a criminal enterprise; they had enough evidence to charge Rosebrook with racketeering.

Putting together such a complex indictment would require additional resources. The chief legal counsel for the Organized Crime Investigations Commission in the Ohio Attorney General's office was finally persuaded to take the case. "This is one of the most extensive cases I've seen," said Carol Hamilton O'Brien, an investigator with the Attorney General's Office. "I have a real strong feeling about people who try to hurt witnesses. This guy had to be stopped."

A national insurance-fraud investigator told a deputy that he considered Rosebrook the most prolific vehicle chopper in the country. An informant told investigators that Rosebrook made about $40,000 a month chopping stolen vehicles.

One key to his success, "He never fished in his own pond, or sold crack on his own corner, so to speak," Stout said. He respected Rosebrook's intelligence and efficiency. "These vehicles would come in overnight and be gone by morning," he said. "He was fast, and that's one reason he was hard to catch. Things that could be identified didn't hang around long."

––––––––

The contents of the five binders labeled "Rosebrook" – thousands of tattered, taped and faded pages stacked in an evidence room – tell one story. But Rosebrook and his supporters tell another. They say Stout and his colleagues targeted this soft-spoken dad. They say deputies threatened, coerced, intimidated, and framed him.

Friends and family packed the courtroom at his April 4, 2005, sentencing. They had placed ads in the local newspaper, publicly pledging love and support: "Thinking of you. We believe in you."

Rosebrook's current wife said he worked long hours nearly every day during the twenty years she'd known him, always fixing, selling or towing cars legitimately. The couple, who had remained married for fourteen years, ran a Bellefontaine car lot for six years in the 1990s.

Her husband would give anything to a friend in need and nearly as much to a stranger in trouble, she said. "That's what he did more than anything – help others."

Rosebrook's twenty-eight-year-old daughter, Penny, said that years of aggressive pursuit by the police took a toll. She recently moved away because she felt threatened by Detective Stout.

————

From jail, Rosebrook said that in his only mistake was that he'd paid money while under house arrest in July to Dan Ott to kill Stout's buddy, the "fixer." A witness in the case, the "fixer" had threatened Rosebrook's family.

For all the talk of cars and trucks and parts, however, Rosebrook's case stopped being about cars for Jon Stout in 1999. According to Stout, that's when a man connected to Rosebrook disappeared.

Michael Lattimer, an eighteen-year-old high-school dropout from the Logan County village of Rushsylvania, had a troubled past. His father hadn't stayed around. His mother had a criminal record. He found a friend in Rosebrook in 1999. At that time, law enforcement suspected Rosebrook and his buddies of breaking into unoccupied homes and stealing antiques from elderly people who had moved into nursing homes.

Lattimer got caught. Stout struck a deal with him, hoping it would lead to Rosebrook. Lattimer told them everything he knew.

"I told him to go home, keep his mouth shut, and no one would ever even know he'd been caught," Stout said. "But the perfect story never has a perfect ending."

Rosebrook learned of the arrest. Stout speculates that Rosebrook suspected Lattimer had given him up.

The cops immediately arrested Lattimer in hopes they could keep him safe. But on November 23, 1999, not long after posting bond at the Logan County jail, Lattimer visited his grandma's Rushsylvania home where he took a phone call from Rosebrook. Donna Huffman, Lattimer's grandmother, said that her grandson spoke of a truck deal. She could see that he didn't want to meet Rosebrook, but Lattimer left the house anyway.

Last seen getting into Rosebrook's car near the Rushsylvania post office, Lattimer missed the family's Thanksgiving dinner two days later. His mom worried. "He wasn't a bad kid," Tina Huffman said. "But I had a bad feeling from the very beginning when he started running with Rosebrook and some of those guys. I don't know what happened, but I don't think he's ever coming back."

Just as they had in Ray Payne's bombing in 1984, the police cited Joe Rosebrook as a suspect in Lattimer's disappearance, but never charged him.

Rosebrook had a different story. He claimed that while the Paynes and the Huffmans and others like them tried to get on with their lives, Stout sat in his office and reread dusty files. Stout posted fresh fliers featuring Michael Lattimer's face. He chased reluctant witnesses, hoping someone would talk. He monitored Rosebrook's visits and illegally listened to his jailhouse phone calls. Rosebrook knew Stout was a crooked cop, a perfect fit for the Logan County Sheriff's Office.

As Joe Rosebrook looked over the papers scattered over his lower bunk in the small prison cell, he had to laugh. He considered Jon Stout a crooked cop, and now Stout found himself in trouble for sexually molesting a fifteen-year-old school girl, one of the victims in a homicide investigation. It couldn't get any better than this.

Rosebrook thought about Jon Stout and his longtime buddy, the "fixer." Rosebrook remembered that on April 20, 2004, a year earlier, Stout had somehow possessed a John Deere backhoe recently stolen out of Union County. When Rosebrook learned of this backhoe on Stout's farm, he contacted his private investigator and had him go to Stout's farm and take pictures of the machine. The investigator took his photographs to the Union

County Sheriff's Office and filled out a theft report, telling one of the detectives where to find the backhoe.

The Union County Sheriff contacted Logan County Sheriff Mike Henry about what the investigator had discovered and, before the investigator had returned to Logan County, someone saw the "fixer" driving the backhoe down the road to his shop in Ridgeway in northeastern Logan County. When confronted by the investigator, Stout made up a story, claiming that he had borrowed the backhoe from Don Hays from West Mansfield.

Don Hays said, "Bullshit, my backhoe was stolen."

Rosebrook remembered threats from the "fixer," saying that if he or Stout got into any trouble over the backhoe, the "fixer" would kill Rosebrook's wife and daughter in front of him and then shoot Rosebrook.

"And guess what," said the "fixer." "Stout would be the investigating officer and would determine that Rosebrook had shot his family and then had committed suicide."

————

Afraid for his life, Rosebrook told several law enforcement officers what the "fixer" had said, and that the "fixer" had even driven to Rosebrook's home and said it in front of witnesses standing in his driveway, in front of his garage.

These threats came the same day that the private investigator, Gary Phillips, went to court in Logan County on another case. When Phillips returned to his car, he found a Logan County Sheriff's Office card – with the name torn off – under his windshield wiper paired with a sticker resembling a bullet hole, with another sticker of a bullet hole on the driver's side window. Phillips took the card to the FBI, but they could only get a partial print.

According to Rosebrook's comments from jail, Stout also had an inmate tell him that if Stout or anyone got into any trouble over the backhoe, Stout would bury Rosebrook's daughter one hundred feet from Michael Lattimer's grave, as well as the little one, his other child, right beside her.

Rosebrook thought about it. If Stout and his buddy, the "fixer," would kill people over a stolen backhoe, then he could only imagine what they might do if Stout faced charges for having sex with a fifteen-year-old school girl.

Chapter Twenty-four

> Doug: *Very good. Now, what do you see on the*
> *screen?*
> Stacy: *There's a gun.*
> Doug: *And what do you see the gun doing?*
> Stacy: *It's pointed at me.*
> Doug: *Okay, what else do you see?*
> Stacy: *There's a man standing there.*
> Doug: *What is it that you see, Stacy?*
> Stacy: *He has short, gray hair.*
> Doug: *Do you have any idea who this is?*
> Stacy: *No.*

– From the transcript of Stacy Moody's hypnotism session, March 6, 2007

With a trial date looming and no certainty as to when the court would rule on Steve Moody's various motions to dismiss the cases against Scott's estate, someone needed to make a decision. What did Stacy really see that early fateful morning? It seemed like grasping at straws, but the Moodys felt they had no other options when they agreed to hypnotism. Even if the judge didn't allow the findings as admissible in court, they would go a long way in confirming what Stacy had told the Logan County Coroner.

When people hear the word *hypnosis*, they may picture the mysterious hypnotist figure popularized in movies, comic books and television. This ominous, goateed man waves a pocket watch back and forth, guiding his subject into a semi-sleep, zombie-like state. Once hypnotized, the subject feels compelled to obey, no matter how strange or immoral the request.

Muttering "Yes, master," the subject does the hypnotist's evil bidding.

This popular representation bears little resemblance to actual hypnotism. Modern understanding of hypnosis contradicts this conception on several key points. Subjects in a hypnotic trance do not act as slaves to their "masters" – they have absolute free will. And they're not really in a semi-sleep state – they're actually hyper attentive.

What is hypnosis? People have pondered and argued over hypnosis for more than two hundred years, but science has yet to explain fully how it actually happens. We see what a person does under hypnosis, but not why he or she does it. This puzzle calls into question a much bigger mystery: how the human mind works. But psychiatrists do understand the general characteristics of hypnosis, and they have some model of how it works.

Hypnotism puts one in a trance-state characterized by extreme suggestibility, relaxation and heightened imagination. The subject doesn't sleep, but instead stays alert the whole time, something along the lines of daydreaming or the feeling of "losing yourself" in a book or movie. The person remains fully conscious, but the person tunes out most of the stimuli around him. The person focuses intently on the subject at hand, to the near exclusion of any other thought.

Whether hypnotism can refresh a witness' recollection in a trial remains a matter of opinion. Stacy saw something. Could the results of any hypnosis session help refresh her memory as to what she actually saw? Some courts allow a witness' recollection to be refreshed by hypnosis and their testimony will be admissible if the trial court determines that, under the totality of the circumstances, the proposed testimony is sufficiently reliable to merit admission. The party offering hypnotically refreshed testimony – here, Stacy – has the burden of showing, by clear and convincing evidence, the reliability of such testimony.

How to do that?

Have Stacy hypnotized by the best experts in the state, two men with more than thirty years' experience working with the Ohio State Highway Patrol. On Friday, March 6, 2009, Douglas Wells and Philip Osborne with Forensic Consultants, Inc., hypnotized Stacy. They held the session in their offices in Columbus. It took approximately one hour. The following is a partial transcript from that session:

Phil: [Addressing Stacy] You warming up? Okay? If you'd like to put your jacket or sweater on, it's okay. But you might become warm or uncomfortable.

Stacy: Okay, I guess.

Phil: You okay now?

Stacy: Yeah.

Phil: Okay. Stacy, everything that's going on here in this room is being recorded. Audio and video, for your protection, for everybody. Okay? I want you to know that. Before we do this, we have to have your permission. Everybody has to volunteer. If you want to go through with this, we'll need you to sign here and down there.

Doug: That's giving us consent to do what we're going to be doing, which is helping you with hypnosis.

Stacy: Okay.

Phil: Thank you. Today's the 6th. The time is 9:59. Are you ready to get started?

Stacy: Yeah.

Phil: What's your middle initial?

Stacy: "M."

Phil: Is your last name Moody?

Stacy: Yeah.

Phil: How old are you?

Stacy: Seventeen.

Phil: Date of birth?

Stacy: September 14, 1989.

Phil: What's your home address?

Stacy: 2765 County Road 21, De Graff, Ohio 43318.

Phil: De Graff, Ohio?

Stacy: Yeah.

Phil: What's your occupation?

Stacy: I'm a waitress.

Phil: Are you building up some muscle?

Stacy: Yeah. [Laughter.]

Phil: Okay, we're here . . . we're going to do some hypnosis here. What do you know about hypnosis?

Stacy: Nothing, except what I've seen on TV.

Phil: Nothing at all? Okay. Let me get some other information that's going to help us to help you for any number of reasons, for recall. Do you have any heart problems, diabetes, asthma, anything? Epilepsy or allergies or anything?

Stacy: No.

Phil: Ever passed out?

Stacy: No.

Phil: You're not under a doctor's care now?

Stacy: No.

Phil: Ever been treated for any emotional problems or anything?

Stacy: No.

Phil: Do you wear contacts?

Stacy: Yes.

Phil: Have them in now?

Stacy: Yes.

Phil: Do you sleep with them?

Stacy: No.

Phil: Will it bother you to have your eyes closed?

Stacy: No.

Phil: Would you rather take them out?

Stacy: I don't have any place to put them.

Phil: All right. Ever had eye surgery?

Stacy: No.

Phil: Any problems sleeping at night?

Stacy: No.

Phil: Walking problems, legs ache?

Stacy: No, only when I work and I'm standing for a long time.

———

Phil: Any fears of heights or enclosed places, elevators, escalators, or anything?

Stacy: Yeah.

Phil: Scared of heights?

Stacy: Yeah.

Phil: When you say heights, like climbing trees . . . things like that . . . scaffolds . . .

Stacy: Sometimes . . . it depends on what it is. Sometimes I get kind of freaked out in enclosed places.

Phil: Like what?

Stacy: Well, I can get in an elevator without any problems.

Phil: Any aches, pains, discomfort anywhere?

Stacy: No.

Phil: You're not pregnant?

Stacy: No. I hope not. [Laughter.]

Phil: Do you ever watch television or watch movies on TV? And stuff?

Stacy: Yeah.

Phil: What do you like to watch?

Stacy: Oh, CSI and chick flicks.

Phil: What kind of movies do you like?

Stacy: Oh, just basically chick flicks.

Phil: What's your favorite color?

Stacy: Pink.

Phil: I can go with that. What would you rather do, take a walk on the beach, in the woods, in a garden, all the above?

Stacy: On a beach.

Phil: On a beach? Go to a beach much?

Stacy: No, I've only been there twice.

Phil: Where did you go?

Stacy: We went down to Florida once to a beach, and then I went to South Carolina in January and we went to a beach.

Phil: Okay. Did you have a good time?

Stacy: Yeah.

Phil: Good. Hobbies? What do you like to do?

Stacy: I like to hang around with old farm tractors.

Phil: Do you drive them?

Stacy: No, I can't do that, but I like to be around and watch my dad work on them. And sleep and eat.

Phil: How many old tractors does your dad have?

Stacy: Probably close to fifty.

Phil: Whoa! Do you take them to county fairs and things?

Stacy: Well, our county fair did away with the old tractors, but we have our festival . . .

Phil: That's quite a hobby. What's he do with them all, does he have them all stored?

Stacy: Yeah. He's got them in the barn.

Phil: Okay. Well, as Doug had said earlier . . . hypnosis, all hypnosis is self-hypnosis. All it is is a mental and physical relaxation. And whether you know it or not, about a couple of times every day we all go into hypnosis. For example, when we get up in the morning, we're sound asleep, we wake up and before we open our eyes in the morning and we're still relaxed . . . we're still asleep, but now we're conscious of what's going on in the house, maybe we hear some noises, we can hear some birds outside, maybe, or hear the dog or cat around or somebody's talking. We're fully aware of what's going on, and that's a form of self-hypnosis. You're totally relaxed. And that's all that hypnosis is, mental and physical . . . it's a sense of relaxation. Do you have any questions?

Stacy: No.

———

Phil: You ready to go? No questions? All right. Doug will take over.

Doug: You already recognize my voice as being different from his?

Stacy: Yes.

Doug: You know both of us are going to be involved in this. So, I want you to welcome the sound of both of our voices as a positive thing. That's the reason I'm talking now so you can get used to hearing how I sound so you'll recognize both of our voices. . .. We're going to start talking to you . . . so that both of us can focus our attention on important factors and not try to do two things at the same time . . . get you thinking on that. Okay?

Stacy: Yeah.

Phil: Okay. All set? Okay. Be relaxed. Put both feet on the floor, there. Lean back in your chair, there. You don't want to put your sweater on? You're comfortable?

Stacy: I think I'll put it on. [Stacy puts on her hooded jacket.]

Phil: Okay. Feel better?

Stacy: Yeah.

Phil: You're more comfortable?

Stacy: Yeah.

Phil: Warmer?

Stacy: Yeah.

Phil: Okay. I think I turned the heat down a little bit so it wouldn't get stuffy. It might get hot in here, but you might be more comfortable with a light sweater on.

Okay. Well, what we're going to do is . . . I'm going to have you just look right straight ahead and I'm going to do . . . I'm going to put my hand on your shoulder, but I'm going to tell you right before that so you'll know . . . you won't be startled, you won't be scared, you didn't expect this. So, I'll tell you before that, Okay?

So, for what I would like you to do, Stacy, is just sit back and relax and just let your mind go, and I'd like you to look right straight ahead and . . . look at the tip of my finger, look at the tip and just concentrate on that, and as it's going to come closer and closer to you and . . . and maybe it will be out of focus and maybe it will get blurred . . . a lot of . . . and maybe you'll see a fingerprint . . . but as it comes closer and closer just keep your eye on the tip of my finger there and at some point in time it will be in focus and sometimes it will go back out of focus, but that's perfectly fine, it's natural.

As I take my finger over the top of your head, just let yourself begin to relax now. Just let yourself go and just start concentrating on the muscles in your scalp . . . all of those muscles on the top of your head . . . just let them completely, totally relax.

And your eyes, your nose, just let everything relax, your mouth, just totally relax. All the muscles around your lips, your chin, your jaw. You may even find your jaw separates . . . that's perfectly fine. You become more and more relaxed.

Just let yourself relax. Deeper and deeper. More and more relaxed, you're doing fine. You're doing great. Very good.

With every breath that you take, just let yourself go deeper and deeper into relaxation. More and more relaxed. Very, very relaxed. Deeper and deeper. Deeper and deeper.

What I would like for you to do is just think of yourself, now, in a very, very large tall building, say up on the 20th floor. It can be any type of building you like. It could be an office building, it could be a department store, it could be any type of building you like it to be. You're in this large building, up on the 20th floor now. Now on the other side of the floor, there is a very large elevator and at the count of three we're going to cross the room and be standing in front of the elevator, at the count of three.

One, imagine you're walking across the room. Two, approaching the elevator. Three, there you are. And in just a moment, Stacy, we're going to take a trip down from the 20th floor down to the first floor. And with every floor that you pass, you go deeper and deeper into relaxation. You'll feel the sensation of going down the elevator and you'll be more and more relaxed with each floor that you come to.

There are the doors of the elevator, sliding ever so gently open, very quiet. And as you just step onto the elevator now, and you feel the carpeting beneath you. . . very, very plush, very soft, very relaxing. The elevator is decorated in all your favorite colors, whatever they may be. Very relaxing. As you turn around toward the doors again, you see them sliding ever so gently closed. You begin to go deeper and deeper into relaxation. Just imagine yourself reaching out to pushing the button for the first floor. And the doors are closing.

With every floor that we pass . . . we go down to the first floor, and every floor that we pass you'll go deeper and deeper into relaxation. Then you'll watch the lights from the buttons as you pass the floors . . . there's the 19th floor, there's the light for the 18th, 17th . . . deeper and deeper into relaxation. 16, 15 . . . deeper and deeper, more and more relaxed . . . 14, 13 . . . deeper and deeper . . . 12 . . . more and more relaxed . . . 11, 10th floor . . . deeper and deeper . . . 9 . . . more and more relaxed . . . 8, and 7 . . . deeper and deeper . . . 6, and 5 . . . and here's the 4th floor . . . more and more relaxed, deeper and deeper . . . 3, 2 . . more and more relaxed . . . and the first floor. And you're completely relaxed.

———

As you walk out into the room there's a big, soft chair, overstuffed chair sitting there by itself. Now you can imagine yourself sitting down in that chair now. You're very relaxed. Deeper and deeper into the cushion. And you become more and more relaxed. Deeper and deeper. More and more relaxed. Very good. You're doing a good job, Stacy. Very good.

Very relaxed. Very comfortable. Deeper and deeper. More and more relaxed. And before you, now, in just a moment you'll be able to see an imaginary ruler. This ruler has numbers on it . . . the numbers from one to four represent a light state of relaxation; the numbers five through eight represent a medium state of relaxation; the numbers nine through 12 indicate a deep state of relaxation. Somewhere on that ruler of relaxation is your state now. And as I said before, it may be fuzzy, it may be obscured . . . the numbers. But I'm going to count from one through 12, Stacy, and when I reach the number that represents your state of relaxation, you'll be able to indicate to me that that's where you're at by moving your left thumb for me.

One, two, three, four, five, six, seven, eight, nine, 10, 11, 12.

[At 12, Stacy moves her left thumb.]

Very good. Very good.

Doug: Stacy, I want you to imagine that you're sitting in this chair, which is very, very comfortable already, but imagine that it's the kind of a chair they advertise on TV, like a mattress that you put air in and take air out to select the type of comfort that you choose. And I want you to imagine that the state of comfort that you're in right now is just like average. But as I count from five to one, it's going to be like the air that's used to inflate your chair. It's going to balance itself out so that it becomes more and more and more comfortable, so that this chair is the most comfortable chair that you've ever imagined . . . that you've ever sat in in your entire life.

———

Now, we know that today is March the 6th in 2009. Now I want you to imagine that you're actually seeing those words on that screen. March 6, 2009. Observing that date on that screen is very, very pleasant because what you can do in your mind is create a design that the words and the numbers are in your favorite way of designing things. Like you were drawing them yourself.

And I want you to imagine now that that number is changing, very slowly, and let's imagine that we're going from March to February. And as you see the change from March to February, you're going to be more and more relaxed. Now, imagine January. Now, I want you to imagine that 2008 is the actual date that you see on the screen. It's changing. Now, in your imagination, it's 2007. And as it's changing, you're becoming more and more relaxed. And now it's 2006. And now it's 2005. And you're seeing that number . . . and just watching that number is making you more and more and more relaxed.

———

Your vision is wonderful. All your senses of appearance of what you can see are working really well, but you're not involved. You're observing, just like when you watch TV or see a movie.

Today is the day of the incident. You're distant. The only thing that's going on is that you're viewing the incident and the things that are going on. You're not there. You're watching it just like you're watching CSI on television and seeing something involving other people altogether, but your vision in your mind's eye is perfect. Absolutely wonderful. Your awareness of what you're seeing is magnificent. You've never been able to see more clearly in your life, and just seeing is a relaxing and pleasant experience. You're completely uninvolved.

I'm going to count from five. And when I get to the

number one, I want you to speak to me. And I want you to tell me where you are, just like you're watching that person. I want you to tell me where that person is physically in the building the day, the place, and the time of the incident that you're observing, but not involved in back in May of 2005. I just want you to tell me the room that you're seeing a person who looks just like you the day of the incident when I get to the count of one. With each number from five to one, you're going to become more and more relaxed and more capable of observing this situation from a distance with clarity and yet relaxing with each number.

Five, four, three, two, one. What's the room, Stacy? [38:42 minutes into session.]

———

Stacy: Bedroom.

Doug: Very good. Now, you're very, very, very relaxed. Everything is in slow motion. Everything that's going on is distant from you, but your terrific vision and powers of observation are just working at the highest level possible. As you sit, uninvolved, in this very relaxing chair, watching these events take place on the screen, there's no participation yourself, whatsoever, no feeling of anything having to do with this situation. I would like you to tell me when I get to the number one what is the first thing that you're seeing on this screen even though you're not in any way involved at all. I'll be counting from five to one. I want you to tell me exactly what you see on the screen as to what is occurring in that bedroom. Five, four, three, two, one. What do you see on the screen?

Stacy: There's a gun.

Doug: Tell me what the gun looks like.

Stacy: It's long, and . . .

Doug: And what do you see the gun doing?

Stacy: It's pointed at me.

Doug: Okay, now, I want you to completely and totally relax as I count once again from five to one. And we're going to do a stop-action. The scene is going to stop. No movement is going to occur, just like when somebody stops the film and puts it on pause. You can still see it, but it's not moving. With each number, you're going to be more able to be clear as to what you see. Five, four, three, two, one. What else do you see in this freeze frame? Looking up at that screen.

Stacy: There's a man standing there.

Doug: Can you tell me; can you tell me what you see. And in as much detail as you can. Remember, it's a freeze frame. You tell me what you see. I don't know what you see. Tell me so that I'll be able to see it, too. Make it that clear for me, please. Now let me also count from five to allow you to adjust your vision so it's the best vision you could possibly have. And in doing so, you'll become more and more relaxed . . . and a sense of complete and total security and safety and no other concerns at all except how well you can see and what you can see. Five, four, three, two, one. What are you seeing on that screen, Stacy?

Stacy: It's a dark figure. [42:14 minutes into session.]

Doug: Describe it to me as best as you possibly can as if I . . . as if you're trying to recreate it in my mind as it is in yours.

Stacy: I'm laying on my bed on my stomach. I try to get up, but I can't.

Doug: Tell me what you see, not what you sense. Now remember, we're removed from everything, all we need to do is see. Let me give you some more memory that will help you relax and make it easier for you to speak clearly. Okay. Five, more and more, four, more and more and more, three, more and more, and two, and one. Remember, I can't see except through your words. Tell me what you see. Describe to me as best you can what you see.

––––––––

Stacy: It's really dark. There's a man.

Doug: Remember, I can't see myself, so you have to be able to explain to me what you're seeing on the screen.

Stacy: He has short, grey hair.

Doug: Do you have any idea who this is? Can you see that person and identify him in some fashion?

Stacy: No. He's got a blue shirt on.

Doug: Is it anybody you've ever seen before?

Stacy: No.

Doug: Is it anybody you've ever seen since?

Stacy: No.

Doug: Have you got any idea if this person has any kind of a name?

Stacy: No.

Doug: I'm going to count to ten, Stacy. And when I get to ten, I want you to project this event that you're watching into motion once again. And tell me what is happening once the freeze frame starts to move again in your mind's eye. And as I'm counting from one to ten, you're going to become more and more relaxed with each number. It will become more clear in what you can see on the screen. One, two, three, four, five, six, seven, clearer and clearer, yet even more relaxed, eight, nine, ten. Imagine the picture on the screen is moving now. What is happening? What do you see?

Stacy: There's a fire, gunfire.

Doug: Do you see it fire?

Stacy: I hear it fire.

Doug: Do you hear fire?

Stacy: Like a gun.

Doug: Do you hear the sound of the gun being fired?

Stacy: Yes.

Doug: Okay. And then what? What do you see? What do you see? Just what you see. You can hear, too, certainly, but you're disconnected from it, you're just observing. What do you see? What do you hear?

Stacy: It's still dark.

Doug: Can you see something now even though it's dark on the screen? That person that's on the screen, does that person look like you?

Stacy: Yeah.

Doug: And is that person that's on the screen that looks like you, what is that person doing? Remember, you're just watching. What is that person that looks like you doing?

Stacy: Laying there.

Doug: Is that person able to see anything?

Stacy: No.

Doug: And why not?

Stacy: Because her eyes are closed.

Doug: Do they open up at all besides that one glimpse that you described before?

Stacy: No.

Doug: What is that person going to do next? Say, let's make this thing go forward, like fast forward. What's the next thing that person is going to do?

Stacy: Get up.

Doug: And do what?

Stacy: Walk into a bedroom.

Doug: To where?

Stacy: Another bedroom.

Doug: Do you see anybody else, anything else?

Stacy: Yeah, there's another body.

Doug: Remember that person that you talked about earlier? Did you ever see that person again?

Stacy: No.

Doug: Where did that person go?

Stacy: I don't know.

Doug: You didn't see him come or go?

Stacy: No.

Doug: You just saw him for a glimpse?

Stacy: Yeah.

———

Doug: Okay, fine. Now, let's do this. Just remember where we are, Stacy. We're sitting on that real big, comfortable chair watching this on this screen. That's where we're at. And what you're describing is what you're seeing and that person that looks like you is seeing. Let's relax some more. From the count of ten to one. Ten, nine, with each breath you take you're going into another level of relaxation . . . eight, seven, relaxing more and more, six, five, four, three, two, one. So very, very relaxing. That chair you're sitting in is so comfortable. You don't care if you ever get out of that chair, it's so comfortable. And that fresh air that's coming into that area, it's the kind of air that you like better than any air on the face of the earth. It's absolutely wonderful. You're so very, very, very relaxed. Are you seeing anything in more detail than what you've said so far?

Stacy: No.

Doug: Is there anything out there in the surrounding area that you haven't told me about so far that you know of, that you're seeing?

Stacy: No.

Doug: Now, you're really doing good, and I really want you to relax, totally and completely. And I'm going to count from one to ten, again, and with each of these counts you're going to find yourself being more and more and more relaxed. One, two, three, four, five, six, seven, eight, nine, ten.

————

Phil: Stacy, you've been very helpful here. You've done a nice job, and you're very, very relaxed. And probably more so than you've ever been.

I'm going to count from ten to one. With every count, with every number I go through, you become more and more alert. When I get to five, I'm going to stop counting so that you count at your own pace. You can count by yourself. At every count, you become more and more alert. Somewhere between three and one your eyes will open, and you'll be perfectly normal in every way. Ten, nine, eight, seven, six, five . . .

Stacy: Four [Stacy lifts her head up], three, two, one.

Phil: Stacy, now remember now, you're in a very, very relaxed state of hypnosis . . . in a state of relaxation. We'll finish this now, but is there anything else you recall? Anything you can see?

Stacy: No.

Phil: Can you identify the person?

Stacy: No.

Phil: Never saw this person before?

Stacy: No.

Phil: How do you feel?

Stacy: Tired. I feel like my eyes are crossed. [Laughter.]

Phil: You were really relaxed, huh?

Stacy: Yeah.

Phil: Now, you're woke up? I'll tell you what you'll feel like, you're going to be very relaxed for a long time. And you're going to feel like you just got up from a real, real long nap. But every single aspect of this . . . is going to be like . . . positive for you. It's going to be like, gee, that was really an interesting and pleasant experience.

If necessary, would you ever like to do this again?

Stacy: Well, maybe.

Phil: You were in a deep state of relaxation.

———

After an hour, the session ended in success. Stacy, Phil and Doug came out of the examination room, looking for the Moodys. Stacy had seen someone with a gun, someone that shot her twice. A gray-haired man wearing a blue shirt.

It wasn't Scott.

Chapter Twenty-five

Ohio Revised Code Section 2117.06© provides, in pertinent part, that " * * a claim that is not presented within **six months** after the death of the decedent shall be forever barred as to all parties." (Emphasis added.)*

Some courthouse observers – and there were many – might say it looked like chaos. To the clerk of court and her administrative staff, and the probate judge and his referee, maybe not chaos, but certainly a unique, extraordinary time. One estate after another was being opened, and all were seemingly contingent on the actions taken by other estates.

Ten years after Wilma Buroker's death, the newly elected probate court judge decided to change strategies. With almost all of those who expected to inherit now deceased, and with a farm and other properties falling into disrepair from lack of clear ownership, the judge made settling Wilma Buroker's estate his main priority and finally ordered the sale of the farm land and rental properties. In addition, the judge ordered the conversion of the life estates called for in Wilma Buroker's will to cash. After more than 100 years, the Fuson/Buroker family farm had come to an end.

But to sell these properties using a conventional real estate broker – listing the properties, waiting for a buyer – would take too much time, much more time than the court was willing to allow. Advertising the properties for sale by auction seemed like the only logical way to proceed.

Several months later, with the various sales finally complete, the Estate of Wilma Buroker filed its last account, transferring its remaining assets to Wilma's daughter's estate – the Estate of Sharyl Shafer – and Wilma Buroker's estate was finally closed.

To courthouse observers, it had been the longest running open estate in the annals of the Logan County Probate Court.

Next, the court turned its attention to the Estate of Sharyl Shafer. Her will left most of her property to her husband, Gary, and Gary's will read the same, giving his property to his wife, which were standard reciprocal wills for a husband and wife. Then, all the assets from both Sharyl Shafer's estate and Gary Shafer's estate flowed to their only child, their daughter, Sheri Kay Shafer Moody.

Flowing from her parents' estates, the Estate of Sheri Kay Shafer Moody ended up receiving one-half of Wilma Buroker's original estate. As called for in her will, the other half of Wilma's estate was going to establish an education foundation for children living in Logan County. Sheri Kay's house on State Route 47 West also went up for sale by auction. And a separate auction sold all of Sheri Kay's household goods and personal effects – her furniture, pots and pans, automobiles and a pickup truck, clothing, and knickknacks. The court had one goal in mind: aside from family heirlooms like Stacy's great-grandfather's saddle, the one he used when he rode in the Rose Bowl parade, the probate court judge wanted everything converted to cash.

———

Finally, turning to the Estate of Sheri Kay Shafer Moody, Sheri Kay's will left all her assets to her two children, Scott and Stacy, to share and share alike, *period.* The will omitted the normal and customary phrase: *or to the survivor of them.*

Lawyers normally include this phrase in drafting wills in an attempt to avoid problems down the road. Years later, one child might have died and his or her family has long departed the area (typically his or her spouse having remarried), and now lawyers must go looking for distant relatives that haven't been close to the decedent for years. That's why probate lawyers suggest to their clients that they review – and possibly rewrite, if necessary – their Last Will and Testament if someone mentioned in their will dies. Because of that person's death, they may want to rethink the distribution of their assets.

Fifty percent of Sheri Kay's estate, now worth several hundred thousand dollars, would go to Stacy, a minor. Her court-appointed guardian, Attorney Paul Kormanik from Columbus, would handle her funds. The other half of Sheri Kay's estate would go to the Estate of Scott Moody, administrated by his father, Steve Moody. Under Ohio law, Steve Moody was the only beneficiary of his son's estate.

"Hold on," cried Stacy's guardian, raising the first of numerous legal arguments requiring a motion hearing and the probate judge's attention.

"Scott's estate can't inherit from his mother because of Ohio's 'Slayer Statute.' Simply put," he said, "a murderer or anyone else who is responsible for taking someone else's life can't inherit from that person's estate."

"Haven't you people ever heard of the Menendez brothers? It would make life too easy for some of these tortfeasors," he wrote in his brief in support of his motion. "Sheriff Henry's official report declared that Scott Moody was the shooter. He killed his mother, Sheri Kay Shafer. Therefore, he can't inherit from his mother's estate."

―――――

"Not so fast," chimed the attorneys representing Steve Moody. "Let's look at what the statute actually says:

> Ohio Revised Code Section 2105.19, Persons prohibited from benefiting by the death of another, states:

(A) Except as provided in division © of this section, no person who is *convicted* [emphasis added] of, pleads guilty to, or is found not guilty by reason of insanity of a violation of or complicity in the violation of section 2903.01, 2903.02, or 2903.03 of the Revised Code or of an existing or former law of any other state, the United States, or a foreign nation . . . shall in any way benefit by the death. All property of the decedent, and all money, insurance proceeds, or other property or benefits payable or distributable in respect of the decedent's death, shall pass or be paid or distributed as if the person who caused the death of the decedent had predeceased the decedent.

According to Steve Moody's counsel, the key word was *conviction*. The sheriff never filed charges of murder against Scott Moody for the death of his mother, nor did a court or any jury ever convict Scott of killing his mother.

After months of delay, the filing of briefs and oral arguments in open court, the probate court judge finally ruled against Stacy's guardian and ordered the distribution of one-half of Sheri Kay's estate to Scott Moody's estate.

Once that issue was resolved and assets were transferred to Scott's estate, the attorneys for Paige Harshbarger's and Megan Karus's families would see an opportunity to persuade their clients to file wrongful death actions against Scott Moody's estate. After all, Scott killed their children, causing unbearable pain and suffering.

Now the question became paramount: Was Scott Moody the shooter? No one in the community thought so, including Scott's father, Steve. With the receipt of funds from Sheri Kay Shafer's estate, this would finally give Steve Moody the opportunity to have other forensic experts examine all available evidence to see if they came up with a different conclusion than what Sheriff Henry, in his hurry to wrap things up, proclaimed. It would be worth the money, and it was a justifiable estate expense. Not only would this investigation and research be used to help prepare the estate defenses from these claims, but it would finally answer the underlying question – whether Scott, in fact, was the shooter.

––––––––

When Scott's estate finally received its distribution from Sheri Kay Shafer Moody' estate, the expected race to the courthouse began. With the estate now having several hundred thousand dollars in assets, attorneys for the estates of Paige Harshbarger and Megan Karus filed their claims against Scott Moody's estate in probate court. In addition, they filed wrongful death actions in the general division of the court of common pleas, where the judges heard personal injury/wrongful death actions like automobile accidents.

The court dockets would be filling up fast with scheduled motion hearings, each one requiring the presence of several attorneys, many from out of town. The clerks became exasperated. The simple telephone calls across the street to the law offices on the courthouse square to schedule hearings would no longer suffice.

"Now comes Plaintiff Mark L. Harshbarger, Administrator of the Estate of Paige Harshbarger, by and through counsel, and hereby requests that this Court stay the distribution of any assets from the Estate of Scott R. Moody for the reasons more fully stated below."

That's how it started. It would be one motion after another, taking months for the legal process to play out in two separate courts.

Scott's father, Steve Moody, had mixed emotions about the lawsuits. As the administrator of his son's estate, he didn't want to face these wrongful death claims, but on the other hand, these lawsuits represented his one opportunity to present in court testimony of other forensic experts to see if they came up with a different conclusion than Sheriff Henry. His son lay in a grave wearing the label of murderer. Perhaps these cases would clear his name.

———

Steve Moody would go on to hire experts to review all the evidence. For the umpteenth time, the Logan County Sheriff's Office's investigative file would be pored over looking for inconsistencies. More than forty witness statements would be reexamined. In preparation for trial, depositions would be taken. All the evidence from this tragedy, some obvious and some not, from photographs, autopsies, toxicology reports, blood spatter and shell casings to corporate records, real estate deeds, and even school attendance records would be up for review. Private investigators would be hired to interview key witnesses, looking for a motive. State crime lab results would be questioned, known criminals with thoughts about the case would be considered. Steve Moody instructed his attorneys, "Leave no stone unturned."

———

To head off distribution of any assets from Scott Moody's estate, the attorney representing Paige Harshbarger's estate put these facts before the court: On May 29, 2005, five individuals, including Paige Harshbarger, allegedly were killed by Scott Moody, who in turn allegedly committed suicide. On April 28, 2006, approximately eleven months after the death of Scott Moody, an attorney on behalf of Plaintiff Mark Harshbarger, Administrator of the Estate of Paige Harshbarger, mailed a letter to the attorneys representing Defendant Steven R. Moody, the Administrator of Scott Moody's estate, requesting copies of 'homeowners' insurance policies as well as any umbrella policies and other insurance policies in the name of Steve Moody. The letter also served "as notice of a claim against Scott Moody's estate for the wrongful death of Paige Harshbarger."

A few weeks later, Steve Moody's attorneys responded and rejected Plaintiff Harshbarger's claim against the Estate of Scott Moody for the wrongful death of Paige Harshbarger. As the attorneys pointed out, pursuant to Ohio Revised Code Section 2117.06(B), effective April 8, 2004, all claims against an estate must be presented within six months after the death of the decedent. (Ironically, the law previously allowed one year for claims to be submitted against an estate, but it had been changed the year before this tragic Memorial Day weekend.) Simply put, the family for Paige Harshbarger, through their attorney, did not present Paige Harshbarger's estate's claim until almost eleven months after the death of Scott Moody, the decedent.

Unhappy with Steve Moody's response rejecting their claim, Paige Harshbarger's family decided to hire an experienced personal injury lawyer, one who would explain to Moody's attorneys and the court that the statute of limitations for wrongful death actions in Ohio was one year. As he would write, "Steve Moody, as administrator of his son's estate, was in error and 'willfully ignorant' of Ohio law."

———

Exactly one year after the death of Paige Harshbarger, Attorney David Rudwall from Dayton initiated a wrongful death action on behalf of Paige Harshbarger's family against the Estate of Scott Moody in the Common Pleas Court of Logan County. The court logged the suit, and now cases were pending in two Logan County courts – probate court and the court of common pleas, the court that would normally handle wrongful death claims.

Two years later, Attorney Rudwall decided to withdraw his wrongful death action against the Estate of Scott Moody because Scott's estate still hadn't received any assets. However, Attorney Rudwall reinitiated the wrongful death action against Scott's estate on October 20, 2008, based upon the discovery that Scott's estate would finally be receiving money from the distribution of assets from the Estate of Sheri Kay Shafer, his mother's estate. With lawsuits now pending in two courts, the paperwork and decrees began flying back and forth.

In December 2008, Steve Moody filed a Notice of Rejection of Claim in the probate court. On December 23, 2008, the administrator of Paige Harshbarger's estate filed a Motion for Stay of Distribution of Assets, asking "that a stay of distribution of the current and prospective assets of the Estate of Scott Moody should be issued by the Probate Court to prevent improper distribution thereof."

Now things really started heating up between the lawyers. On January 5, 2009, Attorney Rudwall filed a similar request in the court of common pleas. Paige Harshbarger's father wanted to bring a halt to all proceedings in both courts, especially as it concerned the distribution of any assets from the Estate of Scott Moody to Steve Moody, until this issue of the statute of limitations regarding the filing of claims against Scott's estate could be resolved.

The counter argument asserted by Steve Moody's attorneys: Plaintiff Harshbarger's Motion for Stay of Proceedings should be denied because any matter related to the administration and distribution of estate assets falls within the exclusive jurisdiction of the probate court. Revised Code Section 2101.24(A)(1)© states that "[e]xcept as otherwise provided by law, the probate court has exclusive jurisdiction...[t]o direct and control the conduct and settle the accounts of executors and administrators and order the distribution of estates." Therefore, any matter "related to the administration of an estate and the distribution of its assets [is] within the exclusive jurisdiction of the probate court."

At this point, Steve Moody was left with no other choice. He needed to finally bring these lawsuits to a close. He needed to file a motion for summary judgment in the court of common pleas, a procedure that basically stated the following: "A party against whom a claim . . . is sought may, at any time, move . . . for summary judgment in the party's favor . . . if the pleadings, depositions, answers to interrogatories, and admissions on file show that there is no genuine issue as to any material fact and that the moving party is entitled to a judgment as a matter of law." As attorneys and judges know, there is usually a high bar to reach this standard.

But the single issue in Defendant Moody's motion for summary judgment, a motion that could finally end these lawsuits in Moody's favor: Did Plaintiff Harshbarger timely file his claim against the Estate of Scott Moody?

The probate court had already said no, rejecting the claim as not timely filed, which left Harshbarger with no recourse against Scott Moody's estate. The probate court judge had ordered that the claims filed by Paige Harshbarger's estate and Megan Karus's estate be dismissed.

But another trial loomed with the same exact question in the court of common pleas. Who's right? Do claims filed against an estate have to be filed within six months or is the statute of limitations for filing wrongful death actions in Ohio one year?

————

The court weighed all the arguments. The prior pleadings in this case clearly indicated that both Paige Harshbarger and Scott Moody died on May 29, 2005. The court could take judicial notice that Steven Moody was issued Letters of Authority by the Logan County Probate Court (now Logan County Family Court, Probate Division) to serve as the administrator of his son's estate on June 10, 2005. Likewise, Plaintiff Mark Harshbarger was issued Letters of Authority by the same court to serve as the administrator of his daughter's estate, but those Letters of Authority were not issued until June 16, 2006. (As an aside, at the time Harshbarger submitted his wrongful death claim against Scott Moody's estate, he had not yet been appointed as the administrator of his daughter's estate.   Only the legal representative of a decedent's estate can file a wrongful death action on behalf of the decedent's statutory beneficiaries.)

As Harshbarger readily admitted, he always believed that "Scott Moody was the wrongdoer." No one blames him for believing that way. After all, that is what the Logan County Sheriff announced in a press conference on May 29, 2005. Five months later, Ohio's Bureau of Criminal Identification & Investigation issued their formal report on October 17, confirming their initial findings. With this report, the sheriff issued another press release confirming his department's initial suspicions and closed their file.

———

Harshbarger claimed that issues regarding whether Stacy Moody deliberately lied to county detectives (Detective Jon Stout), whether the investigation was tainted or corrupt (based on Stout's conviction), the fact that Stacy Moody was recently hypnotized, or that the Moody family placed an advertisement in the local newspaper seeking help from anyone who might have knowledge about the case were issues relevant to the motion for summary judgment pending before the court. They were not. They might have some relevance at trial, but those facts should not be used in considering Defendant Steve Moody's motion for summary judgment.

Harshbarger's primary argument suggested that he had a contingent claim, which would be an exception under Ohio law allowing him one year to file a claim against Scott Moody's estate. Because this claim is supposedly contingent, Harshbarger believed that a cause of action does not accrue until Scott Moody is adjudicated by the court to be liable for Harshbarger's daughter's death. According to Harshbarger's attorney, the most important fact in this case is not when Scott Moody died or when his client filed a claim against the estate, but rather "the most important fact is whether the death was wrongful."

The attorneys for Steve Moody made it clear in the filing of their opposing brief that, "Ohio Revised Code Section 2117.06© provides, in pertinent part, that "* * * a claim that is not presented within **six months** after the death of the decedent shall be forever barred as to all parties * * *." (Emphasis added.) The pleadings in this case clearly indicated that Scott Moody died on May 29, 2005, and that Harshbarger filed a claim against his estate on April 28, 2006, more than six months after Scott Moody's death.

Harshbarger's complaint argued otherwise: "Decedent Scott Moody engaged in a course of negligent, reckless, intentional and/or otherwise wrongful acts and omissions, as a result of which Plaintiff's decedent Paige Harshbarger sustained personal injury, pain, suffering, property damage and loss of enjoyment of life before her death" and that Scott Moody caused her wrongful death. All these causes of action, wrote Attorney Rudwall, are torts and are subject to R.C. 2305.10 calling for a one-year statute of limitations (later revised to two years) to file a claim against the tortfeasor, in this case Scott Moody's estate.

Regardless of the above, Rudwall argued that R.C. 2117.06© spells out exceptions to the six-month statute of limitations where it applies to contingent claims: (A) All creditors having claims against an estate, including claims arising out of contract, out of *tort*, on cognovit notes, or on judgments, whether due or not due, secured or unsecured, liquidated or unliquidated * * * (Emphasis added).' Since Harshbarger's alleged claims arise out of tort, R.C. 2117.06(C)'s six-month statute of limitations dealing with contingent claims applies," which, according to Rudwall, means that the one-year statute of limitations would not begin to run until Scott Moody was declared by the court to be liable for Paige Harshbarger's death.

––––––––

Five weeks prior to the scheduled trial date, the judge conducted a pretrial conference to get an idea from the attorneys about how long each side thought it would take to present their case. How many witnesses would the parties call to testify? Had the parties completed all discovery? What problems did the attorneys anticipate? What motions, if any, were still pending, waiting for the court to issue a ruling?

Personal injury lawyers have a reputation for cockiness and egocentricity. And rightly so. They need an outgoing, boisterous spirit to convince those recently injured – or the families of those wrongfully killed – that they have the wherewithal to fight those despicable insurance companies who refuse to fairly settle their claims. The war stories they could tell, the unbelievable amounts of money they have obtained for their clients. Please, don't call us ambulance chasers!

They need to make an entrance, always the last to enter a room. (Why aren't you standing up for me?) The attorney representing Paige Harshbarger's estate fit the bill.

"Mr. Rudwall, you're late," said the judge as the attorneys took their seats in the judge's chambers. It was crowded, with five chairs placed in a semicircle before the judge's massive oak desk. The attorneys knew they had a lot of ground to cover in that afternoon's conference.

"I'm sorry, judge," exclaimed Rudwall. "I was out in the hallway talking with my client, Mr. Harshbarger. I apologize, I didn't mean to be late."

"No, that's not what I mean. You were late when you filed your claim against the estate. Claims against an estate fall totally within the purview of the probate court, and you clearly filed your client's claim outside the statute of limitations, which gave you six months to file your claim. Clearly, the probate court has jurisdiction over this matter. As a result, I'm granting Defendant Steve Moody's motion for summary judgment. Your case is dismissed."

Rudwall looked dumbfounded. They'd run out of legal options.

Steve Moody would feel relieved that it was finally over, but he'd also feel crushed. It quickly became apparent to him. He'd never have his day in court to try to change the official conclusion, an opportunity to demonstrate to the community that Scott had not pulled the trigger that cold Memorial Day morning. After months of trial preparation, he and his attorneys felt confident that they could prove with clear and convincing evidence that his son was not the shooter. And now he felt he even knew why.

Chapter Twenty-six

What could have set Scott off? He apparently was sleeping when Bret Davidson and Andrew Denny left. Why would he wake up suddenly and go on a shooting rampage? And why did he go to his grandparents' house first? There were too many questions, too many inconsistencies. And no discernible motive.

– From the lawyers' list of inconsistencies

After more than four years from the date of the shootings, all the depositions, interviews, court appearances, and so many other activities that had occupied Stacy Moody and her family were finally over. But the questions – the troubling questions – and the inconsistencies remained.

———

Andrew Denny said that when he left the house, he saw a male lying on the sofa. Bret Davidson slept on the sofa that night, but Davidson said that he had already left. He remembers seeing Denny's big Dodge truck with the smokestacks parked in the driveway when he left. Who's right?

According to Bret Davidson, he looked at his cell phone before he left, and it was approximately 6:00 a.m., while Andrew Denny *and* Stacy Moody said that Denny left a few minutes before seven. If Bret wasn't asleep on the sofa, then who was? Who did Denny see? The murders seem to have taken place immediately after Denny left.

Several reports said that Gary and Sharyl Shafer's house (at least the front door) was locked and that sheriff deputies had to kick the door in to gain access; other reports confirm this, noting that Gary and Sharyl Shafer had an obsession about locking their doors. How did the shooter get in and why did the shooter lock the door when he left?

And who put the Shafers' dog in a bedroom, closing the door? And why?

———

Dave Cusic said that he was not there that Saturday night (and neither Bret Davidson nor Andrew Denny report seeing him there), but later Davidson apparently told Nikki Vagedes, Stacy's stepsister, that Cusic was there. Why the discrepancy? Could Davidson have meant Jason Sutherly?

———

Stacy said that she heard Paige and Scott fighting, that she heard Paige saying something like, "Put it down." If they were fighting, why does it appear that Paige was shot while she lay sleeping? Paige appears comfortably tucked in and it looks like she never woke up or moved around before she was shot.

———

Did Scott have a contact wound behind his ear or not? Would it have been possible for him to shoot himself without having the barrel of the rifle placed up against his skin? And why would Scott switch hands? He was right-handed. The contact wound was behind his left ear, making it difficult to pull the trigger of a rifle with his right hand.

The trajectory of the two bullet wounds in Scott, could he have inflicted those himself?

The temperature hovered in the mid-40s that morning and everybody else wore warm clothes. Why not Scott? If he did take off his clothes, why didn't they have blood on them? Scott always wore a belt because of his skinny waist, so why would he take off his belt and place it on another pair of jeans, the ones seen on the floor?

Conversely, if Scott had worn the jeans on the floor with the belt on, why would he take them off and switch pants? If dirty with blood, wouldn't blood have stained the jeans with the belt?

Scott's muddy boots lay on the floor; how did he not track mud all over the house?

How did Scott's socks stay so clean in a house with dirty floors?

Did the footprints near Sheri Kay's bed match Scott's shoes?

————

Stacy heard two shots – gunfire – between the two times that she was shot. After the second time, she never heard any more gunfire. If Scott did the shootings, shouldn't she have heard two more shots – the shots that took Scott's life?

————

John Martin would have done anything for Stacy. She called him for help that day. Why didn't he go over? Why would Steve Wolf call him to find out if something had happened? Why was Martin too worried to report what he saw that morning, someone he thought he recognized walking across the back of his property?

————

What could have set Scott off? Bret Davidson and Andrew Denny thought that Scott was sleeping when they left.

Everybody else was asleep, so no one else made him go into a rage. Why would he wake up suddenly and go on a shooting rampage?

And why would Scott first track across a one-quarter mile muddy farm field and go over to his grandparents and kill them in cold blood? According to the official report, Scott went into their basement to fetch a .22 caliber rifle, walked back upstairs into their kitchen, and then shot both of his grandparents in the face and behind their ears. He put the dog in the bedroom at some point and then left the house. He walked back over to his own home, took off his sweatshirt, shirt, belt (or changed jeans), and shoes, and then shot everybody else.

———

Scott had a recent injury, probably a hernia, which he complained about to Stacy. It apparently prevented him temporarily from doing farm work. While in so much discomfort, how did he find the energy to trek through muddy farm fields to his grandparents that morning, shoot both of them, and then return home and shoot everyone else?

———

Scott did not like guns or shooting for sport. All the killing shots looked professional, head wounds behind the ear. Why would Scott shoot his grandmother and grandfather in the head and not in the body, especially if he lacked familiarity with guns. It appeared that he shot his grandparents while they stood and moved around in their kitchen.

And where did the rifle come from? Gary Shafer's brother said he recognized and knew all of Gary's guns. He had never seen the .22 before and insisted that his brother would never have bought a used firearm. Guns placed in the property room at the Logan County Sheriff's Office would often end up for sale at Stout's Gun Shop. Did it come from there?

Kevin Miller, the last registered owner of the firearm, recalls that he sold it to Ray Gillenwater, now deceased. What was the chain of ownership? If it belonged to Gary Shafer, where and when did he buy it? Did he register his weapons? If so, why not this one?

———

Witnesses driving by the Shafer property that morning reported someone running *from* the Shafer house. Listeners heard on a police scanner that police were searching by the airport for a man running *away* from the Shafer farm. Who was it?

———

And what about the rumors discovered by Detective Consolo working for the Ohio Attorney General's Office that Stout had been secretly dating Sheri Kay Shafer. Were those rumors true? Did that have anything to do with this?

———

Experts on teen violence remain baffled by the case. Scott Moody didn't fit the typical pattern of the isolated, cult-influenced youths who have pulled the trigger in other multiple shootings. He wasn't a loner with a taste for Nazism like Jeff Weise, the sixteen-year-old who shot his grandparents before firing on his high school in Red Lake, Minnesota, and killing seven others. He didn't face relentless teasing like Charles "Andy" Williams, the skinny, fourteen-year-old freshman at Santana High School in Santee, California, who killed two classmates and wounded thirteen other people in 2001. And he didn't resemble Eric Harris, age eighteen, and Dylan Klebold, age seventeen – the infamous duo who dressed in black trench coats and dreamed of revenge before they killed thirteen people and wounded dozens of others at Columbine High School in Littleton, Colorado, in 1999.

To many, Moody seemed the antithesis of Columbine's self-styled suburban terrorists. A clean-cut teenager, Moody felt so passionate about his farming that not even his allergies could keep him from raking hay for his cattle. He had planned to show his cows at several county fairs that year. Two days before the shooting, Scott went over to his girlfriend's farm to help with chores while her father traveled out-of-state.

"He seemed like a decent young man," said Martha Harshbarger, whose fourteen-year-old granddaughter, Paige, was a close friend of Moody's sister and, in the week or so before the shooting, had become Scott's new girlfriend.

The key question that baffles psychologists: If Scott Moody killed so many, could he have shared with others whatever internal demons tortured him in the days and early hours before the shootings? Did he still hurt somehow from the ugly, three-year custody battle between his mother, Sheri Kay Shafer, and his father, Steve Moody, that ended – at least in court – after he turned seven? Did he have unresolved feelings about his father, whom he quit seeing at age sixteen?

As the new "man in the house" following his mother's second divorce in 2003, did Scott feel overwhelmed by the financial pressures, including $56,000 in back real estate taxes and the repayment of a recent loan, encumbering the family's 445-acre dairy farm? Did he blame his grandparents, Gary and Sharyl Shafer, for the farm's declining fortunes over the past ten years?

Those who knew Scott Moody say they can't reconcile his behavior with the boy they knew. Steve Wolfe, Scott's former stepfather who lived with the family for six years until his divorce from Sheri Kay in 2003, doesn't believe that Scott "could have had that kind of rage in him."

School officials, students and family members all describe Scott Moody as a "quiet" youth. The principal at Riverside High School said she has no reason to believe that Moody suffered isolation or ridicule from his peers. He had an almost unblemished disciplinary record, with one single detention for tardiness during six years of schooling in the district.

Nic Hess, a local teenager who had helped the family bale hay, put it more bluntly: "We knew he was a little weird – he always kept to himself. But we never thought he would do something like that."

The family's two farmhouses, now standing empty and mute on State Route 47 West, once had shiny new aluminum siding and red shingle roofing. But then the homes started to look worn down and in disrepair. In 1997, the grandparents quit paying real estate taxes on the farm, eventually running up $56,000 in arrears. They headed off foreclosure by the county when family members agreed to a payment plan that included selling off part of the 1.3 million dollar farm.

Steve Wolfe said he doubted Scott had many concerns about the future of the farm because it was poised for a comeback. Scott had "worked the ground" that spring, he said, planting feed crops for the family's growing herd. "At the time, they had twenty-two cows, and they had twenty or thirty more that were going to freshen (give birth) in the next two or three months." Wolfe said that Sheri Kay had taken out a loan to repair the tractor and planned on buying even more cows.

Wolfe conceded that Scott and his grandparents may have differed over how to operate the farm, but he doubted it could have triggered such a violent reaction in Scott. Family disagreements over the farm "had been a thing for at least thirty years," he said.

———

Lee Anderson, whose son Bret had been with Moody during the round of graduation parties the Saturday night before the shootings, said his son insisted there was little drinking and no antisocial behavior at the parties. Afterward, Bret stayed the night at Moody's home but left at 6:00 a.m. – just an hour or so before the shootings – because he had farm chores to do before his family left for a baseball game in Cincinnati.

When Bret showed up that morning, Anderson said he scolded his son for staying out all night without telling him, but he saw no signs that Bret had been drinking. "I told him he'd better get his butt moving," Anderson said. "There were sheep to feed, cattle to feed. But he appeared to be normal when he got here. His eyes were a little bloodshot, but he appeared to have had a full night of sleep. He didn't appear to be anything out of the normal."

———

According to close friends, Scott Moody didn't show any signs of depression. Family and school officials agree, saying that they'd seen no warning signs. Nor do they agree to call him a good kid who somehow snapped. Many still think that Moody lies falsely accused in death.

Wolfe said that he never saw a rifle in the family home when he lived with Scott and his mother, and that Scott had only a passing interest in hunting. He wants to know where the rifle came from.

———

Years later, the questions continue to hang over this rural farming community of 13,000 like an oppressive summer haze. Relatives and friends of eighteen-year-old Scott Moody say they still can't believe the quiet farm youth years ago went on the shooting rampage that left six people dead on the Shafer family farm. Some grew tired of remembering Sheriff Henry pointing the finger at Scott Moody, with no credible evidence beyond the teen's body holding a .22-caliber rifle.

At one point Sheriff Henry, backtracking from earlier pronouncements, said that, although the preliminary findings point to Scott Moody as the shooter, the case "is definitely not closed." But, Sheriff Henry conceded that no amount of high-tech sleuthing could reveal exactly what happened on the Shafer farm the morning of Scott Moody's 2005 high school graduation, or what demons may have laid buried deep within him.

"We've concluded we may never know what caused Scott Moody to commit this crime," he told reporters. That explanation, the sheriff acknowledged, probably will never satisfy those with an emotional stake in the case.

Chapter Twenty-seven

"I don't care how much you pay me, I'm never going back to Logan County."

– Sandusky County Sheriff's Office Detective James Consolo, assigned as an investigator to work with the Ohio Attorney General's Office, after discovering all four tires on his car had been slashed

As the day dragged on that Saturday, May 28, 2005, the deputies in the Logan County Sheriff's Office expected the three-day weekend to provide them with many headaches. Another Memorial Day holiday with the phone ringing off the hook. Riverside High School graduation, which meant lots of school kids going to lots of parties.

"Where is everybody?" called Curt, a wannabe deputy sheriff in his late 40s with greying hair, as he walked in through the back door of the Logan County Sheriff's Office to check on things with his buddies.

The phone rang. Nobody rushed into the room to answer it.

As the fifth ring echoed in the silent, still room, Curt picked up the receiver. "Sheriff's Office."

He listened to the irate voice and shook his head at the rage. "No, Sheriff Henry's not here. It's a holiday weekend and just about everybody's gone. You want me to take a message?"

Curt listened patiently for a few moments, then jotted down a name and telephone number on a scratch pad.

"Boy, you're not going to believe that phone call," he said to two deputies walking in from the break room. "Some farmer out on 47 wants to see Sheriff Henry right away. Said he's pissed; he just found out that you lowly road warriors have been out at the high school having sex with his granddaughter and her friends, threatening to arrest those girls unless they went along with it."

The two deputies looked at each other, concerned. This could turn into something serious.

One of them said, "Did he mention anything about drugs?"

The fixer looked down at his notes. 'Shafer. 592-3058.' "Yeah, he sure did. He said someone's going to jail. Wait till Stout hears about this."

Epilogue

We would rather be ruined than changed.
We would rather die in our dread than
Climb the cross of the moment
And see our illusions die.

– W. H. Auden, British poet, b. 1907 – d. 1973

Jon Stout was fired from his position as a senior detective with the Logan County Sheriff's Office for dishonesty and insubordination because, according to the termination papers filed with the State Personnel Board of Review, he spent time alone with a girl on five separate occasions without his supervisor's knowledge or approval, and on one occasion led the girl's parents to believe other officers would be present.

Stout reached a settlement equal to three years' salary with then Sheriff Michael Henry and the Logan County Sheriff's Office. In return for $135,000, paid out over several payments, Stout agreed to resign his position and commission and never again seek employment with the Logan County Sheriff's Office. He did not have to surrender his peace officer's certification and he could seek employment with another agency in Ohio. The county commissioners, who normally would have had to approve the settlement, learned of the payments after Sheriff Henry paid Stout from his discretionary account.

Because Stacy would not testify against Stout, the prosecutor agreed to dismiss certain charges in return for Stout pleading guilty to one count of attempted child endangering, a second-degree misdemeanor. In May 2008, Judge David Faulkner (on assignment) sentenced Stout to 90 days in jail (suspended), one year probation, and a $250 fine.

Then, on July 5, 2008, Judge Faulkner granted Stout's request to expunge his conviction for attempted child endangering, a misdemeanor, on the grounds that Stacy had refused to testify at Stout's trial. The judge granted Stout's request even though the former detective had admitted to the charge. This ended a three-year legal fight that originally included two felony charges of sexual battery. Because Stacy had turned sixteen years of age on September 14, prosecutors couldn't agree whether to charge Stout with the more serious charge of statutory rape – had Stacy been only fifteen years of age – or give him the benefit of the doubt that the sexual acts took place after Stacy's sixteenth birthday.

The resulting outrage led to changes in Ohio's sexual battery law. In 2008, then State Rep. Tony Core sponsored a bill which passed, and the governor signed into law, that added peace officers to the list of people (e.g., teachers, coaches) and professionals who could face charges of sexual battery, a felony, regardless of the child's age if the child was in their care or under their supervision.

———

Stacy woke to a world where the person who'd murdered six people and left her for dead knew where she slept and could break into the Moody house just as easily as he had the Shafers'. As the investigation progressed, Stacy's deepest instincts warned her to fear the sheriff office's lead detective, one she could give no logical reason to flee or evade, the one who rejected her testimony and went to great effort to get her to recant her statement.

Stacy handled the situation in the classic response of molestation victims, by placating the one in power and accepting guilt. Thankfully, years later, Stacy finally found salvation in her faith. She went on to attend a Midwestern Bible college, completing her bachelor's degree. While enrolled in school, where she waited tables in a coffee shop and worked in the school's bursar's office as a file clerk, she met the love of her life.

Stacy's now happily married with two young boys. She and her family live in a quiet rural town in western Pennsylvania. She no longer has any meaningful contact with her former friends living in Bellefontaine, Ohio, and she is estranged from her father and stepmother. Stacy still has noticeable scars from the gunshot wounds on her face and neck. Thanks to her great-grandmother, Wilma Buroker, she is financially secure.

———

Sheriff Michael Henry was forced to step down at the end of his term and did not seek reelection.

After a brief stint at Lowe's selling washers and dryers, Jon Stout found work as a deputy sheriff in another Ohio jurisdiction. He and Curt remain fast friends.

Coda

I've been asked countless times: Do I think Scott did it? The short answer, no. At first glance, most people might assume that the sheriff's investigation was thorough, complete, and the results should be irrefutable. Then why the groundswell of public opinion that claimed Scott could never have been the shooter?

There were so many inconsistencies in the sheriff's investigation that red flags should have been seen by everyone. The most disturbing photograph I saw showed where Scott had been dragged from the top of his bed, close to the headboard, to where his feet were now firmly planted on the ground, as if he might have been sitting at the end of his bed. The "railroad" blood tracks on the bed, from the headboard on down, were clear evidence that he had been dragged from the top of his bed to this new position. With apparently Scott's blood spatter on the headboard (although it was never tested), it would have been impossible for him to have done this himself, especially after he had already been shot in the head.

Then, the first rifle shot, behind the ear. Hold a yardstick up behind your ear and try and figure out how hard it might be to pull the trigger, especially with the end of the barrel not touching your head. Not impossible, but highly improbable. Then, move your body down to the end of the bed and shoot yourself again, this time in the mouth. When convenient, place the rifle in a straight alignment next to your body and put your thumb in the trigger guard. How anyone could accept this implausible explanation is beyond me.

Put simply, I believe the first shot didn't kill Scott, and the shooter found it difficult to stage the shooting to make it appear like a suicide. After Scott's body was dragged to the foot of the bed, he was shot a second time. Now it was easy to place the rifle next to Scott with his thumb in the trigger guard, appearing to be a suicide. Was a silencer or some type of noise suppressor used inside Sheri Kay's house? Probably. That's why no one woke up after the initial shots were fired.

Everyone who knew Scott – from his best friend, other classmates, teachers, those who knew him in the community – all said the same thing. There is simply no way Scott could have done this. I was impressed with the fact that Scott, a farm boy, apparently did not like to handle firearms. And the one mention of Scott stopping his pickup on a country road in order to avoid hitting a rabbit struck a chord with me. This person was simply not capable of being the shooter.

People can have their suspicions regarding Scott's concern about farm finances, discontent with his grandparents, arguments with his mother, but none of it adds up to a credible motive. Mass shootings take something more. Here, considering the time of day when the shootings happened and the prior evening activities, there was nothing that could have triggered this outrage in Scott's behavior.

Do I suspect what happened and who the shooter might be? After all our work was done, we felt that we knew who was responsible for the shootings. We reviewed our evidence with our retired F.B.I. consultant but were disappointed to learn that the F.B.I. would not consider reviewing the case because it was a "state" matter. Only if a law enforcement agency sought their help would they consider becoming involved. How about the Ohio Attorney General's office? Nope. They simply did not feel there was sufficient evidence to pursue another shooter.

Is there is honor among thieves? Who knows, but they're good at recognizing each other. Joe Rosebrook, a convicted felon, knows Stout, and he knows that Stout is a dirty cop. I found Rosebrook's statements about Stout to be credible, confirming our belief as to what might have possibly happened.

If Scott wasn't the shooter, then what was the motive. Theories abound, but most center around teenage sex and drugs. Chapter Twenty-seven is one theory: Gary Shafer became outraged when he learned from his daughter, Sheri Kay, that his granddaughter and others were the victims of "road warrior" sex. He wanted to meet with Sheriff Henry as soon as possible. Now, careers would be on the line. It would be a scandalous investigation with plenty of accusations and denials, all leading to a nasty smear on the sheriff's office. That's just one theory.

Looking at this case from a criminal standpoint, had Scott lived and been charged with five counts of aggravated murder and one count of felony assault (Stacy) for the shootings that took place that fateful Sunday morning, a prosecutor would have had a tough time ignoring all the evidence tainted by Stout's actions. Further, Police Chief Ron Murray uncovered so many inconsistencies in the sheriff's investigation that most members of any jury examining the evidence would have doubt, certainly reasonable doubt, as to Scott's guilt.

But then there is another problem with this case – the Logan County Sheriff's Office. Is it corrupt? Incompetent? Guilty of misfeasance, malfeasance, negligence, untrustworthy? All the above?

As an aside, one of the troubling events discovered during

this period – maybe humorous under other circumstances – deals with Colonel Keith LeVan. He's the number two man in the Logan County Sheriff's Office, right below Sheriff Mike Henry.

Parents in the community hired a babysitter to take care of their one-year-old daughter. Like most parents, they wonder about what takes place in their home when the babysitter is there. Is she doing her job or just watching the soaps all day long, ignoring their baby daughter?

They decide to purchase a "baby cam." Now, they can rewind the tape each night after work and see what's been going on during the day. One evening, while reviewing the tape, lo and behold in walks into their home Colonel Keith LeVan, in uniform. Stunned, the parents look at each other. Why would Colonel LeVan – everyone in the community knows who he is – be inside their house? What could possibly be wrong? After a few minutes, their questions are answered.

With eyes wide open, they watch LeVan embrace their babysitter. (For what it's worth, LeVan is a married man.) After a few moments, LeVan and their babysitter proceed to remove all their clothes and engage in wanton sex on the family room couch. In shock, the parents turn the tape over to the local newspaper, which runs a great sensational story about the affair. LeVan's punishment: Two weeks' suspension, with pay. That story just scratches the surface of the problems discovered with the Logan County Sheriff's Office.

Knowing what we discovered, I believe there is clear and convincing evidence that proves Scott Moody was *not* the shooter. After working on this case for hundreds of hours over several years and discussing the various facts with colleagues and numerous experts, I feel my opinion is justified. Apparently, a great number of Logan County residents concur.

Simply put, there is probably more to this story than the

public will ever know. Unfortunately, although it's considered closed, it's really now a cold case, stuck in the back of some file cabinet in the sheriff office's storage room, probably rubbing up against the "Tootie" Mullet and Marshall Griffin files and who knows whatever else has been buried by the Logan County Sheriff.

Acknowledgments

It is one of the blessings of old friends that you can afford to be stupid with them.

– Ralph Waldo Emerson

Several open banker boxes and scattered files are on my office floor – case summaries, investigative files, written statements, cassette tapes and photographs, memos and pleadings – looking at this organized mess brings back sad memories of the pain suffered by so many people in Bellefontaine because of the Moody shootings.

In looking back at this tragedy – thinking of those events that took place more than ten years ago – one person quickly comes to mind who was instrumental in our success in resolving the many and varied legal controversies that engulfed this case. A young and brilliant lawyer, Charlotte Osmer, began as my associate and then as my co-counsel in attending to all of the details requiring a lawyer's attention – legal research, interviewing witnesses, preparing outlines and questions for depositions, developing strategies, writing trial briefs, motions and memorandums of law, brainstorming motives and avenues to pursue, making countless trips from Columbus to Bellefontaine for depositions and court appearances – even attending funerals – all to try and help solve this case. Her outstanding work was unprecedented.

———

As I used to tell my associates, proofread, then proofread again.

If you must, sleep on it and then proofread it one more time the following morning. Thanks to my number one proofreader – who lived through all the days, months and even years I lived with this case, Mary St. Clair. Of course, any remaining proofreading errors are mine.

Thanks, too, to my son and his wife, Matt and Christen St. Clair, for reading first drafts. No one likes to tell dad not to give up his day job. But grandsons Ollie, Henry and Mason were encouraging. They said, "What's your day job?"

I'm lucky to have a few friends who were willing to stick their necks out and take the time to read early drafts. Thanks to Congressman (Ret.) Jack Brinkley for his wit and wisdom, the epitome of a true Southern gentleman; Brooke Daniel for her graciousness to take the time out of her busy schedule to offer a different perspective; and talented artist Adleyn Scott, for having the patience to listen to one more of my stories without rolling her eyes. For all, I appreciate their keen insight.

Elaine Johnson is a wordsmith. My deep gratitude for her assistance in reworking some of the difficult chapters, adding some meat to the bone.

Finally, I wrote most of this story more than ten years ago, when it was still fresh in my mind. Then the project was put on hold, indefinitely. After moving to Georgia, I kept asking myself: Why was I still lugging around eight banker boxes full of case pleadings, depositions, investigative reports, interviews, autopsies, and a host of other material and not finishing this project? Thanks to Sarah Winchester who finally encouraged me to get back to work. A stern task master (yes, a college statistics professor) with a keen eye, she also took a fresh look at the facts and helped me crystalize my thinking on exactly what took place that fateful Sunday morning, May 29, 2005. Without her encouragement, this project would still be taking up space on the top shelves in my office closet.

About the Author

Rob St. Clair practiced law in Columbus, Ohio, for more than thirty-five years, limiting his practice to probate litigation. He represented Steven R. Moody in his capacity as administrator of his son's, Scott's, estate, defending the estate against two wrongful death actions.

St. Clair is a Vietnam veteran and a retired colonel in the U.S. Marine Corps Reserves. He currently lives in Columbus, Georgia, where he teaches military history. He also enjoys traveling overseas to foreign battlefields, photographing today's landscape, and writing articles about his trips for military publications.

Made in the USA
San Bernardino, CA
01 April 2019